Integrative Health through Music Therapy

Suzanne B. Hanser

Integrative Health through Music Therapy

Accompanying the Journey from Illness to Wellness

Suzanne B. Hanser
Music Therapy
Berklee College of Music
Boston, Massachusetts, USA

ISBN 978-1-137-38476-8   ISBN 978-1-137-38477-5   (eBook)
DOI 10.1057/978-1-137-38477-5

Library of Congress Control Number: 2016940853

Cover illustration: © Fanatic Studio / Alamy Stock Photo

This Palgrave Macmillan imprint is published by Springer Nature
The registered company is Macmillan Publishers Ltd. London

Dedicated to the memory of two mystics,
Sam Hanser and Louise Montello,
And to the mystic within you.

Foreword

One evening while I was serving as the Attending Physician on the Family Medicine Inpatient Unit of Boston Medical Center, I was called to see a patient for agitation. This young gentleman had a history of alcoholism and was showing signs of delirium tremens, a condition where someone experiences severe psychomotor agitation due to biological withdrawal from alcohol. He displayed the hallucinations, restlessness, and combativeness that so often accompany this condition. He was so disoriented and upset that he wanted to leave the hospital and bolted for the door. Due to his mental state, he was not able to make safe decisions for himself and could also be harmful to others. The standard protocol in these situations is to call hospital security who often come and physically need to control the person through restraints. In fact, similar circumstances had occurred already in the previous 48 hours necessitating tense confrontations between the patient and security personnel. Fortunately, at the time of this incident, we were also conducting a research study of the impact of music therapy on hospitalized patients. Although this patient was not enrolled for the study, I quickly called for our music therapist who was on the floor treating other patients. She came with her guitar, and immediately started to engage this man with music. She was able to help him sit down and begin to sing along with her on some rhythm and blues songs which he apparently knew well. At first, he sang very softly with her, and over the course of 10 minutes, became more relaxed and soon was willing to cooperate with the nursing staff. The need to restrain him or call security was obviated. An episode of crisis had been solved in a patient-centered whole person manner.

For me, that was a turning point in how I perceived music therapy. The music therapist played a vital role in that moment for the patient, for me as the treating physician, and for the hospital staff. Over the last decade, I have had the good fortune to collaborate with Suzanne B. Hanser, Chair of the Music Therapy Department at Berklee College of Music, to bring music therapy into our integrative patient care model. Our Program for Integrative Medicine and Health Disparities is based at Boston Medical Center, an urban safety-net hospital that serves a predominantly low income minority population. As a result, together we have enabled music therapists to serve patients who otherwise would not have access to this innovative and effective treatment.

In my role as Director of Integrative Medicine, my goal is not only to cure disease, but also to help others heal themselves through developing a sense of connection between mind, body and spirit. I have personally experienced the influence of music therapy in doing just that. One music therapist participated in our integrative medicine group visit model of care. She used techniques such as guided meditation with live music to enable a group of Spanish-speaking women to better cope with chronic pain. Another music therapist achieved remarkable results with a Haitian cancer support group, where she engaged participants in writing their own lyrics, joyously singing their own songs and playing percussion. I was privileged to both participate and witness a remarkable feeling of community that transpired. In another outpatient music therapy group, a mother arrived with her pre-teen son who had chronic behavioral problems. She was immensely gratified to be able to attend the groups, as she felt music therapy reached her son, while other interventions such as 'talk therapy' had failed. As research collaborators, Suzanne and I have had the opportunity to learn from each other as we have collaborated on studies to document and measure the significant impact that we have observed clinically. This has required quantitative and qualitative measures, and also analysis of song lyrics and musical outcomes that display something beyond the objective data.

The modern healthcare system strives to meet what the Institute for Healthcare Improvement has coined as the triple aim: improve health outcomes for patients and populations, increase patient satisfaction with their care, and reduce overall healthcare costs. Others have suggested there is a fourth aim: enhance the vitality, resilience and wellbeing of healthcare providers so they can carry out the triple aim. For practitioners, researchers, and advocates of music therapy, the challenge is to identify how music therapy truly contributes to any one or more of the four aims. What are the conditions, settings, and patient populations where music therapy, in all its various forms, could make its greatest impact? How can we capture the true value of music therapy? How can we integrate music therapy into a holistic model to meet patient needs and improve the healthcare environment? How can we help patients find comfort, awakening, coping, acceptance and peace?

The average physician has little or no exposure or awareness of music therapy and how it may differ from passive music listening. For those who are aware, I suspect the majority would believe that music therapy would have the potential to be a *nice* service to offer patients. *The challenge for advocates of music therapy is how to influence the health care community—providers, nurses, administrators, payers and many others—to shift their view of music therapy from nice to necessary.*

To address these questions, music therapists, researchers and educators of music therapy need credible expert guidance on the field. Skills, tools, and an attitudinal shift are essential for healing to occur. *Integrative Health through Music Therapy: Accompanying the Journey from Illness to Wellness* prepares music therapists and other practitioners to move music therapy into the mainstream of healthcare. Through the languages of holistic health, integrative medicine, and music therapy, *Integrative Health through Music Therapy* inspires patient and provider along the path to becoming well.

Robert Saper,
Boston University School of Medicine
Boston, MA, USA

Preface

This book is about healing—there, I've said it. I have avoided the word "healing" for my entire career as a music therapist, and I have balked at the use of the term from my clients, colleagues, and students. The word "healing" promises too much. It implies much more than treatment or cure, and tends to be associated with the inexplicable and often spontaneous transformation of individuals to a new state of mind, body, and spirit. Throughout my career, I have limited my professional vocabulary to Western medical vernacular, but in researching and writing this book, I have learned that the historic meaning of the word "health" has been far more holistic and integrated. In fact, *hælan* is the old English root of the words, to heal, hale, health, hail, whole, and wholesome (Daniel, 2010). Its derivation may stem from the Proto-Indo-European root, *kailo*, meaning to be whole, uninjured, or of good omen. So I feel as though I am reclaiming my birthright in dedicating this book to the healing art of music therapy.

My son, Sam, of blessed memory, called me a healer. He spent his short life devoted to becoming one, and he said I was his role model. Sam died just before his 28th birthday, due to interactions between herbs and pain medications after removal of his wisdom teeth. He had just defended his master's thesis in somatic psychology at the California Institute of Integral Studies, had been practicing and teaching Tantra, yoga, meditation, energy work, and other healing modalities, and was ready to launch his idea of building a "Healing Empowerment Center." In his thesis, "Growth and Grace: Human Becomings," Sam wrote:

Life made a promise to us. A promise that we would flourish, blossom, and thrive. It promised us that we could realize the next step in our evolution, that we could keep getting better, keep growing into our next highest vision, our next deepest understanding, our next fullest experience of ourselves. Life promised that this process is limitless and that it never ends.

But it doesn't happen on its own. Life is a relationship and we have a part to play in it. Each moment that we step into our bodies, each moment we expand our capacity to respond to challenges, each time we claim our power and presence just a little more, then life responds with grace, with that delicate but awesome unfolding.

We see this unfolding all around us. Just look at any tree. The force that turns an acorn into an oak I call grace. It's the most natural, organic process. For humans, though, it's a little more complicated. We have a mind and emotions that can often keep us from being in contact with this state of grace. Pain, fear, despair all make it hard to accept what's happening. But the very act of turning towards our experience and becoming present within our own bodies has the power to summon this grace.

In other words, every time we show up fully and completely in ourselves, life fulfills its promise to us. And that is what therapy is about for me. Engaging the dance between presence and grace so that life can fulfill its promise both through us and with us. Therapy is soul work. It's the soul whose presence we are summoning.

By the soul, I mean that essential aspect of our identity that we use to navigate our experience. In my belief, our soul is not our body, it is not our emotions, and it is not the mind, but it uses those things to navigate the world, and it is through those vehicles that it realizes its purpose. While it is not important that the client holds this view or that I use any of these words with them, the orientation in me that holds the soul as the agent of change is what invokes the deep capacity of transformation for the clients I see.

At the other end of this connection, there is also a presence that is bigger than us, something greater than us. One could call it life, one could call it God, one could call it love, but no matter the name, that presence is longing to fulfill its promise to us to help us grow, thrive, and realize our own personal potential. In my orientation with clients, I am also reaching for that greater presence in the room with them.

And so, therapy for me is a dance supporting life giving life to itself. (Samuel Hanser, 2009, p. 1).

This book is a tribute to Sam's unfinished life and work, and to his wisdom and inspiration. Sam showed me that there can be healing for individuals who suffer, and that the purpose of my work as a music therapist is to serve as a guide for those navigating the path from illness to wellness. Although Sam helped many people along this journey, he did not live to fulfill his dream of establishing a center to empower others to heal themselves. This book proclaims my work and that of fellow music therapists as healing, and acknowledges our clients and patients who have claimed that music therapy transformed their lives. It articulates many of the empowering practices that I have learned from my son Sam and applied as a music therapy clinician and researcher.

Now that I have established my newfound identity as a healer, I will admit that I am also a scientist. I have never trusted my biased observations to reveal the true outcomes of music therapy, nor have I assumed that my work was the cause of improvement, never mind transformation. So this book presents some evidence-based strategies that colleagues and I have researched, and techniques that have not been tested in clinical trials but that have passed the test of time—that is, those ancient techniques from indigenous and traditional forms of medicine that have been practiced for thousands of years.

It may seem counterintuitive to publish a book that boasts a holistic approach to healing, while also valuing scientific evidence. But this is familiar territory for me, having straddled those two worlds constantly by adjusting my lenses, telescoping in to develop an intimate relationship with clients and zooming out to objectively view client change and improvement. Negotiating this balance is what makes music therapy both an art and a science. For me, the process engages my intuitive sense to identify the most potentially effective technique for my client or group, while I draw from established strategies that have been tested in a growing body of evidence.

In the context of this book, music therapy is not intended to heal disease or cure illness. Rather, it is a means to treat people as developing beings who are capable of healing themselves. Music therapy harnesses the positive forces of creativity, ability, and potential within every person. Music therapists teach people how to listen to the music that is innate and expressive of who they are, and to the music that is a source of comfort, awakening, hope, identity, coping, peace, or emotions yet to be named or defined. They use music and sounds of the natural world in their awe and splendor, to enable each person to begin to work through those places where they get stuck. Sam said:

> We all get stuck sometimes. For some, what's stuck shows up as a physical issue like pain or illness. For others, what's stuck has more to do with patterns in their life—ways of relating, working, and playing. And for others, what's stuck feels more like a hunger for something deeper yet hard to name. For all of us, if we work only at the level of the issue being presented, we end up missing the bigger picture of what's actually happening. That's why I work with clients at every level of their being.
>
> I think of myself as a dance partner. In making contact with the body, the mind, and the soul, we learn ways of meeting those places that don't feel good, finding flow, and then feeling love. It may sound funny but that's what my work is ultimately about, dropping into love—body, mind, and soul (http://www.healingempowermentcenter.org).

The integration of body, mind, and soul is the focal point for the musical experiences described in this book. Guided by a competent and empathic therapist, the intersection of these three avenues for healing can ignite in a single instant of connection between the person, therapist, and the sound or music that brings meaning to that moment. As the journey to wholeness unfolds, music accompanies the individual, like a good friend whose presence transmutes mood, evokes joyous memories, and personifies all that is beautiful in life. Music therapy offers a complementary but divergent journey, one of creation as opposed to loss. As people manage the ebb and flow of their physical conditions along the path toward wellness, music therapy can help them find the inner resources that support their abilities to cope. By identifying the musical and creative potential that they may not have known they had, they focus on the positive, expressive media that allow them to process and communicate their experiences.

References

Daniel, E. (2010). *The grammar, history and derivation of the English language, with chapters on parsing, analysis of sentences, and prosody.* Charleston, SC: Nabu Press.

Hanser, S. [Samuel]. (2009). *Growth and grace: Human becomings.* San Francisco, CA: California Institute of Integral Studies.

Acknowledgments

In the preparation of this book, I have been blessed to visit exotic and beauteous lands. My travels have taken me to China, Japan, India, and Thailand, where I found remarkable guides: Gao Tian, Liu Ming Ming, Song Boyuan, Kazuko Murata, Russill Paul, Sumathy Sundar, and Patravoot Vatanasapt. They built the roads to holistic and integrative music therapy that I followed.

The most strenuous journey, however, did not require airfare. The search to find greater meaning in my work and life has led me to wise spiritual teachers: Sally Blazar, Stephen Cope, Suzy Conway, Shefa Gold, Roz Heafitz, Robin Jacobs, Sheila Katz, Barbara Penzner, Rebecca Perricone, Elana Rosenbaum, Margie Sokoll, and Lorel Zar-Kessler.

I have taken the hand of many dear colleagues who have demonstrated the impact of music therapy on the mind, body, and spirit: Cheryl Dileo, Amy Furman, Maria Hernandez, Deforia Lane, Colin Lee, Joanne Loewy, Wendy Magee, Suzi Mandel, Jayne Standley, and an entourage of Berklee music therapy faculty: Donna Chadwick, Peggy Codding, Kathleen Howland, Kimberly Khare, Karen Wacks, and Julie Zigo. My students have energized me with their passion for exploration and their curiosity about new ways of thinking and being. Others, like Jeannie Gagne, Jon Hazilla, Chigook Kim, Steve Wilkes, and Lisa Wong, have opened my mind and heart to new directions for music and healing. Nicola Jones at Palgrave Macmillan encouraged me to contribute to the integrative health revolution with a book on music therapy. Astute editors Susan Lindsay and Katya Herman crafted my words and figures into this guidebook for the journey from illness to wellness.

The love of my family, Leora, Graeme, Jack, David, Eli, Shira, OB, Gabe, Jessie, Raviva, and Tova, and their faith in my abilities have accompanied me all along the way. My beloved husband, Alan, gave me the space to go inward to find my voice, inspired me when I surfaced, and enthusiastically welcomed my emergence as an author. He taught me the healing power of unconditional love.

The spirits of my son of blessed memory, Sam Hanser, and my dear friend, Louise Montello, empowered my journey and channeled wisdom that I could never have found without them. I am deeply grateful to all.

Contents

List of Figures

1

Introduction

To be human is such a twisted blessing. We have an embodied existence
with all the horrific and ecstatic feelings that come with it. But as we learn
to find presence within the range of all of it we can discover a power to
change our destiny. What can seem like a curse of pain can transform into
an experience of empowerment (Samuel Hanser, 2009, p. 20).

Music immerses us in the range of feelings that guides self-discovery
along the path to healing. It also anchors us, as we grasp the meaning of
music in our lives and create new ways of expressing ourselves. While
we access, explore, and communicate the deluge of emotions that can
flood us when we are ill, it is possible to become well, even if we are not
healthy. Music therapy empowers us to embark on a sacred quest to find
the healer within, and come to peace with our physical conditions and
their psycho-spiritual concomitants.

The purpose of this book is to explore ways to reveal this inner healer
through combining empirically verified music therapy techniques with
holistic practices, two seemingly dichotomous approaches yoked together
in the loving presence of the music therapist. The book is designed to
guide you as a music therapist to unearth the creative, healing capacity

within yourself and within every individual you encounter along a path to wellness. It addresses you, as music therapist, musician, therapist, and evolving person who is privileged to witness the journeys of others who are ill. It is written for your patients or clients, whom I call companions on the journey, who can benefit from being privy to how clinical choices are made in music therapy. The book is also written for those who are not ill but are seeking a musical path to wellness or optimal health for themselves or in the service of others. Because not all of the interventions require music therapy expertise to implement, integrative practitioners will also find ways to apply music in their work.

This book's vocabulary originates in Eastern philosophy and embraces Western science. Its methods derive from ancient sources, nascent ideas, scientific method, and contemporary thinking. Its inspiration springs from the vision of healing empowerment that my son, Sam, of blessed memory, crafted in his short lifetime. Its core is music and the awe that can emanate from engaging in music.

The ocean that divides East and West has become a symbolic chasm for the ways that these continents have viewed disease and health, as well as treatment and wellness. Because the traditional medical model in the West rejects interventions that are not scientifically verified, the wisdom of Eastern health practitioners has not been widely accepted. Yet complex healthcare systems, such as Traditional Chinese Medicine (TCM) and Ayurveda, have flourished in the East for centuries. Thankfully, the emerging field of "Integrative Health" recognizes the validity of these holistic models among more reductionist treatments for individual symptoms. It is the basis for this book's philosophy.

In the field of music therapy, a dichotomy exists between those strategies that have been scrutinized in Western research literature and those that derive from less scientific sources. Sound healing and energy work have existed for many generations, but have not been conducive to experimental validation. The elusive nature of energy and its manipulation cannot be clearly observed and measured, and its impact cannot always be explained. As a result, Western research and medical science does not acknowledge the possible influence of this phenomenon. However, in holistic health systems, these invisible influences are not ignored. On the contrary, they are honored and revered as the life forces that they represent. In *Music: The New Age Elixir*, Lisa Summer (1996) differentiates between those who apply sound and music in healing and those who are trained and qualified to provide professional music therapy services. Summer urges us to challenge unfounded claims of twentieth-century New Age practitioners who prescribe certain tones and vibrations to heal disease. She says, "The vast majority of New Age music healing philosophy is fatally flawed by the oversimplification of the complex psychological, physiological, acoustical, and musical phenomena" (p. 9).

Just like energy, there are aspects of living that are difficult to comprehend, and yet as human beings, we *feel* them and know them to be true and powerful. The powers of music and of the human spirit have been rhapsodized in poetry and philosophy, but are considered far from the domain of scientific inquiry. However, if we are to derive true healing in our work in the more holistic sense of the word, then we cannot discount those things that cannot be measured and seen. It is often the unseen that brings us the greatest advancement on our journeys from physical, emotional, and spiritual illness to wellness. This book, though written by a trained musician, therapist, and scientist practitioner, suggests that true healing can be found when we practice with a new openness to strategies that are as yet undocumented, in deep respect for their origins and sometimes inexplicable mechanisms.

A Music Therapist on a Journey

I was introduced to the language of the piano soon after mastering the alphabet, and this magnificent instrument has accompanied my life. At the piano, I am decidedly unscientific, and, on occasions, imbued with supernatural powers. At least that is how I feel when I sense an indescribable connection with a composer, or when I am able to express something musically that I could never express in words. While growing up in New York City, I became privy to the secrets of music through classes at the Preparatory Program of the Juilliard School, where I learned composition, theory, harmony, ear training, sight-reading, pedagogy, and the fundamentals of violin, flute, and contemporary dance. I also learned who I was and who I wanted to be.

When I began my career as a music therapist in 1971, there was little empirical research to support or explain the techniques I was implementing. Trained in behavioral music therapy at The Florida State University, I learned the science of human behavior, and observation and assessment guided my work. I went on to graduate school at Columbia University, where I was a Fellow in the Center for the Behavioral Analysis of School Learning, specializing in methods of music-enhanced learning. As a scholar and researcher, I approached music therapy with a discerning eye and devoted much of my career to assembling data on its impact in a variety of clinical populations. When feasible, I conducted randomized controlled trials, the gold standard of research methodology, to test the efficacy of music therapy and to contribute to its body of evidence. A post-doctoral fellowship from the National Institutes of Health (NIH) enabled me to engage in biomedical research at Stanford University School of Medicine, where I honed the science of music therapy within the Western medical model.

Still, I was never content to simply practice, research, and teach. I felt that the training that had been gifted to me obligated me to work more diligently to establish music therapy as an evidence-based and widely accepted practice within medicine. As President of the National Association for Music Therapy (currently the American Music Therapy Association) from 1992 to 1994, and President of the World Federation of Music Therapy from 2002 to 2005, I dedicated my efforts to advocate for the profession as a science as well as an art. Throughout my formal and informal education, I filled many bookcases: with medical science and research methodologies on the shelves by the window; musicians' perspectives and aesthetics nearby; psychological theories and treatises next to those; and, closer to my study, texts on the cosmos, the mystical, the ancient, and the spiritual. Five years ago, I added to that collection when I inherited Sam's library, and as I read through his books, I became enlightened to esoteric, energetic practices and healing literature. Thankfully, as I have run out of empty shelves, I now have access to vast virtual collections that integrate the disparate syntaxes of these disciplines into a unified dialect to complement my clinical thinking as a music therapist.

All of these volumes have informed my work. In my practice, I have applied the evidence-based techniques that my colleagues and I have investigated so carefully and systematically over the years. But I have also implemented strategies that are not found in the technical literature. These strategies have led to defining moments in music therapy, when I have stood in awe of the inexplicable process that unfolded before my eyes and the subsequent transformation that transcended verbal description. While my personal journey has wandered into spiritual realms that address the meaning of these experiences and beyond, my publications have largely avoided the vocabulary of the soul and spirit. In my urgency to convince the scientific community of the value of music therapy, I have been extremely cautious about how I communicate. However, my clinical experience has been informed and delighted by introspections and insights that defy explanation.

Fortunately, the current climate in the West is one of great curiosity about the ways of the East, and the integrative health movement has spawned cross-continental exploration and research. As a Western-trained music therapist, I have been grateful to participate in some of these collaborations and have benefited significantly from Eastern wisdom. At this time, I am empowered to write this book, not only because of lessons learned from my son and my own experience, but also because of the respectable status that music therapy has gained for its research and clinical practice in medicine.

The Journey

The book escorts you on an expedition whose mission it is to inculcate the experience of illness with meaningful and creative coping strategies. The journey refers to the experience of someone from the first signs of discomfort to a point of wellness, wholeness, acceptance, or optimal health. This is the journey of an individual, and its cartography reflects that. Its maps are conceptual, holistic, and integrative networks, drawn for navigating this multifaceted and individualistic journey. On the road, there are often common steppingstones, like first signs and symptoms, diagnosis, treatment, recovery and resilience, and acceptance of condition or wellness.

Yet death is the inevitable destination of every life's journey, and we music therapists can carry the person through life's final moments. Before guiding our companions through these passages, however, we must also prepare ourselves for piloting this exploration. Our own journey is one of self-analysis and awareness before coming into therapeutic relationship with the person in need. As we accompany the person in whatever direction they take, we are integrating music into holistic approaches to pain, anxiety, and resistance, and methods that work through the body and breath, mind, and spirit. With such attention on music, it is important to acknowledge and include silence in the lessons along the way, and to glimpse the uncharted, future journeys that lie ahead.

Parts of the Journey

This book is divided into three parts that track the journey. Part I presents a technical introduction to health, wellness, integrative health, and the roots of healing music. Part II is written through the eyes of music therapists and companions who become fellow travelers along the journey from illness to wellness. Part III describes music-facilitated and music therapy techniques designed to accompany the journey. Each chapter follows its own distinct outline, in order to best mirror the variety of paths that travelers follow in their quests for wholeness.

Part I charts the journey with conceptual maps that explore the meaning of health, integrative health and medicine, holistic healing, and the foundations of integrative music therapy. This section introduces the technical vocabulary, history, and underlying mechanisms that explain holistic approaches and potential roles for music therapy. In the journey idiom, holistic health and wellness, optimal health, and acceptance offer goals or destinations for the person who is ill or suffering.

Chapter 2 describes what it means to be well, and suggests ways to thrive and achieve a state of flow, even when we are sick. Engaging in music offers an outlet for creativity, while focusing on the parts of the self that are active and healthy.

Chapter 3 explores how alternative and complementary medicine began to include wisdom from healing traditions around the world and embrace ideals from integrative health and medicine. Advances in technology and psychoneuroimmunology have also informed the healthcare community that mind and body are intimately connected and that an eclectic network of treatments can guide the process of becoming well.

Chapter 4 scrutinizes maps for the journey and investigates the holistic health systems of Traditional Chinese Medicine and Ayurvedic medicine. These models exemplify Eastern ways of enhancing health and offer frameworks for treating the whole person, not just the ailing physical body. Holistic health delineates expectations for the healing process that include emotional and spiritual growth, not just physical health and wellbeing.

Chapter 5 follows the history of musical healing practices. True to its word, an integrative model of music therapy draws from multiple cultures, traditions, and ways of communicating through music.

Part II is about the journey and the process of journeying. Health and wellness take on new meaning when a music therapist brings out the creative talent within each person who is on the journey to wellness. As a guide for one who is suffering, the wise music therapist arrives equipped with the presence of body, mind, and soul to accompany a person through the voyage. This section of the work offers techniques to help the music therapist become that ideal.

Chapter 6 includes activities that prepare you, the music therapist, physically, emotionally, mentally, existentially, spiritually, and musically for the journey with another. It all starts with the self.

Chapter 7 explores the evolving relationships between you, the music, and your companion—the person who is ill or suffering—from the initial preparation for a session to its conclusion.

Chapter 8 presents case studies, telling the stories of a few special individuals as they begin the journey. Sally's initial discomforts and concerns about signs or symptoms lead to worry, stress, and entry into the medical labyrinth. Diagnosis brings challenges to Helen's identity that will follow her throughout her life.

Chapter 9 continues the journey to wellness through additional case studies. Treatment is often accompanied by side effects, pain, and suffering, as told through Shula's story. Accepting the diagnosis and understanding its ramifications can be a source of additional challenges.

Recovery may be accompanied by rehabilitation and new lifestyles and habits, but it may also spawn a period of hibernation to prepare for re-entry into the world of the healthy. Garrison's experience is one of shock and acceptance. Arthur's story exemplifies resilience after serious illness. Sometimes our companions have no treatment options or do not recover. In this case, acceptance of a chronic condition or loss of functioning may be the focus of music therapy. Karl contemplates the final destination of his life.

Part III is devoted to the musical pathways through the journey, including interventions that address some of the problems often plaguing a person who is hospitalized or ill. Music therapy supports many body-mind-spirit practices and also stands on its own, as an influential source of healing.

Chapter 10 provides specific techniques to use music to comfort and soothe, including breath work, facial massage, progressive muscle relaxation, drummassage, imagery, meditation, mantra, listening, toning, and singing.

Chapter 11 shows ways to awaken with music, including more active breath work, focusing, movement, yoga, drumming, imagery, lyric analysis, humming, singing, and chanting.

Chapter 12 explores the musical identity that becomes embodied through the journey. Brad's and Darcie's original approaches help them find their musical selves, while confronting the challenges of their conditions. Songwriting, lyric substitution, and clinical improvisation round out a series of strategies to explore a parallel musical journey.

Chapter 13 presents coping techniques that attempt to merge the head and heart. The process of singing and writing songs is described, in addition to emotional-approach coping and pain management strategies.

Chapter 14 discusses the path to peace, when the end of life is near and the meaning of life becomes a central theme. Legacy work through music therapy may involve songwriting, reminiscence, ritual, engendering gratitude, and being in silence. The future is an uncharted journey, with both endings and beginnings, and a continuing path for music therapist and companion.

Part I

Maps for the Journey

2

In Sickness and in Health

My son, Sam, was not a healthy child. He had his first respiratory virus at a few weeks of age and was diagnosed with asthma and eczema before he could walk. As a result, throughout his childhood, Sam and our whole family had to pay attention to the state of his health, potential limitations, and warning signs. Sam would feel inadequate when his peers went running out for recess while he followed behind, huffing and puffing. He felt isolated when he was home from school due to another infection or skin flare-up. As a side effect of his asthma medication, he found it hard to control his emotions. I recall him running to the refrigerator, saying, "I feel really hungry, and I can't help it." Later, he claimed, "I need to move around, I don't know what's going on." As Sam's mother, I needed to be vigilant, constantly checking on his condition, doling out the appropriate meds, and helping him regulate his physical activity. I watched him maneuver his teetering moods and wondered whether I could teach him how to understand his condition.

For Sam, being in "good health" meant that he could breathe and function well at school and home without the need for supplementary medication. But it was clear that his health affected and was affected by cognitive, social, and emotional factors. When he wasn't well, he couldn't

© The Editor(s) (if applicable) and The Author(s) 2016
S.B. Hanser, *Integrative Health through Music Therapy*,
DOI 10.1057/978-1-137-38477-5_2

think very clearly or relate to others in his customarily cheerful way. When he was down, everything was down. Only when I saw that he was content and accepting of whatever came his way could I say that he was healthy. As a mother, it was not enough to know that he was free of symptoms of asthma and eczema; I wanted to know that he was happy and free of concerns that he might start wheezing and alarm his friends, or that the itchy irritation of an eczemic episode might churn up apprehension and emotions beyond his control.

In the medical vernacular, health has been defined as the absence of illness. But, as a mother and as a music therapist, I am fully aware that this definition is inadequate to describe the world of a sick child or any person who suffers with a physical illness. Fortunately, more contemporary thinking about health is encompassing the concept of wellbeing as well as physical status. Wellbeing can refer to overall satisfaction. But for the purposes of this book, it means multiple states of contentment, resourcefulness, resilience, and good health, within social, existential, affective, cognitive, economic, psychological, spiritual, and physical domains.

Today good health is in jeopardy. Prevalence of alcohol use and obesity is on the rise, with a more dangerous and steep trajectory for minority groups. Physical inactivity, smoking, and obesity account for approximately 40% of premature deaths in the USA (Harris, 2010), and this translates into greater disparities in health for members of minority cultures. There is increasing evidence that lifestyle, diet, and exercise are all important determinants of health for everyone. Is it possible to envision a time when musical experiences are so much a part of our lives that we feel no need to smoke, eat compulsively, or drink excessively? What if we could infuse our habits with more pleasurable, energizing, relaxing, and creative activities?

Positive health places recovery from illness and resistance to disease at the forefront, focusing on prevention. In their book, *New Horizons in Health: An Integrative Approach*, Burton Singer and Carol Ryff (2001) advocate for enhanced funding from governmental agencies, such as the National Institutes of Health (NIH) in the USA, to invest in studies on resilience, primary prevention, and the promotion of optimal human functioning. They promote a research agenda that identifies the biological, behavioral, genetic, and psychosocial mechanisms underlying health and wellness, examines relationships and interpersonal communication as potential predictors of health, and recognizes the environmental and communal factors that affect health outcomes. They urge researchers to integrate their theories and findings across disciplines. They define the essence of "health" as a human being who is thriving and flourishing.

Sam's definition of optimal wellness also referred to flourishing, blossoming, and thriving. He believed that optimal wellness reflects a balance in a constellation of factors affecting mind, body, and spirit. Homeostasis is another term that describes an ideal balance, whereby the complex chemical reactions in our bodies are regulated to facilitate healthy functioning. Homeostasis is achieved when there is complete stability, control, and maintenance of equilibrium across the life cycle. Conversely, lack of homeostasis causes disease. Reaching a state of full homeostasis means that there is an integration of our innate potentials leading to self-actualization, with full recognition and use of our talents, abilities, and skills.

I learned about self-actualization in one of my first music therapy classes. My teacher, Dr. Don Michel, drew a triangle on the board and passionately described why music is so important in our lives. The triangle was divided into a hierarchy of needs, first proposed by Abraham Maslow in 1943. Figure 2.1 displayed the most basic physiological needs, such as breathing, food, sleep, and shelter at the base, then safety and security, followed by love and belonging, then self-esteem, and finally at the apex, self-actualization. While most people were able to have their basic needs met, it was most challenging to find people who felt as though they were truly self-actualized. Dr. Michel circled the pinnacle of the triangle and explained that self-actualization could be achieved at the peak of creativity, with the mastery of musical performance or when an "aha" moment sparks with discovery or insight.

I instantly understood that something like this "self-actualization" must be happening when I mastered a challenging passage at the piano. At those times, my fingers seemed to glide across the keys without my control or effort. And there were also those moments when I listened to the most beautiful music I had ever heard, at a piano recital of Vladimir Horowitz. I felt as though I were in a different world, experiencing the utmost beauty and sheer joy. This was my form of self-actualization, and

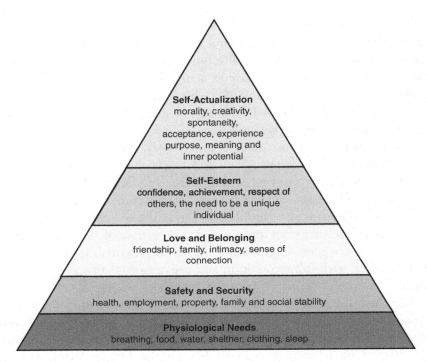

Fig. 2.1 Maslow's hierarchy of human drives

I anticipated immersing myself in more of these experiences in the process of becoming a music therapist. Now after decades in my career as a music therapist, my moments of self-actualization come mainly from witnessing transcendent responses to music by the people with whom I work—people who are suffering from chronic illnesses or life-threatening conditions, people who are patients in hospitals, or passive recipients of painful treatments.

Having had several surgeries as a child, I have always had considerable empathy for people who are ill. When I was seven years old, I had surgery to build a canal for my left ear that was deformed at birth. I recall arriving at the hospital, greeted by masked faces and enormous needles. My clothes were stripped off, and I was wrapped in cold white sheets. I felt sharp punctures, first in my arm, then in my thigh. I jumped in surprise, but found myself restrained. When I opened my eyes, my parents were gone, and I was alone in a gray hallway. The only sounds were metallic and they reverberated against the rails of my bed. I was drowsy, but felt myself moving toward an immense light. Someone cupped my nose and mouth, and I breathed a sickly, burning syrup, the ether anesthetic used at the time.

When I woke up, I felt raw with pain from my neck up. I was the only patient in the hospital ward, so echoing footsteps meant they were coming for me. Because my eyeglasses could not fit over the turban bandage around my head, I did not see very well. When a fuzz of white leaned over me, it was to undress me, squeeze me, or stick me. No one spoke to me until the next day.

Only one of my possessions was allowed on the ward. It was a music box clock, adorned with a pink ballerina that danced when the alarm went off. The opening notes of Beethoven's "Für Elise" would play, the ballerina would twirl, and I would feel embraced at last.

Fortunately, medicine has changed, hospitals have changed, and healthcare is changing. However, the challenges of being sick remain largely the same. Kathleen Galvin and Les Todres (2013) argue for a humane and holistic view. They advocate for caring for a *person* who is ill, rather than using the reductionist model that defines the patient as a series of signs and symptoms that affect different parts of the body. In preparing their case for a "lifeworld" approach to care, they describe the same sorts of dehumanizing assaults to dignity and lack of personal control that I encountered as a child. They recognize the infantilizing experience of an ill person who must take on the role of being "sick," and submit to the orders of physician and nurse. Sickness "manifests in an excessive emphasis on *how* the person is, not *who* the person is" (p. 16), and personal identity becomes embroiled in disease and physical condition.

Their analysis reminds me of an article I read long ago that had a significant effect upon me. Written by anthropologist Horace Miner in 1956, "Body ritual among the Nacirema" researched the medicine men of the Nacirema tribe whose temple, the *latipsoh*, houses dehumanizing and humiliating ceremonies.

Few supplicants in the temple are well enough to do anything but lie on their hard beds. The daily ceremonies, like the rites of the holy-mouth-men, involve discomfort and torture. With ritual precision, the vestals awaken their miserable charges each dawn and roll them about on their beds of pain while performing ablutions, in the formal movements of which the maidens are highly trained. At other times they insert magic wands in the supplicant's mouth or force him to eat substances which are supposed to be healing. From time to time the medicine men come to their clients and jab magically treated needles into their flesh. The fact that these temple ceremonies may not cure, and may even kill the neophyte, in no way decreases the people's faith in the medicine men (p. 717).

Of course, if you read the names of the tribe and temple backwards, you realize that this primitive and inhumane system is none other than the American hospital.

Galvin and Todres see the need for new ways of dealing with sickness. They believe in the importance of retaining and maintaining the self, along with the embodiment of a "lived body" that relates to the world and others in meaningful ways.

To be human means to live within the fragile limits of human embodiment; our insiderness reveals the human body as tiredness, pain, hunger, loss of function, excitement, vitality, and other experiences of the human body's being in the world. When un-preoccupied with the vicissitudes of bodily attention, embodiment supports us in moving out into the world, attentive to people, places, and tasks in life. On the other hand one's attention can be dominated by bodily messages that announce dis-ease and are a reminder of the limits of our everyday possibilities and potentials (p. 19).

While illness can bring separation and isolation from familiar places and loved ones, wellbeing refers to connection, vitality, movement, and peace. Within the "lifeworld" model, the active, healthy individual is one who engages in a rhythmic and balanced life. Healthy rhythm refers to steady breathing and gait, and responsiveness to the seasonal changes and other cycles of life. The individual is capable of sensing peace, accepting what exists, and paying attention to the present moment. The future is seen as one of possibility. Wellbeing is "independent of health and illness, but is a resource for both" (p. 76).

Wellbeing does not require excellent physical health. In fact, many individuals who have terminal illnesses, or are in the process of dying, often experience the sort of peace and acceptance that defines wellbeing. In fact, they often report appreciating these transcendent states for the first time, when they have become ill or find themselves close to death. This sense of transcendence has been described by contemporary psychologists as a higher state of being than Maslow's self-actualization. In the context of health, self-transcendence refers to finding meaning in life that is "manifest in several ways: giving creatively to the world, inspirational experiences, and attitudes when faced with unchangeable situations" (Matthews & Cook, 2009, p. 718). The optimistic attitudes that are inspired by self-transcendence lead one to apply appropriate problem-focused coping strategies, and to experience positive emotional wellbeing.

Resilience is another concept that reflects the ability to adapt to ill health or adversity, to cope effectively, and break through these challenges. According to the American Psychological Association (http://www.apa.org/helpcenter/road-resilience.aspx), resilience can be fostered in different ways:

- staying connected in relationships with significant others and in the community; doing for others
- changing the interpretation of problems as insurmountable
- accepting that change is part of life
- developing goals and moving toward them
- taking decisive action rather than avoiding problems
- finding a sense of self-discovery in the opportunities that adversity can bring
- developing self-confidence and positive self-identity
- maintaining perspective on the bigger picture
- keeping positive and optimistic
- taking care of yourself
- finding new ways to build hope

This is where music comes into play. Music therapists can help individuals work through and toward these goals. Through engagement with musical and artistic media, individuals identify the creative parts

of themselves that build self-confidence, and process lessons of acceptance that offer perspective and hope. I am reminded of Sam's interest
in playing the trumpet, and the concerns I had that his asthma would
prevent him from being able to play a brass instrument. With permission
from his physician, he began breathing exercises prepared by a respiratory therapist to build breath control slowly and gradually. When it was
deemed feasible to begin putting lips to trumpet, he did so with such
a huge smile that it was difficult to place his mouth with the appropriate embouchure. Producing a strong tone and subsequently performing
in the school band also produced a strong sense of self-confidence. He
worked as hard on monitoring his ability to play the musical phrases with
just the right amount of breath as he did on creating a pleasing, musical
tone. Sam became a trumpet player rather than an asthma sufferer. He
was acutely aware of his abilities and limitations, and played them to the
hilt in his joyous trumpet blowing. I would say that Sam not only demonstrated resilience in coping with his asthma, but also had an optimal
life experience.

Sam was certainly experiencing flow, a concept that has been studied
by Mihaly Csikszentmihalyi throughout decades of research. His popular
book, *Flow: The Psychology of Optimal Experience* (2008), describes the
experience that I labeled earlier as self-actualization. When musicians like
me, Sam, or anyone who plays or sings, encounter a peak experience or
flow state, they typically enjoy the following:

• complete focus, involvement, or engagement
• a sense of ecstasy
• deep inner clarity
• confidence that they have the skill to master the activity
• a sense of serenity, with no concerns
• timelessness, thorough focus on the moment, and a sense of being part
  of something larger
• intrinsic motivation that whatever creates flow is rewarding on its own

One of Csikszentmihalyi's research subjects was a composer who described
his experience creating music:

You are in an ecstatic state to such a point that you feel as though you almost don't exist. I have experienced this time and again. My hand feels devoid of myself, and I have nothing to do with what is happening. I just sit there watching it in awe and wonderment. And (the music) just flows out of itself (http://www.ted.com/talks/mihaly_csikszentmihalyi_on_flow?language=en).

While musicians do not always experience expansive joy, this man achieved an extreme state of flow when composing music. The good news is that one does not have to be an expert to experience flow. In fact, it is possible for almost anyone to reach this extraordinary state. But activities that produce the greatest flow are generally challenging, and require

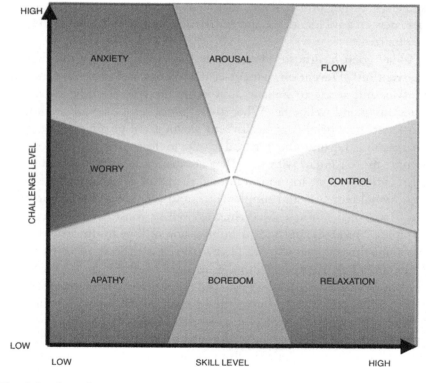

Fig. 2.2 Flow chart

a high degree of skill. Figure 2.2 displays a chart of psychological states, based on level of challenge and skill.

As shown, activities that require low skill and low challenge, such as a beginner's practice of the C scale on a piano, can reap apathy. Playing a piece that is more challenging can produce anxiety for the amateur musician. But after practicing and attaining greater skill, it may become boring to play that piece again. Performing a very difficult piece that requires just the right level of skill for mastery is the recipe for maximum flow.

It follows that when music therapists teach their clients new music skills and challenge them to use their creativity, they are greatly facilitating the flow of flow. (Flow is as flow does!) Under ideal conditions, this sort of optimal experience breeds a state of holistic wellbeing. Rather than existing solely in their roles as invalids, "inpatients" can spend time in the hospital focused on becoming "composers," "improvisers," or "singers." As they pursue their musical and creative talents, they explore these new creative identities, and experience unexpected benefits to being hospitalized.

Today good healthcare means more than pills, surgery, and medical interventions. Prevention, patient-centered compassionate care, healthy lifestyle, and access to holistic approaches are contributing to optimal functioning and wellbeing. When these forces combine with traditional treatment, new heights of health and wellness are possible. Consumers are reaching beyond the medical clinic to learn healthy habits, and become more content with life. They are demanding services and insurance reimbursement for nontraditional therapies like acupuncture, massage, herbal remedies and supplements, and treatments from Ayurvedic and Traditional Chinese Medicine, as well as music and creative arts therapies. Music therapy adds the dimension of flow to the goal of treatment, moving people who are ill toward self-actualization or transcendence and a new, creative identity. As medical science increases longevity, or *quantity* of life, music therapists and other holistic partners are aiding *quality* of life. Meanwhile, the medical community is procuring scientific evidence to support therapies with roots in ancient or Eastern traditions that are now the basis for the evolving field of integrative medicine. As clients learn and practice mindfulness meditation, yoga, the arts, and many other creative healing modalities, they are also capable of reaching new levels of potential.

Although Sam was a frail child, he became a strong and healthy adult. He ate fresh, organic food, and worked out regularly. He weaned himself off the steroids and pharmaceuticals that treated his asthma and eczema, and took Chinese herbs in their place. He worked and played with passion and gumption. In addition to meditation and yoga, his daily routine included a stop at his local café, where he held court at a back table for whoever needed to talk or be heard. He listened to great music of many genres, and continued to create graphic designs. While he left his trumpet behind, he studied piano and kept a keyboard handy for musical experimentation to stir his creativity. While on a path to becoming a healer, he was able to achieve an optimal state of health and wellness.

Sam's experience helps us to understand that, while we cannot always be healthy, we can become well. The mind and spirit affect the body dramatically, and may be responsible for the sense of wellbeing that can arise even as the body falters. The dynamic connections between mind, body, and spirit are investigated in the next chapter as we examine an integrated model of medicine, health, and empowerment. Let us now explore the vocabulary of psychology, neurology, and immunology to further allow us to view mechanisms that underlie the impact of music and music therapy upon the mind, body, and spirit, and ultimately, our health and wellness.

3

Integration: Medicine, Health, and Empowerment

Sam was not an artist. As a child, his doodles and drawings rarely made it to the refrigerator door, while his two sisters' artistic marvels were mounted regularly. It wasn't that he lacked talent. He never took much interest in art, choosing theater, piano, and trumpet as his creative outlets. So when he decided that he would attend art school for college, it came as a shock. But he had a goal: He revealed that he had a plan to build a Healing Empowerment Center, and attending art school would help him develop the skills to do so. He enrolled in the Massachusetts College of Art summer program to develop a portfolio, applied to 18 art colleges, and was accepted to all of them. Sam chose the program in Interior Architecture at Parsons The New School for Design, and began developing his proposal for a thesis on a healing space. He wrote:

> I propose to design and build a Healing Empowerment Center. This will be a metaphysical clinic founded upon a true synthesis of Eastern and Western wisdom. Rather than generate dependent victims of health mythology, the center will utilize a dynamic model of integrated holistic therapies based on power and responsibility from within. It is the goal of this center to give people back to themselves by helping them to build consciousness and create their lives anew.

© The Editor(s) (if applicable) and The Author(s) 2016
S.B. Hanser, *Integrative Health through Music Therapy*,
DOI 10.1057/978-1-137-38477-5_3

The mission:

> To provide resources, education, direct service, and support to those who wish to reclaim their power in creating their lives, day by day, breath by breath, lifetime by lifetime.
>
> To support clients in taking back their ability to heal themselves and the world in which they live through drawing upon power and responsibility from within (Samuel Hanser, 2004, p. 13).

Sam's goals seemed ahead of their time, but there is a revolution afoot. Traditional ways of practicing Western, or allopathic, medicine are being challenged on all fronts. Burgeoning scientific evidence is documenting the impact of age-old Eastern and Ayurvedic approaches to health, such as acupuncture, yoga, and meditation. The connection between mind and body has been soldered through major research investigations over the past several decades. Consumers are demanding new models of healthcare that treat the whole person and take into account health disparities in accessing treatment options. "Heal" is not the four-letter word that it once was in the established healthcare community. People are reclaiming their abilities to help themselves by changing their lifestyles and sampling unconventional forms of treatment.

This revolution became fully charged when individuals, particularly those with incurable or untreatable illnesses, turned to alternative therapies. It was difficult to establish the safety and efficacy of approaches that had not undergone the extensive scrutiny of medical science, so these consumers could be at significant risk. Yet many of them discovered unconventional treatments that helped or healed them. In 1992, the Office of Alternative Medicine (OAM) was founded in the National Institutes of Health (NIH) in the USA, in order to study and inform the public about these increasingly popular medical treatments. Indeed, there were many benign remedies, such as relaxation training and exercise, that clearly aided symptom relief and pain management. Other more invasive treatments, like acupuncture and Chinese herbs, required more supportive research before they could be used by consumers. These interventions and many more like them, used side by side with conventional medical treatment, became known as complementary therapies. The establishment of the National Center for Complementary and Alternative Medicine (NCCAM) under the auspices of the NIH came about in 1998, and in December 2014, its new title became the National Center for Complementary and Integrative Health (NCCIH). The modification of the term from "Alternative Medicine" to "Integrative Health" exemplified the value of an amalgamation of healthcare practices as an integrated whole, in order to improve overall health. There is also a Consortium of Academic Health Centers for Integrative Medicine that currently includes 57 established medical schools or centers, several of which offer music therapy services.

Integrative medicine (IM) is an evidence-based approach that includes nontraditional therapies in a comprehensive treatment plan to heal the whole person, not just the diseased part of a patient. It calls upon the relationship between physician, professional team, and person to form a community that can attend to the person's needs. Its practices are based on the complex interactions of mind, body, and spirit. It takes into consideration lifestyle as well as treatment. Integrative health (IH) emphasizes a wider field of wellness, lifestyle, health promotion, prevention, and community-based programs outside of medical establishments.

IH is now fueling the healthcare revolution with impressive data that support the natural healing power of the whole person, not just a symptom or diagnosis. In her book, *Holistic Pain Relief*, Dr. Heather Tick (2013) defines IM:

> IM focuses on the patient and not the problem. Practitioners of IM spend more time listening to patients' concerns and pay attention to factors affecting the mind, body, and spirit. They recognize that medicine rarely "fixes" what ails the patient. They focus on healing, which allopathic medicine often ignores. Let's not forget, there is a lifelong natural inclination of the body to heal. This health-focused approach affects the questions we ask of our researchers and colleagues, and it changes the conversation with our patients (p. 22).

With more and more healthcare practitioners professing IM and IH as their philosophy of care, services like music therapy are becoming integral to the model. Because there is strong evidence that the mind, intention, and belief act on the body, these factors can also affect immunological functioning. It stands to reason that because music affects the mind in similar and even more complex ways, music can also affect health. The field of psychoneuroimmunology (PNI) is demonstrating precisely how this phenomenon works.

The Counterpoint of Connection

The roots of PNI and the mind-body connection were planted long ago. In *The Cure Within: A History of Mind-Body Medicine*, Anne Harrington (2009) follows healing narratives from ancient stories of possession by demons to modern-day theories on the meaning of brain wave fluctuations in meditators. In the early history of medicine, Hippocrates (460–370 BCE) rejected notions of magic and the supernatural, and professed that the goal of medicine was to bring harmony and balance to the four humors of man: blood, phlegm, black bile, and yellow bile. Aristotle (384–322 BCE) proclaimed that both physical and spiritual elements were relevant to the human condition.

Eugene Taylor (2002) catalogued the strong lineage of physiologists, physicians, philosophers, and others who have forged bonds between disciplines to understand these mechanisms. Notable figures included a line of Harvard Medical School (HMS) professors, beginning with its dean and professor, Oliver Wendell Holmes (1809–1894), who looked at disease recovery, as opposed to disease itself. William James (1842–1910) was a medical doctor who trained at HMS, but moved on to specialize in the fields of philosophy and psychology. He is known for linking emotions with activity of the autonomic nervous system. In 1915, Walter Cannon developed the theory of the fight-flight response, connecting psychology, neurology, and immunology in his explanation of the response to threat. The Cannon-Bard Theory, developed with Cannon's graduate student Phillip Bard, challenged James' findings by pointing out that emotions can occur independent of physiological arousal. Then, in 1956, Hans Selye defined the General Adaptation Syndrome, and used the metallurgic term "stress" to denote the body's response to a demand. Selye's theories contributed significantly to the new interdisciplinary field of psychoneuroimmunology by demonstrating the impact of stress on the organism. By then, psychosomatic medicine was in vogue, popularized by Freud's theories, and became widely accepted by the public and medical community alike. In the next generation of HMS medical mentors, physiologist A. Clifford Barger (1917–1996) found a direct relationship between hypertension and coronary heart disease. He taught cardiologist Herbert Benson (b. 1935), who is now Director Emeritus of the Benson-Henry Institute for Mind-Body Medicine.

Meanwhile, neurologists and brain scientists were identifying how the mind and brain interacted. Some highlights include: MacLean's discovery of the direct connections between the sensation of emotions and the brain's limbic system and cortex, in 1958; Fischer's brain maps of states of ecstasy, in 1971; Ader's finding that behavioral, neural, and endocrine factors affected the immune system, in 1981; and Stefano and colleagues' investigation of the neurophysiology of the placebo effect, in 2001.

In the 1970s, the popular press began to translate this research into accessible language that could inform consumers about how they could call upon their own resources and the principles of the mind-body connection to heal. Biofeedback was shown to be an effective way that people could control their own physiology. Jogging was promoted as a healthy sport to combat heart disease. As communications and relations between the USA, Russia, Eastern Europe, and Asia warmed, Westerners learned about how the rest of the world practiced medicine and healing. In 1972, President Nixon's trip to China spurred interest in acupuncture and herbal medicine, while yoga studios began to appear in storefronts. In 1975, with the publication of his best-selling book, *The Relaxation Response*, Benson (with Klipper) birthed a progeny of popular literature and a research agenda on the impact of activities, such as meditation, that elicited the relaxation response. Norman Cousins, a highly respected political analyst who was diagnosed with ankylosing spondylitis, a type of arthritis that carries a poor prognosis and results in severe spinal pain, left the hospital to explore his own self-healing. In 1976, Cousins chronicled how he used positive thinking and laughter to cope successfully with this debilitating condition. In an article published in the *New England Journal of Medicine*, entitled "Anatomy of an Illness (as Perceived by the Patient)," he reflected on the impact of turning his attention away from symptoms and toward joke books and television comedies. Impressive research on the influence of mind-body practices on heart rate, brain activity, metabolism, and most recently, genomic activity, continues to be documented in fruitful scientific investigations.

Indeed, positive mental attitude was seen as the next panacea. Research on the placebo effect, from the Latin for "I will please," offered convincing evidence that an inert substance could exert healing properties on a person who believed strongly in its medicinal value, especially when prescribed by a trusted physician. A *Journal of the American Medical Association* article by Brody and Miller (2011) suggested ways to exploit the power of the placebo effect in ethical clinical practice. Today all randomized controlled trials are strongly urged to include control groups that use placebos.

Meanwhile, yoga was gaining popularity in the West, and meditation was introduced as an accessible strategy for coping with the stresses of everyday life. In 1979, Jon Kabat-Zinn developed a set of practices known as mindfulness-based stress reduction (MBSR) at the University of Massachusetts Medical Center, where he and colleagues taught patients at the hospital how to manage stress through meditation. This technique has now been implemented in many centers of integrative medicine, and has been shown to be extremely effective in dealing with a wide variety of medical conditions.

Surgeon Bernie Siegel's 1986 book, *Love, Medicine and Miracles,* urged cancer survivors to heal by investigating the meaning of illness in their lives and the meaning of life. Today there are entire sections in bookstores devoted to mind-body techniques and healing. Benson's book with William Proctor, *Relaxation Revolution* (2010), offers perspective on current findings:

> Your mind can actually alter your genetic activity—in ways that may significantly improve your health and heal you of a number of diseases…We now know that your mind can help control your body—all the way down to your genes' activity—because scientific research has proven this to be the case. Furthermore, your mind can influence your body for good or ill, and you can learn how to effect beneficial changes and achieve better health… Ironically, these genetic findings help bring back into play certain tradi-

tional mind body practices—such as meditation, yoga, prayer, repetitive-worship music and rituals, and seemingly simplistic relaxation techniques—that modern mainstream medicine has dismissed or neglected as superstitions or relics of the unscientific past. Many ancient practices and rituals have been rejected by modern science, only to be resurrected from the grave by that same science (p. 20).

The Psychoneuro...of Music

The threads of psychology, neurology, and immunology that weave theories of psychoneuroimmunology (PNI) are complex and fascinating. Owing to technological advances that enable scientists to examine the brain more thoroughly and noninvasively, new cross-disciplinary specialties, such as psychoneuroendocrinology and neurocardiology, are inventing new vocabularies and solutions to scientific enigmas and medical conditions. A more intense look at PNI research reveals what is known and yet to be known that will explain the impact of music therapy.

Music therapists are perhaps most familiar with the psychological aspects of music therapy, as the literature is replete with studies that show significant effects of music on such varied states as cognition, awareness, self-esteem, mood, motivation, and arousal, as well as improvement in clinical outcomes in treating conditions such as anxiety, relaxation, depression, distress, and pain. The *Handbook of Music and Emotion: Theory, Research, Applications* (Juslin & Sloboda, 2010) and *Music, Health, and Wellbeing* (Macdonald, Kreutz, & Mitchell, 2012) provide comprehensive perspectives on the various roles that music can play. Neurologic music therapy (NMT) has firmly established clinical protocols that address the relationship of musical interventions to complex neurologic functions and conditions, thanks to pioneering research by Michael Thaut (2005). In one of many investigations in this robust line of research, Thaut et al. (2009) documented improvement in executive function and emotional adjustment in individuals who underwent NMT after suffering from traumatic brain injury.

The research relative to the influence of music on immune function is likewise mounting, but more challenging to interpret. The autonomic nervous system provides a model to study the mechanisms of psychoneuroimmunology because the sympathetic autonomic nervous system (SANS) is the home of arousal, the fight-flight response, and its associated hypervigilance, elevated heart rate and blood pressure, muscle tension, and activation of neurochemicals such as norepinephrine. At the other end of the continuum, the parasympathetic autonomic nervous system (PANS) activity is initiated with rest, relaxation, and recuperation, and results in diminished heart rate and blood pressure, and release of acetylcholine.

SANS and PANS teeter in my daily life as I begin a typical workday. As the number of e-mails on my desktop multiplies, I begin to feel like each entry elevates my blood pressure by a notch. By mid-day, I realize that I must complete end-of-day reports, but I have appointments all afternoon that prevent me from completing them. I have to leave the office early in order to run some errands, and make dinner for the family. My SANS is working overtime. By 5 p.m., my heart is racing, my palms are sweaty, and it is hard to catch my breath. I feel sick to my stomach because the SANS is sending blood to my muscles to prepare the fight-flight-freeze response, but muscles cannot help relieve the kind of stress I am under. This sympathetic arousal and its ensuing circulation to the extremities rob my vital organs of blood, but how can I activate my PANS? It is not until I return home and clear the dinner dishes that I can sit down, listen to some music, and clear my head of the pressures and missed deadlines. PANS comes to the rescue at last. I am breathing deeply, my circulation is aiding digestion, and I feel more relaxed. It is too early to sleep, so I decide to play the piano for a while. As I play the pieces that I know well and can play without thinking, my autonomic nervous system is coming into balance. I achieve homeostasis, a pleasant activation of energy and contentment, mastery, and calm. I am in my favorite flow state.

Chronic activation of the SANS takes its toll and results in illness, while PANS activity can allow for recovery. Benson's relaxation response has been shown to elicit the PANS, and I know that listening to music that has personal meaning to me has the same effect. Researchers are also looking to PNI mechanisms to document and explain the effect of music and music therapy on various types of stress.

Health psychologist Dr. Ann Webster is an instructor in medicine at Harvard Medical School, and has worked side by side with Dr. Benson at the Institute for Mind-Body Medicine at Massachusetts General Hospital. She said this about the benefits of music therapy:

> Music is meditation. It calms down the sympathetic nervous system. Because it reduces stress, it boosts immune functioning, improves mood, and regulates blood pressure. Music therapy is a much more interactive way to elicit the relaxation response. When people use a meditation CD to relax, it's one size fits all. People enjoy listening to music, but what one person might resonate with, another person won't. So, with music therapy, the process is highly individualized. Music helps people get through scary medical procedures, and it's very spiritual. Music can often allow one to feel connected to a higher power (personal communication, March, 2015).

Dr. Webster has witnessed music therapy in action. Her observations include the spiritual in addition to the psychoneuroimmunological outcomes of music therapy interventions.

In "The Neurochemistry of Music," Mona Lisa Chanda and Daniel Levitin (2013) assert that engaging in musical experiences has an impact on health through four major neurochemical pathways:

1. Music results in pleasure, reward, and motivation, as documented by the release of dopamine and various opioids, or peptides, that are endogenously produced in the body.
2. Music affects stress and arousal through demonstrated changes in stress hormones, like cortisol, adrenocorticotropic hormone (ACTH), and corticotrophin-releasing hormone (CRH).
3. Participation in musical activities initiates release of serotonin and neuropeptides, including beta-endorphins and alpha-melanocyte stimulating hormones that work on the immune system.
4. Changes in oxytocin as a function of music reveal a sense of belonging and social affiliation.

There are three primary neurological axes, or interconnected areas of the brain, that cooperate to determine how the individual will react to stressors: the hypothalamic-pituitary-adrenocortical axis (HPA), the endogenous opioid system, and the sympatho-adrenomedullary system. These pathways work in concert, resulting in a multitude of specific and unique responses to music and musical involvement.

Chanda and Levitin pose an interesting theory:

> (T)he brainstem interprets music as signals related to survival, and then initiates corresponding physiological responses. For example, music commonly classified as "stimulating" mimics sounds in nature, such as the alarm calls of many species, that signal potentially important events (e.g., loud sounds with sudden onset and a repeating short motif). Interestingly, positive affect and reward anticipation have also been associated with high frequency short motif calls (e.g., Knutsen et al., 2002). This, in turn, heightens sympathetic arousal (heart rate, pulse, skin conductance, and breathing). By contrast, "relaxing" music mimics soothing natural sounds such as maternal vocalizations, purring and cooing (soft, low-pitched sounds with a gradual amplitude envelope), which decrease sympathetic arousal (p. 186).

Fancourt, Ockelford, & Belai, (2014) performed a systematic review of 63 studies on the psychoneuroimmunology of music over the last two decades. This research links psychological reports and vital signs with the release of various neurotransmitters, cytokines, lymphocytes, immunoglobulins, and hormones. Unfortunately, the authors found a dearth of explanations as to the mechanisms underlying the response to music, and criticized the extant research on its lack of specificity in types of music and musical participation. They point out that the endocrine, immune, central nervous, and autonomic nervous systems are at the nucleus of a web that is affected by external stimuli, such as stress and music. Both stimuli can lead to physiological and psychological arousal that influences these central human systems. It will be up to future researchers to continue to investigate the complex interactions between biomarkers in order to untangle the specific psychological, neurological, and immunological responses to music.

Integrative Music Therapy

Dr. Joanne Loewy is the Director of the Louis Armstrong Center for Music and Medicine, and Associate Professor of the Icahn School of Medicine at Mount Sinai Medical Center. She leads a team of music therapists in clinical services and research throughout the center. She commented on the role of music therapy in integrative medicine:

> The music therapist can gain a sense of what might be usual and customary to the person's lifeworld which is distinctly different from what is brought out related to the hospitalization. Through a live music experience, music therapy as integrative medicine can fuel life energy that accesses resilience and sparks hope, or conversely provides permission to let go.
>
> Music can ignite memories and situations distinctly related to a person's belief system. In building trust within a dynamic music psychotherapy relationship, we provide a platform for the integration of culture, history, and clinical inference. (Loewy, personal communication).

Supported by research on the potential health benefits of music, music therapists have a strong case for the integration of music therapy into healthcare services and systems. An integrative approach to health will include those services and interventions that have an evidence base to support their clinical outcomes, and those that demonstrate efficacy will thrive and mature.

The Institute for Healthcare Improvement, a Cambridge, Massachusetts firm dedicated to worldwide resources for enhancing health services, is pursuing a triple aim that they believe will enhance healthcare. These goals include: improving patient satisfaction; managing symptoms, such as pain; and reducing healthcare costs through decreasing length of stay and need for medication (http://www.ihi.org/Engage/Initiatives/TripleAim). I am fortunate to be part of a research team at Boston Medical Center that is examining the outcomes of three conditions: music therapy, massage therapy, and usual care, on these outcomes. This project has recruited 90 patients, and the positive response from medical staff is already supporting the feasibility of introducing these services on the Family Medicine Unit.

This research has enabled me to work with Dr. Robert Saper, Director of Integrative Medicine and Health Disparities at Boston Medical Center. Because Dr. Saper is also the Attending Physician on the Family Medicine Unit, he has been able to witness the benefits of music therapy and massage therapy firsthand. At the conclusion of daily board rounds that chart each patient's status, he escorts the medical residents to a consultation room and guides them in a meditation exercise to prepare them to meet patients on the unit. One day, after seeing a particularly agitated and confused patient, the medical residents shook their heads in frustration at this man's inability to cooperate and comply with the prescribed treatment. Dr. Saper noted the symptoms and knew the immediate remedy. He promptly ordered music therapy.

4

Holistic Healing

Healing is not an ability reserved for the educated elite or specially gifted but rather an innate capacity available to us all. Everyone is a healer.

Healing is an experience of re-member-ance. By shedding the light of our consciousness on those aspects of our Self that we have forgotten we bring ourselves to a place of at-one-ment. Healing is thus a re-cognition (reknowing) of our oneness.

All that is required for healing to take place is a loving space where we can be fully and completely ourselves. Such a space becomes especially potent when it is supported by a person willing to understand and accept our process exactly as it is. When a practitioner and client engage this space with a posture of receptivity, healing occurs naturally (Samuel Hanser, 2004, p. 16).

Sam advocated for the power of self-healing, and articulated some of the conditions that would facilitate the healing process. Sam believed that really knowing or "re-member-ing," as he called it, leads to the truth. According to Sam, finding the true self, which is often in itself an act of remembrance, is a vital part of healing. He believed that everything we need is within us waiting to be discovered and realized. In *Many Blessings: The Remembrance of One*, he said,

© The Editor(s) (if applicable) and The Author(s) 2016
S.B. Hanser, *Integrative Health through Music Therapy*,
DOI 10.1057/978-1-137-38477-5_4

Only you can decide the truth for yourself. In fact, you already know every-thing you'll ever need to know. That is why I call this process re-member-ing. It really is a putting back together of the Self. There are many paths to the truth but the truth is one. And you must walk your own path for only yours can lead you to this truth (Samuel Hanser, 2010, p. 1).

Sam's notion of re-member-ing is not new. It was also referred to mil-lennia before in Plato's *Dialogues* (399–387 BCE). Plato presents the concept of *anamnesis*, the idea that all learning is a rediscovery of what we already know. Plato's student, Socrates (469–399 BCE), further devel-oped this ideology, claiming that the soul is immortal and eternal, and through reincarnation, we reclaim knowledge that was forgotten through the trauma of birth. This thinking is expressed in the Socratic method of teaching, one that questions the student rather than revealing the answers. The student works to retrieve the knowledge that is already held within. In much the same way, everyone already has what they need to heal themselves.

Over thousands of years, great philosophers have formed taxono-mies that attempt to create a sense of order in the world and to under-stand the relationships between natural and supernatural phenomena. Based on Plato's foundations and the *scala naturae* (scale of nature) of Aristotle, the Great Chain of Being of the NeoPlatonists presents a hier-archical structure. With the omnipotent being of God at the apex, angels appear at the next level, followed by humanity, animals, plants, and min-erals (see Fig. 4.1). Contemporary philosopher Ken Wilbur bases his integral approach on this Great Chain of Being, articulating a holistic view of human consciousness through the levels of matter, body, mind, soul, and spirit. His hierarchy holds absolute spirit at the apex, followed by the spiritual, existential, mental, emotional, and physical domains. He contends that in order for self-understanding to take place, one must be fully aware of each of these levels of being. One then differentiates, transcends, and integrates what is known at each stage in a process of transpersonal analysis in order to achieve optimal health (Wilbur, 1984).

In *The Inward Arc: Healing in Psychotherapy and Spirituality*, Frances Vaughan (1995) discusses a similar transpersonal journey toward whole-ness. She believes that when a person takes responsibility for self-healing,

Fig. 4.1   Great Chain of Being

that person can expand his or her awareness through personal reflection in each of the physical, emotional, mental, existential, and spiritual realms. In order to maintain emotional health, for example, Vaughan suggests that one must acknowledge and fully experience the feelings that bubble up at any time, be able to communicate them verbally or nonverbally, and then learn how to consciously expand them and release them.

To the music therapist, this is a recognizable process. We are accustomed to guiding individuals as they become receptive to a particular piece of music, and we encourage them, through discussion, to process any associated feelings that come up. The music therapist can then help the individual to discharge these feelings through active music making or improvisation.

Healing from the Heart

In *Freedom from Anxiety: A Holistic Approach to Emotional Well-being*, Marcey Shapiro and Barbara Vivino (2014) express their theory:

> All real healing is self-healing. True healing, though, may look different than a medical cure. Conventional medicine offers many simple and elaborate "band-aids," but these heroic efforts are almost exclusively aimed at managing symptoms rather than examining or shifting underlying causes. Healing, on the other hand, requires a transformation of consciousness, an "ah-ha" moment where we understand ourselves anew. Healing is entirely an "inside job" providing a fresh comprehension that shifts our experience of reality.
>
> All healing is inevitably heart-centered. It is through our heart that we connect with our inner divinity, sense of knowing, and deepest wisdom. As we nourish our heart space, we come to an increased sense of unity with our inner being. We allow the wisdom of the heart to guide us in the direction of wholeness (p. xvii).

Interestingly, there is a research foundation devoted to the wisdom of the heart. The HeartMath Institute (HMI) in Natick, Massachusetts, has been researching potential methods for managing stress and engendering optimism and fulfillment through bridging heart and mind (http://www. heartmath.org). Toward its mission to establish "heart-brain coherence," HMI is examining the relationship between cognition and emotions, specifically through the cardiovascular and nervous systems, alongside the specialty of clinical neurocardiology (http://intra.ninds.nih.gov/Lab. asp?Org_ID=82).

Meanwhile, noninvasive measures, such as heart rate variability (HRV), are providing clues for balancing the autonomic nervous system, and helping bring the body to homeostasis. HRV is a measure of sympathetic nervous system activity, and a lower HRV is a predictor of mortality associated with heart arrhythmias or cardiac disease. Results from studies of the impact of music listening and music therapy on HRV are varied, but promising (Bernardi et al., 2009; Chuang et al., 2011; Iwanaga, Kobayashi, & Kawasaki, 2005; Orman, 2011; Roque et al., 2013; Umemura & Honda, 1998).

Healing from the Numinous

Psychologist Carl G. Jung knew one of the keys to the experience of homeostasis and wholeness. He called it the "numinous," defining the term as something appealing to the highest standard of aesthetics, and that holds mystery and awe, as well as the expansiveness of divine presence. He claimed that numinous experiences, such as engagement in and creation of music and art, held great potential for healing (Jung & Franz, 1964). Thus, the sensations that are elicited by the most divine music and extraordinary creative acts can transcend normal expectations, accessing a spirit that is capable of releasing the inner healer.

In *The Healer Within* (1997), author Roger Jahnke recommends some "powerful medicine" to maximize the ability to heal one's self. The first is choosing to think positively and letting go of worry and the mentality of victimhood. Jahnke's assertion has been supported by research by Segerstrom and Sephton (2010) linking optimistic thinking to improved immune function. Jahnke also suggests that one should enhance one's lifestyle with things that feed the mind, body, and soul, such as good nutrition, exercise, play, and spiritual practices. A wide array of studies support this, including a study of 20,000 men and women in Norfolk, United Kingdom. Khaw et al. (2008) found four healthy behaviors (avoidance of smoking, moderate alcohol intake, physical activity, and a diet inclusive of fruits and vegetables) to be predictive of significantly greater longevity. Jahnke also advocates for some of the ancient methods that enhance health, such as meditation, deep relaxation, breath work, gentle movement, and self-applied massage. As you will see in subsequent chapters, music can enhance each of these practices and also provide a creative lifestyle choice. Jahnke reminds us of the ancient derivation of some of these "new" ideas, by quoting the Yellow Emperor of China:

> The physician who teaches people to sustain their health is the superior physician. The physician who waits to treat people until after their health is lost is considered to be inferior. This is like waiting until one's family is starving to begin to plant seeds in the garden. —Yellow Emperor's *Classic on Internal Medicine*, 350 BCE (p. 8)

The Terrain of Holistic Healing

Traditional Chinese Medicine

When invited by Professor Tian Gao to lecture at the Central Conservatory of Music in Beijing, China, I was surprised to find extensive course offerings in the foundations of Western music as well as traditional Chinese music. It was 2006, and by then, a true integration of Eastern and Western music was possible, thanks to collaborations forged by this excellent conservatory with notable patrons such as violinist Itzhak Perlman.

Knowing my interest in methods of healing, Professor Ming Ming Liu took me on a tour of the Traditional Chinese Medicine (TCM) hospital, where I witnessed lines of people waiting to have their pulses taken, tongues examined, personal histories revealed, and prescriptions of herbs filled. I observed treatments of acupuncture, moxibustion, and cupping. There was no Western medicine here, but Professor Liu said that the Chinese people, particularly the younger generation, were increasingly rejecting traditional forms of medicine in favor of the Western clinics and new technologies that promised new therapies and cures. She was anxious to show me the newly built Children's Hospital. There, only a small suite of rooms was devoted to traditional methods, and the rest of the hospital was much like the institutions I knew in the USA. The neonatal intensive care unit boasted the most contemporary and expensive incubators anywhere, including a sophisticated screening room where parents could see their babies via video projection, avoiding the contact that might introduce germs into the sterile nursery. Their emphasis on modernization and technology could hardly have been more extreme.

Examining the political history of China added perspective on the confusing interplay of Eastern and Western approaches that I encountered at each healthcare setting. During the Qing Dynasty in the 1800s, while borders were closed to external affairs, Chinese leaders prized the past and mistrusted the modern. But when Sun Yat-sen and Kuomintang (the Nationalist Party) took over the Republic of China in 1911, and later under Chiang Kai-shek (1928–1949), a reversal of this philosophy resulted in great interest in Western culture, medicine, and industry. The party went to such extremes as to prohibit the standard textbook of modern Chinese history, and, by 1928, the practice of Traditional Chinese Medicine was banned in hospitals and clinics. It was this same year that Alexander Fleming discovered penicillin, and, clearly, Western medicine was making great strides in fighting infection among other impressive advances in treating illness.

The second Sino-Japanese war intervened in 1937, and, by the end of World War II, rising tensions led to the Chinese Revolution of 1949 and the formation of the People's Republic of China under the leadership of Mao Zedung. Meanwhile, the Chinese people were suffering the consequences of war, poverty, sickness, and, eventually, famine during Chairman Mao's "Great Leap Forward" in 1958–1963. Mao's failure resulted in drastic measures, and, in 1966, he instituted the Cultural Revolution as an attempt to regain control and rid China of all things that represented its past. He started a campaign to destroy the "Four Olds," consisting of old customs, culture, ideas, and habits. Medical schools and music conservatories closed, including the Central Conservatory, many scholars and artists were imprisoned, and links to learning Chinese traditions were severed. With the reopening of these institutions in 1976, new discoveries enabled China to compete in this new world of massive change and development. But as a result, manuscripts of traditional practices that were not approved by the Communist Party were destroyed, and only those treatises that were consistent with contemporary thought and the "New China" were included in curricula. It is ironic that the integrative medicine and health movement in the West is championing efforts to preserve traditional Eastern medicine. Unfortunately, the theories that survive are those that are supported by Western scientists and that fit biomedical research models, while more esoteric texts have been lost.

It is estimated that sometime during the Han Dynasty, between 206 BCE and AD 220, the great Yellow Emperor Huang Di wrote the classic book of Chinese medicine, *Neijing Suwen Lingshu*, which describes the original "integral way" to live life and be in harmony with nature. It was also during this time that Taoist philosophy was recorded in such timeless manuscripts as the *Tao Te Ching* and *I Ching*.

From a Western perspective, TCM may appear to be the use of acupuncture, herbs, and a series of techniques that have passed the test of time, but this perception is incorrect. While these modalities may be part of treatment, the practice of TCM is actually a comprehensive system that integrates the laws of the universe and environmental influences, such as seasons, climate, and geography, into the intricate balance of human functioning.

*Niejing*內經 is divided into the *Suwen* 素問 (*Questions of Organic and Fundamental Nature*), and the *Lingshu* 靈樞 or *Zhen Jing* 針經 (*Classic of Acupuncture*).

In a new translation of the text, Maoshing Ni (1995) defines the essence of TCM:

> Health and well-being can be achieved only by remaining centered in spirit, guarding against the squandering of energy, promoting the constant flow of qi and blood, maintaining harmonious balance of yin and yang, adapting to the changing seasonal and yearly macrocosmic influences, and nourishing one's self preventively. This is the way to a long and happy life (p. xiii).

Here *qi* (or chi) refers to the universal life force and vital, metaphysical energy that flows through the body. Various types of qi circulate out from different parts of the body:

* *jin qi* from the kidneys
* *shen qi* from the heart
* *go qi* in the digestive system
* *do qi* from the lungs
* *wei qi*, a protective force that fights environmental stressors.

Within Traditional Chinese Medicine and philosophy, optimal health depends on the delicate balance of two complementary inner forces, the feminine *yin* and masculine *yang*. These invisible and dynamic influences contribute to health and illness, and are affected by social, emotional, and spiritual factors, in addition to nature and environment. According to the Taoist alchemy, Traditional Chinese Medicine draws its foundation from the *Five Elements*, or *Wu Xing* (五行). These make up all life, and describe the interrelationships between phenomena. Certain characteristics are attributed to each element, including directions, seasons, colors, systems of the body, and others. The elements represent:
* *Gong*宫, earth, the center, core, yellow, digestion
* *Zhi* 徵, fire, south, summer, red, heart and central nervous system
* *Shang* 商, metal, west, autumn, white, lungs
* *Yu* 羽, water, north, winter, black, kidneys
* *Jue* 角, air, east, spring, blue, liver, blood flow.

The interactions between *these* attributes offer a template for diagnosis and treatment, and affect the mind, body, and spirit.

Neijing Suwen Lingshu is devoted purely to acupuncture, with a description of a vast network of *meridians*, or energy channels, that thread through the body. Qi flows through these channels through lines of yin (for heart, lung, and pericardium) or yang (for large and small intestine, and "triple heater," the temperature meridian), but the entire web of meridians is extensive (see Kaptchuk, 2000 for a thorough rendering). To treat an imbalance in the flow of energy, the acupuncturist inserts thin needles at specific points on the skin, known as *nodes*.

Because of its specific protocols, acupuncture is perhaps more amenable to scientific research than other aspects of Traditional Chinese Medicine. As a result, it has been studied rather extensively in the West. Experiments have shown that there is a direct relationship between these acupuncture points to sites of convergence in the planes of connective tissue that interlace through the body. Furthermore, it has been shown that acupuncture needles may produce changes at the cellular level and play "a key role in the integration of several physiological functions with ambient levels of mechanical stress" (Langevin & Yandow, 2002, p. 263). The literature reveals an impressive body of experimentation to support the efficacy of acupuncture, with particularly strong evidence for postoperative pain, chemotherapy side effects, headache, low back pain, alcohol dependence, and paralysis due to stroke (Mayer, 2000; NIH Consensus Conference, 1998).

Obviously, this meta-system differs significantly from Western, or allopathic, medicine's emphasis on treating specific symptoms, organs, and diseases. However, with mounting evidence for both its outcomes and mechanisms, TCM (particularly its tangible treatments like acupuncture and herbology) is achieving respect as an important guide and partner in integrative medicine and healthcare.

Ayurveda

For many years, I ached to venture to India to find the secrets of healing that Sam seemed to have understood so instinctively after he was initiated into Swami Rama's lineage of yoga, Vedanta, and Tantra practices. So, in 2012, when Dr. Sumathy Sundar asked me to visit the Chennai School of Music Therapy, I accepted with enthusiasm. Aware of my desire to meditate in the spiritual land of India, she took me to the Sri Ramakrishna Math, in the sacred Ramakrishnananda Mandapam in Mylapore. It was New Year's Day, and the neighboring crowds were being fed pungent curry out of large vats. Children circled and screamed, people chatted and ordered each other about, and tin plates clanged as I tried to gain my composure in this outdoor venue designed for contemplation. It was evident to me that going deeply inward was the only way to escape the cacophony. I meditated there as I have never before.

Three years later, I entered an ashram in Tamil Nadu, still seeking the healing energy of India. This time, I slowed my pace significantly and lived close to nature along with 20 fellow pilgrims, guided by Russill Paul, a gifted musician, monk, and native of Tamil Nadu. The ancient mantras we learned were meant to connect us with the 5000-year-old heritage of India and our own sense of the Divine in the temples of our bodies. Mantras are repeated words or phrases, from manas, the Sanskrit word for linear, thinking mind, and tram, to protect, to go across, to save or free. I found that these mantras captured my attention fully, and the effect was mesmerizing. When we stopped chanting, Paul instructed us to listen to the silence of our minds and focus on the breath entering and exiting our nostrils. Then we turned our bodies slowly in a circle, in the clock-wise direction for orbiting each temple we visited. I immediately recalled Sam's design of the Healing Empowerment Center. The center of Sam's proposed building had a central core, like the Native American sipapu, that is meant to be an entrance to the Divine. Sam said, "Organizing the building around a single focus creates a center of gravity that draws energy to it. Because all circulation is really circumambulation around this core, the simple act of walking through the building becomes a meditation itself. In this way, the practice of the building becomes an inescapable constant, a mantra as it were, as well as a map for the direction of energy to flow within those who place their focus on the center" (Samuel Hanser, 2004, p. 12). I imagined the Sufi dervishes and wild dancers of the tarantella, as I created my own very deliberate, circular movements. The slight dizziness did induce a trancelike state, and I felt a bit giddy. It was hard not to analyze and think, but after some practice, I merely enjoyed the dance and the chanting. I felt deliciously "in the moment," something I had been driven to achieve at home. I discovered the circular reasoning behind the experience. "Being" means being present, and "being present" means being aware of our inner experiences. Witnessing our inner experiences allows us to be ourselves—in other words, to be. It was then that I knew that there was something in these practices that I could bring back and share with people who are on their own journeys, whether their paths lead from illness to health or to inner discovery.

During my time at the ashram, I was also introduced to several sacred Hindu texts: excerpts from the *Vedas*, the *Bhagavad Gita*, and the *Upanishads*. I was honored that Russill read from Sam's book in between quoting the ancient scriptures. The teachings confirmed that Ayurveda is more than a form of medicine in India and that yoga is much, much more than the *asanas* that I performed faithfully back home.

Ayurveda is the *veda* (science or knowledge) of *ayur* (life), so its translation from the Sanskrit can be the "science of life" or "universal knowledge." Its precepts are drawn from ancient Hindu texts, the *Vedas*, which have been passed down from generation to generation orally over the past 5000 years. These most significant Hindu scriptures in Sanskrit are part of the *shruti* (hearing or listening) literature and are considered *apaurusheya* (composed by the Divine). *Smriti* (remembered) literature is the philosophy that is "remembered" transcendentally and interpreted by the *Rishis* (poets, seers), a sort of commentary on the divine *shruti*. Together these scriptures inform Hindu practices, from the earliest sources of knowledge to the later *Upanishads* (or *vedanta*, the end of the *Vedas*).

The *Vedas* are divided into four major parts: *Rig Veda, Yajur Veda, Sama Veda,* and *Atharva Veda*. Ayurveda is founded mainly in the *Rig Veda* and *Atharva Veda*. At some time between the fifth and second century BCE, the *Bhagavad Gita* was composed. This epic account of Arjuna's and Krishna's journey illustrates many Hindu principles, like *dharma*, one's purpose in life, and suggests ways to address questions of living through life's struggles. There are also more contemporary, practical medical textbooks, like the *Charaka Samhita* for internal medicine, dating back to about 1000 BCE, and *Ashtanga Hrdayam*, a compendium of known healing practices from about 1000 years ago.

Ayurveda's primary tenets that guide practice today include the *tridosha* (three imbalances): *vata, pitta,* and *kapha*. These dynamic energies sustain, support, or suppress the body's *functioning*, as necessary to bring it into balance. The *doshas* have particular functions in the mind and the body, and every person expresses a combination of these in a unique way. Individuals can assess their own constitutions as a ratio of the three *doshas*, and are required to adjust their diets and living habits accordingly.

As in TCM, there are five great elements in Ayurveda. Ayurveda's elements are the ones that are said to have created the universe. They are:

earth, fire, water, air, and ether, and each of the three *doshas* are composed of two primary elements. While the first four are material elements, ether is meant to represent the esoteric constituent that is beyond the material world. The human body is made up of *saptadhatus* (seven tissues) that refer to various elements: *chyle* (lymphatic fluid), blood, muscle, marrow, bone, brain/spinal cord, and sperm/ovum, each with its own special treatment. *Ojas* refers to the vitality or immunity of the body that can be enhanced through lifestyle and diet, as prescribed by Ayurvedic texts. The *ashtangas* (eight parts) include a medical textbook for treating the *saptadhatus*, as well as various diseases and psychological conditions. Surgery, detoxification, and the use of aphrodisiacs are also addressed.

Yoga (to yoke, as in body, mind, and Divine) is one of the *darshanas* (viewpoints) expressed in the *Vedas*, but aspects of its wisdom appear in the *tantras, agamas, puranas*, special *Yoga Shastras*, and other texts. While Ayurveda is designed to heal the body, yoga is primarily for the mind. This is in contrast to a common perception in the West of yoga as a means of physical conditioning. It is Hatha yoga that is popular in the USA, but there are five other types with their own domains and purposes:

- *Hatha Yoga* includes *asanas* (postures), breathwork, and meditation
- *Raja Yoga* contains all yogas, and seeks *samadhi* (one-pointed, concentrated mind)
- *Bhakti Yoga* is one of devotion and worship of the Divine
- *Jhana Yoga* seeks concentration and stillness of the mind
- *Karma Yoga* emphasizes altruistic service and perfection in action
- *Tantra Yoga* involves expanding awareness at all levels of consciousness.

One extremely influential text that came later is the *Yoga Sutras* of Patanjali. It describes eight limbs in the study of yoga:

- *Yama* (virtuous self-restraints)—morality in relation to interactions with others and in the world
- *Niyama* (virtuous observances)—personal ethics and morality toward self
- *Asanas* (staying or abiding)—postures of the body
- *Pranayama* (extension of life force)—breathing and control of prana, to discipline the body and mind

- *Pratyahara* (withdrawal of senses)—control of senses through focus of mind
- *Dharana* (hold, retain, resolve)—single-pointed concentration and cultivation of inner perceptual awareness
- *Dhyana* (meditation)—devotion and worship to the Divine
- *Samadhi* (merge)—union with the Divine.

Lest one think that Ayurveda and yoga are defined by the techniques that are described in this seriously abridged chapter, or solely by the principles that are accessible to Western practitioners, it is important to return to the underlying philosophies, as expressed in the ancient *Vedas*. *Sankhya* (perfect knowledge) is the ideology that pure awareness and primordial physical energy united to create the world. According to the *Vedas*, the universe is composed of *prakriti* (matter) and *purusha* (spirit), while the human being has *ahamkara* (sense of I-ness or ego consciousness) and *buddhi* (spiritual consciousness). *Moksha* (freedom) is the state of liberation achieved when imbalances in these factors are overcome. In her discourse on Ayurveda, Judith Morrison (1995) describes the relevance of this philosophy to the present day and the present moment:

> Primordial energy gives rise to cosmic consciousness or intelligence, which is the universal order that pervades all life. Your individual intelligence, which is different from your everyday intellectual mind, is derived from and is part of this cosmic consciousness. It is your inner wisdom: the part of your individuality that cannot be swayed by the demands of daily life or by ahamkara, your sense of "I-ness."
>
> …In reality, creation, or manifestation, is now and in the present, without past or future (pp. 20–22).

The idea of subtle energies and energetic balance is one that has enjoyed popular success in the West, as interest in spirituality and Eastern traditions has burgeoned.

Energetic Therapies

I didn't need to travel far to learn more about energy work. The basics were in Sam's undergraduate thesis:

The journey toward mastery (of inner resources) leads us all eventually to a place where we understand ourselves as energy. We all have the ability to sense this energy, for it is our very being. With the practice of focused attention (or meditation) we can all increase our perceptive capacity to include this type of awareness.

The human energy field, or aura, as it is often referred to, has been documented across the world throughout all cultures. It includes several interpenetrating layers which, for the sake of simplicity, include emotional, mental, and spiritual bodies. Every thought and feeling we experience expresses itself as energy, and to a trained practitioner, can literally be seen within the human energy field.

If you put your hand on your child's knee the next time they bump it, let yourself feel the love for your child and notice what happens. Your hand will get hot. Why? Because the healing energy of your energy field is flowing through your hand and helping the knee to heal. You might feel the healing energy as wind, pulses, or even electric-like tingling. This type of perception is called kinesthetic sense and we all have it. The human energy field can be sensed in just this way, through touch, and it is a method common to energy-focused healers (Samuel Hanser, 2004, p. 23).

Spheres of life energy that emanate and stream through the body have been studied in treatises of the occult, the *Kabbalah*, Sufi texts, Chinese theses on qi, Himalayan Bönpo manuscripts, writings by the Greek philosopher Herodotus, and other works from around the world.

The idea of *chakras* (wheels or disks), or vortices of energy, converging at salient points in the body, appears in the *Vedas, Upanishads, Yoga Sutras*, and Sanskrit tantra texts. Chakras are sources of spiritual energy and manifestations of how we live, and yoga practice often includes the balancing of chakras as a healing art. In Indian philosophy, each chakra is associated with a location, color, element, archetype, polarity, psychological function, and other assets. In energetic thinking, the chakras vitalize and transmit energy between the physical body, consciousness, and the aura surrounding the body. Energy pulsates up and down the spinal cord, and courses out in key regions:

- *Muladhara* (root of spine): earth, life/death, predator/prey
- *Svadhisthana* (sacrum, sexual organs): water, pleasure/pain, male, female
- *Manipura* (solar plexus, navel): fire, gain/loss, success/failure
- *Anahata* (heart): air, rescuer, rescued, liberator, liberated
- *Vishuddhi* (throat): ether, found/lost, trust/distrust
- *Ajna* (third eye): nether (below earth's surface), sage/fool, objective observer, deluded participant
- *Sahasrara* (crown): cosmic universe, beyond form.

These polarities represent issues that can cause blockages that must be worked out in order to achieve balance. Chanting through each chakra brings renewed energy to each area, and is said to offer a way to work out the tension produced by these psychological themes, as shown in Fig. 4.2.

Working with the chakras is a form of healing that has entered the West, with champions like Anodea Judith, who wrote *Wheels of Life: A User's Guide to the Chakra System* (1987). This detailed guide offers

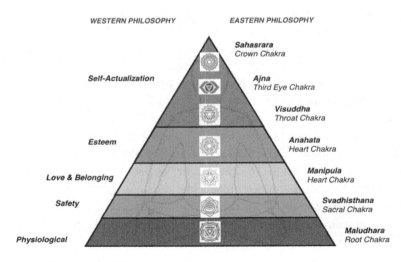

Fig. 4.2 Alignment of Chakras and needs

exercises for bringing energy into each of the chakras. Another energy healer, Barbara Brenner, wrote *Light Emerging* (1993) and *Hands of Light* (1988). Brenner (1988) states:

> (W)e see that we are much more than our physical bodies. We are composed of layer upon layer of energy and consciousness.
>
> Our inner spark of divinity exists in a much higher plane of reality and advanced consciousness than those of our everyday consciousness. We are this higher consciousness just as much as we are our everyday consciousness. This higher consciousness can be tapped into with practice. Once it is found, it is no surprise. One has the sensation of "Oh, yes! I knew that all along." Our divine spark has supreme wisdom; we can use it to guide our daily life, growth and development (p. 137).

Contemplative Wisdom

The inner spark of divinity was said to be ignited through contemplation. However, in prehistoric times, India was a culture of hunter-gatherers who required heightened awareness and the accompanying fight-flight-freeze response to be alert to the many threats to survival. But when it became an agrarian culture, its population was able to relax and let go. With farming, they could turn to a more meditative way of life, and watch the seasons change and the seeds grow. Yoga, as the derivation of the word implies, "yoked" the oxen to the plow and "yoked" the people to nature and a higher source. Rituals developed around the fruits of nature, the senses of the body, and the sounds of the universe.

The origin of meditation as a form of contemplation harkens back to the birth of the Buddha, Siddhartha Gautama, perhaps as early as the sixth century BCE in the Lumbini gardens of southern Tibet. Buddhism then spread throughout India, into Sri Lanka and southeast Asia, and later, via the Silk Road trading path to China, Korea, Japan, and beyond. Zen, Theravadan, and Tibetan forms of meditation developed over time throughout many traditions. In the words of Osho (2004), "Zen was born in India, grew in China, and blossomed in Japan... It became a great tree in China, but could not blossom there... And in Japan it blossomed like a cherry tree in thousands of flowers" (p. 8).

In other traditions, the book of Jewish mysticism, the *Kabbalah*, taught meditation on Hebrew letters and words, while the repetition of Biblical phrases gave the Jewish people a path to contemplate their existence and its meaning. The Christian religions also incorporated meditation in their religious services, and in the seventh century, Islam developed it in their prayers.

The contemplative arts are currently an amalgamation of ancient and modern philosophies, as realized through decidedly disparate approaches, such as neuroscience, mysticism, psychology, the arts, and physics. The field of "contemplative studies" exists today to examine the impact of introspection, including meditation, reflection, and other ways to quiet the mind in order to alleviate suffering and enhance wellbeing (https://www.mindandlife.org/). Many of the techniques in this book are based on contemplative practices that have evolved through the ages and made their way into modern life.

The Ways of Healing

While I have always considered myself to be an evidence-based practitioner, there is much to be learned about the impact of what cannot be observed regarding the health and wellbeing of human beings. From shamans who commune with the spirit world to affect cures, to the native peoples who worship nature and use natural remedies from the earth, the vast wisdom of every culture cites many paths to healing. Being open to the practices that have existed on each continent from times of antiquity can breed deeper curiosity, an awareness of possibility, and the positive intentions that bring growth, change, and health to both the practitioner and the ill person. At least, it has for me.

With Hippocrates and the advent of Greek medicine, the supernatural gave way to a more mechanistic model of illness and health. It is not only the Hippocratic Oath of ancient Greece, "Do no harm," that guides Western medicine today. Since the sixteenth century and Descartes' compartmentalization of body and mind, this Cartesian foundation of medical science has divided the field into specialties and subspecialties, in self-contained systems that may or may not interact. Ironically, in societies that place a high premium on individual choice, such as the USA, treatment focuses on a diseased or compromised part of the body and not on the personhood of the one with the condition. In contrast, medical practices in countries that have valued the collective good, such as China, consider each personal case with its unique history and constellation of experience and view the person as a whole, inclusive of body, mind, and soul (Beinfield & Korngold, 1998).

Louise Montello was a visionary music therapist who valued Eastern philosophy and Western innovation. She worked within a larger universe of practices, placing music and art at the core of her integrative thinking. She saw the essential musical intelligence of every person:

> Eastern practitioners believe that true healing takes place at a subtler level—that of the energy body, the vehicle of consciousness and mental events. If you could actually see and hear the human energy body, you would be privy to the most amazing constellations of melody, rhythm, light, color, and wave—energetic mandalas in constant motion (Montello, 2005, p. 51).

When I remember Louise, I can almost feel the dance of that energy surrounding her spirit.

How fortunate we are to live at a point in history when we can experience many ways of knowing and healing from different parts of the world. While each culture is unique in its practices, Traditional Chinese Medicine and Ayurveda are complete systems that treat the whole person. Thus they lead the way for understanding holistic ways of approaching health and wellbeing. The wisdom of these philosophies has strengthened our understanding of the connections between mind, body, and spirit, and opened our minds to new models of wellbeing. While both systems identify energy as the source of life and its flow as a determinant of health, the role that energy-focused healing might play in health and how it could be integrated into Western treatments remains to be seen. Mind and body are bonded in the medical literature. Spirit and its energies are on their way to finding their place in health and medicine. Contemplation has become a key to unlocking the inner healer.

Ancient texts and rituals are the sources of many integrative healing practices, including music. Like energy, music's influence on the individual is not always clearly observable. However, with its expanding research base, music therapy is now establishing itself as an evidence-based service in medicine and integrative health. The next chapter describes the origins of healing music, those techniques that have been debunked by contemporary scholars, and those that are part of current practice.

5

Roots of Healing Music

Sam was into musical theater. He was short in stature and generally quiet and introspective, but he came alive onstage when he joined the Palo Alto Children's Theatre. He sang with spirit, gusto, and a twinkle in his eye. Singing taught him how to be assertive. His clarity and range offered a rich language for him to express different personae in song. He could hardly hold back a giggle from his gut when he sang and performed. He would smile and guffaw, sob and gasp, all in the course of belting out a showstopper. This experimentation surely fed his curiosity as well as his soul. While his philosophies of life were percolating in his mind, his singing let him try out a full assortment of emotions. Concomitantly, he was hatching a profound spirituality through the language of music.

It is easy to recognize some of the mechanisms underlying music therapy in Sam's story. Creative experimentation with identity, communication of feelings through singing, embodiment of many ways of perceiving the world, and finding a spiritual connection through the arts contributed to the growth of a future healer.

In this chapter, theories about the beginnings of sound and early writings on music offer a glimpse into how sound and music offered spiritual bonding and came to be universal healing modalities. While not

© The Editor(s) (if applicable) and The Author(s) 2016
S.B. Hanser, *Integrative Health through Music Therapy*,
DOI 10.1057/978-1-137-38477-5_5

intended to be comprehensive, the historical narratives presented here derive from diverse cultures and carry lessons on the potential of music to heal. As contemporary music therapists, we can adapt some of these practices to our modern routines and begin to dissect the many claims of their medicinal value. This chapter reminds us of the origins of our precious music and is intended to provide clues behind music's influence on mind, body, and spirit.

Music as Essential to the Human Spirit

In the Beginning

It all began with *"Om,"* or *"Aum"* (ॐ), or so it appears in Hindu cosmology in Sanskrit. Om is described in the *Mandukya Upanishad* as the Eternal itself, the Supreme Unity, the Absolute, the core of existence. As the seed of everything in the cosmos, within and beyond perception, it is also the creation of the universe and all that there is. Swami Krishnananda (1996) interprets the original text:

> OM! This Imperishable Word is the whole of this visible universe. Its explanation is as follows: What has become, what is becoming, what will become verily, all of this is OM. And what is beyond these three states of the world of time, that too, verily, is OM (p. 10).

OM is not simply a sound or word. It is an intonation that has been passed down through oral transmission for many thousands of years. In contemporary parlance, it is considered the sound of interconnectedness, and begins many mantras. When chanted with extended phonation, the sound of AUM is perhaps the most important of mantras, as it invokes the universe: the sound of A (pronounced with a short a) represents the sphere of the sun and the place of waking consciousness; U, the sphere of the moon and the place of dreaming consciousness; M, the sphere of fire and place of dreamless sleep; with silence at its conclusion, the sphere of silence and place of spacious consciousness. The mantras in Hindu scriptures begin with OM.

Modern science explains the beginning of the universe as an energetic cataclysm called the Big Bang. Perhaps, then, it may not be so farfetched to consider the claim that a great energetic force (OM) begot the world. Alain Daniélou (2002) elaborates:

> Hindu philosophers consider that the Universe, starting from an initial manifestation of energy, develops according to the principles contained in its germ, according to a kind of genetic code based on mathematical data.
>
> It is the basic identity of the energy components of matter, life, thought and perception that allow us to establish relations, analogies, between one and another. In this way, a visual or sound language can help us to evoke certain aspects of thought, feeling, emotion, and the harmony of forms. If there were no relationship, one language could not serve as a vehicle for the other.
>
> Our auditory perceptions, particularly in music, are extremely important, because they are what we can most easily analyse in terms of frequency ratios, in numerical terms. Through the phenomenon of language, whether musical or articulated, we can discover something about these equations that are the basis of the structures of matter, life, perception and thought. This is why the ancients always considered music as a sort of key to all sciences (p. 182).

When early civilizations attempted to bring order to the world, they found order in music. Music is a numerical system of energy, time, and space that is also defined by form and perception. This integration of science and art guided acoustical experiments with the first stringed instruments through dividing the strings in half, thirds, quarters, etc. to identify the building blocks of musical sounds. In approximately 500 BCE, Pythagoras calculated the effects of these ratios and created the Pythagorean scale, which divides the octave into hemitones. He also developed the *Musica Mundana* (Music of the Spheres), a treatise on the ratios of distances from the earth to the planets. Passed on orally and later written down by the Neo-Platonists, his theories posed that this cosmic music determined the rhythms of nature. The musical modes owned special healing powers, and ancient hospitals, such as the Sanctuary of Asclepion (the God of healing) in what is now Turkey, touted medicine through music.

Hindu philosophy supports the belief that harmony is the force behind matter and perception, and that sound elicits emotion and thinking, making it an ideal tool for communicating with the Divine and supernatural. *Nāda* (the Sanskrit word for primal sound, tone, river, or stream) is seen as the basis for creation and the central ingredient of life. As such, it is believed to be capable of connecting human beings with the Absolute.

Nāda yoga provides a metaphysical taxonomy of sound and music for achieving awareness of one's luminous, internal, and external consciousness for personal awakening and for creating healing music. Instructions are found in the Hindu *Vedas*, particularly the *Rig Veda* and the *Upanishad*. The *anahata* (inner music or unstruck sound) is the uniquely personal, sacred sound that opens the chakras and unites the individual with the cosmos. The *Rig Veda* urges the spiritual seeker to listen, and the sound will become clear. Of course, the *anahata* is also the name for the heart chakra, and it is through this vortex of energy that such internal music can be found. The *ahata* (external music or struck sound) is perceived through the ears, and processed in the brain. The voice is the mechanism through which *anahata* is transformed into *ahata*; *nādanusandhana* (meditation practice) also brings one's own *anahata* to fruition. In this way, the heart becomes whole.

Ahata developed into a formal schema of Indian music, with *śrutis* (interval categories) and *rāgas* (coloring; scales depicting states of mind). According to tantric texts and *Sama Veda*, the transcendent sounds of Indian classical music emanated from the Gods. The *Silapadikaram*, a pre-Aryan text on Carnatic (southern Indian) music, stipulates the directions for using a microtonal scale, coupled with advice on the environmental acoustics to create the best aesthetics. Certain virtues are attributed to each rāga, for instance, pentatonic with a virile magnetism, and heptatonic with a feminine mystique. Each one is a mode that uses certain *swaras* (tones) to evoke a particular mood. Sensitive to the delicate cyclic balance in humans, every rāga is designed to be performed at a specific time of day or season of the year for maximum impact on its listener. The ancient world, including Persia and Greece, recognized the psychological value of these prescriptive rāgas, and used them to heal and balance the inner nature of the listener.

Mantra is also considered "a mystical energy encased in a sound structure" and an invocation to God (Vishnu-Devananda, 1995, p. 47). A true mantra is one that has been revealed to a teacher, who subsequently achieves self-realization through its repetition and passes it down to disciples or students. This mantra has a *bija* (seed) of power and itself has *shakti* (divine power). It is chanted in a distinctive rhythmic meter, preferably in Sanskrit, the root language used in Hindu rituals and spiritual practices. In Sanskrit, the mantra is afforded even deeper strength, as this language is based on the fifty primeval sounds of the physical world.

When I was in residence at the ashram in India, my teacher Russill Paul pointed out that the *Vedas*, like other sacred verses and poetry, are themselves mantras. "Mantra cultivates the voice of the soul," he said. We pilgrims chanted throughout the day, singing Sanskrit *kirtans* (praise, often part of bhakti yoga) in the typical call-and-response format, and intoning mantras from various scriptures and contemporary sources. Chanting in a language other than English allowed my mind to be free of the associations and intellectual connections I had with the words that I use every day. We chanted the *Gayatri Mantra* three times every day. This mantra is considered the "mother of all mantras," a petition to all the planes of the cosmos:

Oṃ bhūr bhuvaḥ svaḥ
tát savitúr váreṇyaṃ
bhárgo devásya dhīmahi
dhíyo yó naḥ pracodáyāt
The essence of everything: The physical, astral, and celestial planes
That One, Creator, fit to be adored,
Light Divine, we meditate on
Thoughts which may enlighten us.

Hindu mythology asserts that this mantra was whispered into the ear of a boy entering manhood by his father, from generation to generation. Exemplary of the way in which ancient traditions have been reinterpreted for use in the present day, I was taught the *Gayatri Mantra* by my son, Sam, through a playlist he provided for my iPod. Knowing that he chanted this daily in his meditation practice yokes me to him, in the true spirit of yoga. I chant it when I have trouble sleeping, when I experience turbulence during a plane flight, and when I want to feel closer to Sam.

The Chinese Yue

The Chinese character for music (樂 *yue*), with the additional character for herbs, creates the Chinese character for medicine (藥 *yao*). This is often cited as evidence for the ancient use of music to heal. But, according to legend, in the third millennium BCE, a member of the court, Ke T'ien Shih, created special music to praise the Emperor, heaven and earth, birds and beasts. After a great rain, it is told that the people became depressed and lethargic, so dances were created to energize them. Stories like these appear in written form on oracle bones in the second to first millennium BCE, so it is clear that music was a significant part of the early totemic traditions in China.

It is also apparent that the author of the ancient *Classic on Internal Medicine*, the Yellow Emperor, valued music and was intent on identifying music that would harmonize heaven and earth. In one of the Taoist rituals that offers incense and wine to the spirits to unite human beings with the Tao, called *Jiao* (醮), the master meditates to a drum beat. In another part of the ritual, a drum accompanies moving meditation (*Taiji* 太極) and the visible Tao (*Youwei* 有為之道). Yin (earth) is represented by wind instruments, and yang (heaven) is represented by stringed instruments in this meaningful musical tribute.

Confucius (551–479 BCE) taught that music is an essential part of life (Davison & Reed, 1998). In fact, it is necessary to achieve *jen* (absolute virtue and beneficence). In teaching the "six arts," music was second only to ceremony/ritual, followed by shooting, driving, writing, and mathematics. Music, after all, was capable of bringing people into harmony (*he* 和) with each other and with the universe. Among the prolific works of this great philosopher are a large collection of folk songs in the *Classic of Poetry* (*Shi Jing* 詩經), and *Youlan*, or *Solitary Orchid* (幽蘭), thought to be the oldest piece of written music.

Although the Chinese were probably aware of the Greek system of creating musical scales from the divisions of strings, they developed their own scales and modes, based on the pitches of a set of pipes. To create the mode for a piece of music, one pipe was selected to serve as the "yellow bell" (黃鐘) pitch, which established the tonal center for a 12-note scale. These tones corresponded to the months of the year and the hours in a day. Later, a pentatonic scale of five tones came into use, with two additional changing tones for effect. Each note of this scale was built on ratios of fifths and came to be associated with the *Wu Xing* (五行), the five elements. Contemporary sources have claimed that, if the tonic is C, then the tones are said to represent:

- C—*Gong* 宮
- G—*Zhi* 徵
- D—*Shang* 商
- A—*Yu* 羽
- E—*Jue* 角.

It has been argued that songs based on each note as their center bring balance and harmony to the physical system with which it is associated. There has been such interest in this notion by modern-day researchers that, in 2013, Liao and colleagues conducted a randomized controlled trial on the impact of this five-element music. In a well-controlled study of 170 Chinese patients with advanced cancer, one group listened to five-element music, another heard Western music regularly, and a control group did not listen to music at all. Results indicated that those who listened to the five-element music scored significantly higher than those who heard Western music or those in the control group, on measures of quality of life and functional impairment, as well as symptoms entered in their diaries (Liao et al., 2013). It is not known how familiar or enjoyable this Western music was to the participants or their prior experiences with either form of music.

Intrigued by these results, and having heard various renditions of the sounds of five-elements music, I went about researching the topic. On my visit to China in 2014, I met Song Boyuan, a lecturer at the Jiangxi University of Traditional Chinese Medicine. She attended my workshop in Beijing and told me that she had recently delivered a paper on *Flaws of Five-Element Music Therapy* (2014). Her conclusions are as follows:

According to Western music theory that the mode of a song is named in accordance with its tonic note, the theory of five-element music therapy ignores the fact that traditional Chinese music does not completely belong to functional harmony, like music in major or minor tunes with a dominating note surrounded by others. The five-element music used in current clinical practice is not what it is referred to in *Yellow Emperor's Cannon of Internal Medicine*, but a misunderstanding that five scales are interpreted as five modes, and five-element music therapy is a clinical practice lacking proper theoretical basis…There was no record about music treatment based on five-element theory in ancient medical literature (p. 1).

Obviously, the impact of five-element music is controversial in modern-day music therapy, but within an integrative model for medicine, it may receive more attention. There are, of course, other descriptions in historical records of the strong influences of music.

In approximately 100 BCE, Yo-Ki's *Record of Music* described the effect of music on emotions as sympathetic resonance. It went a great deal farther to warn the musician about the consequences of a poor performance in the imperial court. As quoted by Daniélou (2002):

If the tonic is not clear, there is disorder, the prince is arrogant; if the second is not clear, there is dishonesty, the officials are corrupt; if the third is not clear, there is anxiety, the people are unhappy; if the fifth is not clear, there is danger, resources are exhausted…In a period of disorder, the rites deteriorate and music is licentious, the said tones lack dignity, joyful tones lack calm…When music exercises its action…the blood and vital spirits are balanced…the empire is peaceful (p. 31).

Entrancing Music

In Mali, West Africa, music has always been central to the Minianka traditions. It is integrated into community life, work, ceremony, and education. Musicians are healers, and healers, musicians. While they bring life into harmony through their music, these musician-healers also diagnose psychological and physical ailments by watching for the imbalances in community dances. Yaya Diallo and Mitchell Hall (1989) describe the process, in *The Healing Drum: African Wisdom Teachings*:

> When an individual becomes disturbed, the Minianka look to disturbed relationships as the cause, since psychological imbalance is seen as a symptom of social imbalance and possible disharmony with the invisible world. The Minianka regard their musicians as having the necessary skills of intelligence, memory, observation, and social interaction required to bring a person back into tune with self and others in their playing. Musicians need a sense of harmony, proportion, balance, and social tact so that their interactions with fellow musicians and dancers contribute to the harmony of the whole. Musicians need sensitivity and the ability to respond appropriate to the demands of the moment. Regular accompaniment of dancers attunes musicians to the manifestations of individuality through movement (p. 82).

The complex timbres of the drums and xylophones in Africa, gongs in China, and horns in Tibet were also used in prehistoric animistic religions to attract or frighten spirits and Gods. Shamanic cultures around the world recognized the ability of music and dance to induce a trance state, in which the shaman could access helpful spirit guides and coax evil spirits to leave an infirm body. Power songs, arresting percussion, and impassioned dances summoned the spirit world to cure disease. The Native American shamans treated disease as spiritual imbalances, and after fasting, would enter a dream state to receive the song designed to cure the ill member of their tribe. According to Dr. Wayne Peate (2003), they believe in sacred paths to health, related to the four directions:

- North: The healing spirit runs through the body. Native healers believe you have everything you need inside you.
- East: The healing power of relationships. Everyone needs a community.
- West: Restoring healing balance. Native healing requires active participation by the one to be healed.

- South: The healing life cycle, from birth to death to the next world. Native healing is a partnership for life between healer and patient (pp. 3–7).

This wisdom carries a contemporary message about the integration of self, community, investment, and relationship. With the addition of music, it strikes a consonant chord with many cultures that share these values. While each healing tradition boasts its own tracts and practices, the importance of music appears to be ubiquitous.

In the Middle Ages, tarantism was said to be caused by the bite of the wolf spider (tarantula), resulting in uncontrollable urges to dance that could only be cured by exorcism through dancing the Tarantella. Stories originating in southern Italy have, over time, assumed mythic proportions of passion and the supernatural, and inspired many a classical composer to use this as a musical form.

One branch of Sufism still uses a ritual dance, the *Sema* (listening), in which the *semazen* (whirling dervish) turns the body in an attempt to unite body, heart, and mind. While the purpose for the ritual is to harmonize with nature, not necessarily to induce trance, the spinning movements are hypnotic and bring the spiritual seekers together as one entity in the dance. Repetitive movement is recognized as a way to create a sense of mysticism or otherworldliness. In addition, the complex rhythms and timbres of certain ceremonies are combined to transform or purify the soul. Chant, dance, and music are the vehicles to transport the participant to a realm far away from earthly experience. According to *Essential Sufism* by Fadiman and Frager (1997),

> The Sufis attempt to practice unity of breath, sound, and movement… Unity among the dervishes can bring them closer to God, Who is Unity. Ideally, the dervishes move as if there were only one dervish moving, chant as if one dervish were chanting and breathe as if just one dervish were breathing…As the meaning and power of the words repeated begin to sink in, hearts become filled with joy, longing for God, and other spiritual feelings (pp. 16–17).

There is a lovely saying, attributed to the great Persian poet, Rumi: "We rarely hear the inward music, but we're all dancing to it nevertheless" (trans. 1994, p. 106).

Contemporary ethnomusicologists have studied the notion of musical trance with critical eyes. In *Dancing Prophets: Musical Experience in Tumbuka Healing*, Steven Friedson (1996) describes the Malawian *vimbuza* ritual, where drums and hands beat out multiple rhythms. Polyrhythms combine triple with duple meter. He states:

> The metrical doubling inherent in vimbuza drumming is mirrored, in a sense, in the consciousness-doubling of the healer's divinatory trance...The same rhythmic figures that initially helped to bring on a total spirit possession now act as a kind of anchoring of consciousness, a focusing device that helps to stabilize the trance state (p. 162).

Does the music cause the trance state? Friedson suggests that music plays more of a supportive role in inducing trance, through its ability to focus attention, much like the mantras of India.

In *Masters of Mahāmudrā: Songs and Histories of the 84 Buddhist Siddhas* (Dowman, 1985), the story is told of Vināpā, a young prince who became obsessed with playing the beautiful Indian stringed instrument, the *vīnā*. A yogin was called in to teach the prince *sādhana*, a method for achieving Buddhahood through disciplining the mind, but the prince refused to leave his beloved *vīnā*. The wise yogin offered these instructions:

> Meditate upon the sound of your instrument free of all distinction between the sound struck and the mental impression; cease all mental interference with the sound, all conceptualization and all critical and judgmental thought, so that you contemplate only pure sound (p. 92).

Indeed, through this practice, the prince achieved *Mahāmudrā*, the highest tantric path to Buddhahood. The legend of Vināpā was told to teach this important tantric methodology, one that carries lessons for the contemporary music therapist as well.

Soothing Music

Other evidence for ancient roots of music's healing powers is seen in the Middle East. A variety of musical instruments, including woodwinds, trumpets, percussion, and harps are inscribed on Egyptian tombs and temple remains. Harps have been traced back to 3000 BCE in Egypt, and it is likely that Israelites brought lyres to this kingdom by 1580 BCE. Some attribute the birth of music therapy to the well-known story of David's soothing Saul. In *David's Harp: The Story of Music in Biblical Times*, Sendrey and Norton (1964) elucidate:

> Nowhere in the Bible is music's power to exorcize evil spirits more explicit than in the report of David's playing the lyre to restore the ailing Saul. By the time this tale was set down in written form, music had long lost its primitive function as an element in magic. Yet the carry-over was still strong enough for Saul's relief to be attributed to music's magic power. Ancient belief held that music not only had a sedative effect but was able to bring the morbid impulse to a climax, after which the afflicted one might recover. In Saul's case, music not only drove out the demon but acted as a healing agent, thus combining the offices of magic and medicine, as even today among primitive peoples for whom the priest is at once magician and medicine man. The idea of music's healing power was widespread among the Jews until late Talmudic times. We find in the Talmud mention of a song that was thought to provide protection in times of epidemic (p. 202).

Music was seen as medicine and a gift of God, and musicians were prophets as well as poets. As in other cultures, music summoned the Divine in sacred rites and accompanied songs of gratitude and exaltation. In the mystical Kabbalah, music and chant were central to prayer and to bringing the community together in unison.

Music and relaxation may have the most primal relationship of all. A mother's singing of a lullaby to her baby may be the first experience of the manipulation of emotion and the relief of distress by music. Mood regulation often occurs instantaneously and continues over time with the active interplay of mother and child, providing signals of understanding and comfort, also known as love. More simply, lullabies pacify and relax; mothers are intuitive music therapists.

In *Healing Songs*, Ted Gioia (2006) speaks of the derivation of lullabies:

> The Temiar people of the Malaysian rainforest believe that a hypnotic state is evoked by sounds that move in tandem with the beat of the heart...The Temiar hear these rhythms in certain sounds of their native rainforest, in the calls of birds and sounds of insects. They try to emulate these same rhythms with their bamboo tube percussion, alternating high and low tones to create a throbbing back-and-forth pulsation. Here music finds its greatest fulfillment by returning to the comforting, organic rhythms taught to us by our own bodies.
>
> Our first awareness of this rhythm of flow and continuity begins even before we are born, in our mother's womb. There a rich universe of sound establishes our initial contacts with the external world. Our mother's heartbeat is the primary auditory anchor of our prebirth life, but other sounds soon begin to intrude, exerting their own influence (p. 6).

It may also be that lullabies are rituals for bringing the sacred into daily life. The synchrony of mother and child's movements, the call and response of "Motherese" (infant-directed speech that carries strong inflection), and the emotional impact of the singing initiate the deep connections that ensure the safekeeping of the helpless infant. This profound capacity of song has served an evolutionary purpose and today informs music therapy practices.

Generations of mothers have sung instinctively to calm their infants, as I did with Sam. As he grew, Sam's own singing became the modern ritual he used to find himself, or maybe it was the Divine within him. While the true impact is unknown, he would say that singing was capable of renewing his spirit and healing his soul. Throughout millennia, music has transported us inward, upwards, and to the Divine. As a music therapist, how will you find this music? How will you prepare yourself to guide others on the journey? Read on.

Part II

The Journey

In Part II, I shift the voice to first person and the focus toward you, the music therapist, as the locus of healing. With that shift, I move away from the empirical toward a more personal approach. This necessitates a new vocabulary, as well, away from the traditional medical model of therapist/patient toward a relationship of greater equanimity. From here, I shall avoid referring to the people you serve as patients or clients, as these labels do not value the importance of the inner healer. When the healer comes from within, the music therapist is a guide or facilitator to accompany the person's journey from illness to wellness, and the person is a companion on that journey.

The relationship of facilitator to companion is synergistic and dynamic, and the roles are more integrated. To fully guide an individual on a journey toward wholeness, the music therapist must be patient, listen, and comply with the person's needs. Music therapists witness who their companions are, beyond their diagnoses and symptoms. They nonjudgmentally tune into the feelings that underlie the companion's statements, and guide them toward optimal physical, mental, and spiritual wellness. As such, it is more accurate to use an alternative term for the person who is on the journey from illness to wellness. In the ensuing chapters, I will refer to this individual as your companion on this sacred journey.

In the remaining chapters, I address you as music therapist or as fellow traveler on the journey. You may be preparing yourself for your own journey or that of your companion, but it is important to your success that you see yourself as a whole person with many roles and perspectives, not just a collection of traits, characteristics, and symptoms.

In the process of identifying the steps of this journey, I settled on five:

1. initial signs and symptoms;
2. diagnosis;
3. treatment;
4. resilience and recovery;
5. acceptance or peace.

When one encounters the "dis-ease" of problematic signs and symptoms, the response can be fraught with panic or agitation. Discomfort is a sign of imbalance in the body, but when the cause is unknown, the ensuing anxiety alone can exacerbate the person's physical condition. Diagnosis may bring some answers, sometimes eagerly awaited and sometimes dreaded. The diagnosis will map the rest of the journey, or at least the next steps and a final destination, or prognosis.

Treatment is an active time for the person diagnosed with an illness. It often means making decisions and enduring treatments that can be painful or unpleasant. The recovery period may be a time to replenish energy, renew one's sense of perspective, and prepare for a new healthy identity. In the event that recovery is not possible, the end of life's journey offers an opportunity to find meaning, acceptance, or peace.

As a music therapist approaching a new case, you may or may not have access to a medical record, and you may or may not have a formal referral order. But neither of these sources of information will tell you what you really need to know. As you accompany this person on the journey from illness to wellness, you must first know yourself. You must then be prepared to be present for this person no matter what he or she brings. As companions, you will learn about and from each other, and you will be changed as a result.

6

Tuning in: The Music Therapist's Journey

Sam's master's thesis from the California Institute of Integral Studies (CIIS) was a case study of Debra, who experienced frequent and severe migraine headaches. In the thesis, Sam speaks about a special moment of connection that soldered their therapeutic relationship:

That moment showed me how therapy has nothing to do with having the answers or even knowing where to go. It's just about stepping toward all those places inside of ourselves and facing the feelings there. One of my teachers at CIIS said in class one day, "what's shareable gets bearable," and that was exactly what was happening with Debra and me. Within the container of our relationship, of an empathic bond in which she knew I cared about her, she had someone to be in the pain with. And that's the power that therapy can offer—just having someone to be completely in it with you is healing.

The relationship Debra was having with me on the outside was also modeling a relationship for her on the inside. Through the practice of my empathic listening, attunement and support—something novel to her history—Debra could develop a new relationship with herself. Instead of being at war with the emotions she had been carrying, she had surrendered into them. This moment was one of many in which Debra was turning her

S.B. Hanser, *Integrative Health through Music Therapy*,
DOI 10.1057/978-1-137-38477-5_6

body from an enemy into an ally, and as she cultivated an experience of peace in her body, her experience of pain diminished (Samuel Hanser, 2009, p. 4).

This chapter is all about you. It is about preparing yourself as a music therapist to journey with your companions. It seeks to enrich your formal training as a music therapist, taking you beyond the skills-based training in musicianship and therapeutic techniques. It addresses your preparation as a whole human being and an emotional and spiritual guide to your patients, whom I now refer to as companions. It will help you to become more effective as a therapist, and help you to be, as Sam said, "completely in it."

Becoming a Music Therapist

As the chair of the music therapy department at a few colleges over several decades, I have had the good fortune to interview hundreds of prospective music therapists. In these conversations, I hear countless stories of how these students uncovered their true selves through music, and how original compositions captured their essences. Some found these experiences so profound that they felt a sense of transcendence or a higher calling to pursue a music therapy career. Many had personally journeyed to a place of wellness after crisis or trauma, by first immersing in music as a safe container for processing their distress. Then, music became the medium for transporting them to a new place of insight and optimism. They wrote songs about their challenges, performed pieces that passionately narrated their journeys, and created soundscapes for describing their inner worlds. In the process, they surrounded themselves with beautiful music, undoubtedly experienced flow, and spawned a vision for helping others as they had been helped themselves. They also spent a massive number of hours perfecting their art.

I believe that music therapists are the luckiest people in the world. They have excavated their passions, uncovered their talents, and unearthed their *dharma*. My good friend and dharma teacher, Stephen Cope, refers to *dharma* as true vocation or calling. In *The Great Work of Your Life*: *A*

Guide for the Journey to Your True Calling (2012), he refers to something that I think you as a music therapist can relate to:

> People actually feel happiest and most fulfilled when meeting the challenge of their dharma in the world, when bringing highly concentrated effort to some compelling activity for which they have a true calling...For many of us, the challenges of our vocation in the world require the development of a profound degree of mastery. Those who have had a taste of this kind of mastery have experienced moments when effort becomes effortless: joyful, gifted, and unbounded. These moments of effortless effort are so sublime that they draw us even more deeply into the possibilities of our vocations (p. xxiv).

This "effortless effort" sounds much like Csikszentmihalyi's flow and Maslow's peak experience that we entertained in Chap. 2. Stephen Cope asks us music therapists to bring these moments to bear in our own destinies, by considering the deeper possibilities. For me, this means continually reminding myself through discipline and practice that I am capable of this sense of unbounded awe and that I must bring this into my work as a music therapist.

Training to become a music therapist requires intense mastery of many elements of music, including theory, harmony, ear training, composition, conducting, form and analysis, acoustics, and other subjects that train the student in the rational order of sounds, harmonics, intervals, modes, scales, and phrases. Most music therapy curricula include foundations in these subjects during formative years of study, so music therapists-in-training become hardwired to process music analytically and formally. Students are taught to make the finest discriminations regarding the key, mode, modulations, harmonic progressions, genre, and any number of classifications and analyses. When they hear a piece of music, their brains immediately signal those well-learned connections within a massive network of analytical music data, and spew messages about the form and formulation of this music.

Sadly, for the trained musician, referential associations to music that conjure up pictures in the mind's eye of memory and dreams tend to remain backstage while the brain works front and center to analyze and perform. When musicians process music, the volume of grey matter in their brains in the auditory, motor, and visual-spatial regions is actually greater than in those with less musical background and training (Gaser & Schlaug, 2003; Koelsch et al., 2005). Musical training places emphasis on the technical aspects of art, becoming a better musician, and judging performances and musicianship. Ultimately, for some, these habits endanger the musician's happiness and self-acceptance. The emphasis on the ideal self in the striving toward perfection of the craft robs one of the authentic and real self behind the struggle.

Of course, as a music therapist, you must be such a competent musician that you can instantly furnish a favorite song and, a moment later, create a magnificent musical offering to yield a deep emotional response. Meanwhile, you are juggling a collection of musical instruments, electronics, and music, and of course, you are listening to your companion on the journey. Preparing for this journey may not be easy, but the groundwork may serve your personal development as well as the person you are accompanying. A key question is: Are you able to suspend this judgment, and are you caring for your whole self as strongly as you care for others?

Preparing Yourself for the Journey

In Ken Wilber's adaptation of the Great Circle of Being, the individual can gain insight at every level, from the physical to the emotional, mental, existential, spiritual, and absolute spiritual states of being. Your preparation for accompanying a companion on the journey can work its way through this same hierarchy. Let us explore some established approaches and look at how you can be prepared, while incorporating healthy practices into your own life.

Physical Preparation

Your physical wellbeing is fundamental. As someone who is serving others, you must first take care of your own body. You probably know what to do to care for yourself, but are you paying attention to your physical needs as you move throughout your day? Are you ready to make a commitment to treat your body with the respect and devotion that it deserves? My teacher, Russill Paul, was constantly reminding us to worship the temple of our own bodies. After all, these are sacred vessels that carry us through life, and they require care and feeding. Adopting healthy habits and practices may assist you in ensuring that you are being good to your body.

Sleep

Are you getting sufficient sleep? If not, how can you adjust your daily habits and sleep hygiene in order to get a good night's rest? Do you value your need for rest, and sacrifice those things that may interfere with restful sleep? There are certainly some simple guidelines for efficient sleep, such as avoiding caffeine and too much alcohol, and engaging in a restful activity before retiring for the night. But you know your challenges better than anyone. Sleeping well requires much more than making time for a solid night's sleep, so you will have to identify the barriers that interfere with peaceful slumber.

Body Awareness, Posture, and Composure

It is possible to develop tendencies in the way you align your posture or move your body that are detrimental to your physical wellbeing. If you are plagued by performance anxiety, your body is accustomed to tensing up as you begin to play or sing. If you tend to bend over your companion's bedside, you may also be straining your back and constricting your organs. There are many body-oriented and massage therapies that can help you as well as your companions. Some methodologies are particularly indicated for musicians, such as the *Alexander Technique* and *Feldenkrais Method*.

   The Alexander Technique. F. Matthias Alexander was a "reciter" who, in the process of repeatedly projecting his voice, abused and damaged it. The method that bears his name was helpful for him and now many others, particularly musicians. Teachers of the Alexander Technique show their students how to notice the ways they habitually move, and how to improve alignment and posture, while relieving tension. Body mapping is one Alexander practice that has become particularly popular. The body map is the perception of one's experience as the joints move and the body operates. When there is incongruence between the person's perceptional map and the actual map of the working body, it is possible to identify the sources of ineffective posture and movement, and hone the kinesthetic sense to develop awareness of proper and efficient positioning and coordination (Barlow, 1991).

The Feldenkrais Method, as detailed in many texts, including *Awareness through Movement* (1972), is a form of somatic education developed by Moshe Feldenkrais. His method, also prescribed for musicians, focuses on flexibility and range of motion, through a series of gentle, slow exercises. Among others, older adults have similarly benefitted from this method, specifically in their balance and mobility, while decreasing their fear of falling (Ullmann et al., 2010).

Derivatives. New methodologies and amalgamations of old ones appear every day. During a recent visit to Israel, I sampled a derivative of Feldenkrais, reflexology, and bioenergetics, known as Ilan Lev bodywork (which left me feeling immensely limber), then met with Leah Reznikovich (2014) to sample her "Thou Shalt Not Diet" diet, and observed the krav maga martial arts, self-defense curriculum, all of which are expanding to the USA and UK. My research uncovered endless options for improving nutrition and exercise, thus contributing to the healthiest body and mind possible. Identifying triggers for unhealthy eating patterns may help you make better choices. Applying alternative ways to move and exercise may keep you dancing for physical fitness and maximum energy. Fortunately, there are plenty of books, classes, and lifestyle consultants to help you select a program to suit your needs and interests.

Be Prepared

Commit to making one change in your life that will enhance your physical health. Think small and realistic. This decision does not have to be something as grand as smoking cessation or joining a gym. In fact, when you witness the impact of one small change each day, like taking a few deep breaths during your workday or walking instead of riding in the car or elevator, it may be easier to make more significant commitments to change your lifestyle and take good care of your body. There are plenty of available options for healthy living. Whether it is running, dancing, lifting weights, yoga, massage, fitness classes, sports, or specialty training, there awaits a salubrious practice for you as soon as you are ready.

Emotional Preparation

When you are present for someone who is suffering or in pain, it can be difficult to recognize the feelings that are evoked in yourself. This is one of the reasons that supervision is important for every practicing clinician. Your supervisor's perspective may help you expose underlying issues that contribute to your own doubts, for which personal psychotherapy may be indicated. But you will generally know when you need to reach out for help in understanding and dealing with your own emotional responses.

Acknowledging your feelings is a significant first step to working through them. Obviously, your session with your companion is not the time and place to process these. But, as a natural tendency is to block or suppress unpleasant emotions that surface during a session, it is easy to shove them aside and allow them to fester. This approach may be self-protective in the short-term and necessary while you are with your companion, but can be risky over time. Investigating and exploring what you are feeling while preparing for a session or meeting an ill companion will help you understand yourself better, while you learn how to be authentically present with another. Notice feelings that emerge, be kind to them, and show compassion for yourself. Just as you might suggest to a good friend, allow yourself to feel, communicate, and express these feelings. Process your reactions more fully after the session, and explore them in whatever medium feels right. You can sketch them, write in a journal, or compose them into a song. Better yet, try all three, and share these expressions with trusted confidants or professionals. Frances Vaughan (1995) suggests that you pay close attention to a feeling that arises and purposely intensify or release it. In this way, when you put your mind to it, you can see it change before your eyes.

In supervising trainees in clinical practice, I encounter many student music therapists who claim they are not ready to address the feelings that bubble up unexpectedly during sessions. I hear statements like, "There is just too much going on in my life right now to deal with this," or "I can handle it. I am good at not letting this bother me." Inevitably, these attitudes are not beneficial, and some students end up in considerable distress or drop out of the field. There appears to be no viable alternative to acknowledging and working through the feelings that are bound to show up in a sensitive and caring therapist-in-training. Supervision, therapy, and supportive resources strengthen every music therapist's ability to bolster self-awareness, emotional health, and personal insight.

In *The Untethered Soul*, Michael Singer (2007) reinforces this approach:

> Because people don't deal with fear objectively, they don't understand it. They end up keeping their fear and trying to prevent things from happening that would stimulate it. They go through life attempting to create safety and control by defining how they need life to be in order to be okay. This is how the world becomes frightening.
>
> When you have fear, insecurity, or weakness inside of you, and you attempt to keep it from being stimulated, there will inevitably be events and changes in life that challenge your efforts. Because you resist these changes, you feel that you are struggling with life…You see situations that happened in the past as disturbing, and you see things down the road as potential problems (p. 72).

There is no way to hide feelings, however hard we may try.

Be Prepared

One strategy my students have adopted is to write letters addressed to themselves. Many of these students are perceptive observers of others, astute helpers, and empathetic listeners, but tend to be self-critical and judgmental about their own actions and behaviors. It is a sad reality that many of us who are supportive therapists and loving friends treat ourselves as we would never treat anyone else. We rarely show ourselves the patience, understanding, and compassion that we so generously offer others. I ask students to identify a time when they did not handle a situation effectively or were disappointed in themselves. They meditate on the feelings they experienced at that time. Then they write letters to themselves, acknowledging and confirming their good points and suggesting alternative ways to view the situation. As authors, they see how capable they are of being kind and gentle, and how they can benefit from an inner critic turned empathetic. Several students save these kindhearted letters, reading and rereading them when they are lacking confidence, questioning their actions, or just feeling poorly about themselves. After all, if you can be your own best friend, you are always there to help. So sit right down and write yourself a letter. If this agrees with you, and you enjoy songwriting, turn your words into lyrics, and compose a new song of inspiration for yourself.

Mental Preparation

Whatif

Last night, while I lay thinking here,
some Whatifs crawled inside my ear
and pranced and partied all night long
and sang their same old Whatif song:
Whatif I'm dumb in school?
Whatif they've closed the swimming pool?
Whatif I get beat up?
Whatif there's poison in my cup?
Whatif I start to cry?
Whatif I get sick and die?
Whatif I flunk that test?
Whatif green hair grows on my chest?
Whatif nobody likes me?
Whatif a bolt of lightning strikes me?
Whatif I don't grow tall?
Whatif my head starts getting smaller?
Whatif the fish won't bite?
Whatif the wind tears up my kite?
Whatif they start a war?
Whatif my parents get divorced?
Whatif the bus is late?

Whatif my teeth don't grow in straight?
Whatif I tear my pants?
Whatif I never learn to dance?
Everything seems well, and then
the nighttime Whatifs strike again!

—from Shel Silverstein's "A Light in the Attic" (1981)

In this delightful poem, Shel Silverstein jokes about the extremes of asking, "What if things were different?" It seems to be human nature for people to question their actions, sometimes endlessly, about things that cannot be changed. They tend to beat themselves up about past actions and worry about the future, rather than staying present and appreciating what is happening in the moment.

Cognitive-behavioral therapists have developed myriad techniques to challenge dysfunctional thinking and to substitute more adaptive ways of handling life's challenges. Many of these methods derive from the *Vedas*, the Grecian stoic philosophers, and other sources of contemplative wisdom that attempt to regulate the busy mind (Hanser, 2014). In the contemporary vocabulary of cognitive behavioral therapy (CBT), the focus is on staying in the here-and-now, controlling thoughts and actions, learning to be mindful, and using affirmations to engage positive thinking. These are direct descendants of the yoga, meditation, and mantra practices of ancient India.

Cognitive approaches maintain that negative events do not cause unpleasant emotions; rather, it is the associated irrational thinking that results in distressing emotional outcomes. After all, many people can experience a single traumatic event, but only some will be affected pathologically. The behavioral side of CBT holds that actions and behaviors are learned and can, therefore, be unlearned and modified. Behavior is conditioned by environmental contingencies, and change comes about through observing and managing its antecedents and consequences. Thoughts and behaviors that are negative may easily spiral down into depression or escalate into anxiety. Alternatively, positive thinking and pleasant activities can lift moods and result in satisfying experiences.

One straightforward technique for managing emotions is the ABC method (Ellis & Blau, 1998), where ABC stands for antecedents, beliefs, and consequences, respectively. The procedure is as follows:

1. Create a form with three columns, labeled A, B, and C.

2. Think about a time, preferably recently, when you experienced distress, and write down the emotional consequences of this event in the Consequences (C) column. Perhaps you felt anger, frustration, sadness, guilt, anxiety, fear, or being out of control. Write any unpleasant emotion you felt in that C column.

3. Note the Antecedent (A) in the A column by thinking about the conditions that preceded this feeling. This antecedent event might have been an argument, confrontation, disturbance, or anything that occurred just prior that could have triggered your emotion.

4. Picture yourself back at this time, and notice the negative thoughts that automatically came to mind. Recount these thoughts in the Belief (B) column.

The next step is to dispute each negative or irrational thought by labeling the cognitive distortions that were at play, and then challenge their veracity through a more rational response. David Burns recommends an Automatic Thought Record (Burns, 1999) to record these cognitive distortions and more rationale responses. I completed such a thought record when I became highly emotional and anxious after my physician ordered a biopsy. My notes appear in Fig. 6.1.

As you can see, my cognitive distortions were rampant, but I was able to argue with myself and produce a more sensible and positive, rational statement. I also realized that my worrying was completely unproductive. If I had cancer, I would be wasting precious time, and if I didn't have cancer, any worry was completely unnecessary. So every time I caught myself worrying, I told myself, "Worrying is pointless. I'm not going to worry." That thought-stopping approach worked wonders and halted my obsessive concerns for the moment. Over time, I found myself focusing more on the present and less on the upcoming biopsy.

Another effective strategy for developing a peaceful presence is *mindfulness*. In this approach, you learn to recognize when your mind begins to gush negative or dysfunctional thoughts, gently bring your attention back to the present moment, and treat these distractions with compassion and without judgment. Like other CBT approaches, this one borrows from ancient contemplative wisdom traditions, and has now been extensively researched in the West. As a solution to facing

Automatic Thought Record Sample		
Activating Event: Physician orders biopsy, suspecting possibility of cancer. **Emotional Consequence**: Extreme anxiety, feelings of panic, desperation, hopelessness.		
Automatic Thought	**Cognitive Distortion**	**Rational Response**
"This is it. I know I have cancer."	All-or-nothing thinking	"I don't know that I have cancer. Physician only suspects it and is checking it out."
"Things were going really well. Lately, things have been starting to go really wrong."	Overgeneralization	"A couple of things have got me down. But, there are not a whole string of things."
"My mother had cancer so I must have it, too."	Mental filter	"My father did not have cancer."
"The physician must be convinced it is cancer to have ordered a biopsy."	Disqualifying the positive	"Physician said there is a good chance that it is not cancer."
"I am going to be totally on my own. There is no one to take care of me."	Jumping to conclusions: Mind-reading	"My daughter or my friends would probably take care of me—*if* I needed that."
"I am not going to be able to take care of myself or my children."	Fortune telling	"I might not be that sick, *even if* I do have cancer."
"This is the worst thing that could happen to me. I am going to fall apart."	Catastrophizing	"I have not fallen apart when I have been sick or in crisis before."
"I know this is cancer and this is the way I am going to die."	Emotional reasoning	"There is a *chance* that I have cancer. I am frightened that it will be terminal, but *if* I have cancer, it is probably early and treatable."
"I should be able to be stronger about this."	Should statements	"I am afraid and do not need to feel strong right now. It is important to acknowledge my true feelings."
"The whole world is getting cancer. We are being poisoned through what we eat and drink."	Overgeneralization; labeling	"There is a high incidence. The evidence shows that genetics is the greatest risk factor."
"I have done something terrible to deserve this."	Personalization	"I have not done anything terrible. This is just something that needs to be checked out."

Fig. 6.1 Automatic thought record

stress, pain, and illness, in *Wherever You Go, There You Are*, Jon Kabat-Zinn (1994) recommends practicing patience, acceptance, and letting go, as you sit quietly and compassionately watch where your mind travels.

One variant of CBT is dialectical behavior therapy (DBT), an approach that emphasizes learning skills to tolerate distress, regulate emotion, enhance mindfulness, and expand interpersonal relationships. (For more on DBT, see Linehan, 1993; McKay, Wood, & Brantley, 2007.) Radical acceptance is a DBT technique, poignantly imparted in Tara Brach's book (2003) *Radical Acceptance: Embracing Your Life with the Heart of a Buddha*. This philosophy encourages you to accept that which you cannot change, practice forgiveness, and awaken compassion. Brach encourages us to face unresolved issues by exploring the emotions that gird the issue and then show lovingkindness and compassion to every aspect of the struggle.

One technique for enhancing calmness or acceptance within is to compose a statement that challenges your thinking and acknowledges your current situation without being self-critical. Just as I repeated "Worrying is pointless" as I found my mind wandering into anxious territory, you can write your own self-acceptance statement to meet your needs. In *Lovingkindness: The Revolutionary Art of Happiness*, Sharon Salzberg (1995) recommends repetition of the following phrases, which originated in the Pali scripture of Buddhism as *metta*, and serve as fundamental concepts in *tonglen*, the compassion practice of Tibetan Buddhism:

"May I be free of danger."
"May I have mental happiness."
"May I have physical happiness."
"May I have ease of well-being."

These words, or any variant that carries personal meaning and intention, become a personal mantra to help you cope with unwanted feelings or other forms of distress. You can also adopt personal affirmations, words, or short phrases that bring significance to the moment. "Peace," "hope," "love," "I can do this," "I am okay," and "I am grateful for today" are examples.

Eric Maisel (2002) wrote a book entitled *The Van Gogh Blues*, in which he addresses the behavioral tendencies of artists, such as self-criticism and perfectionism, that can lead to depression. He reminds musicians that the music they perform, compose, or sing may be beautiful, but they are the ones who make the music beautiful. His suggested affirmation of radical acceptance is: "I am the beauty in life. It took a whole universe to create me and here I stand, fully human" (p. 121).

Your affirmations may address the musical you, you the therapist, or just you the human being. Whatever the words, you may wish to set your personal statements to music. Then you can chant them to simple tunes that elicit positive associations, or sing them to songs you love. Of course, you can also compose a new melody for your special phrase. Brief affirmations become personal jingles that you take with you anywhere and sing whenever you want to prompt a positive attitude or reinforce your self-worth. Sing yourself a love song; you deserve it!

Be Prepared

Create or adopt a personal affirmation, mantra, or acceptance statement that you can say, chant, or sing to yourself at times of trouble. Post the words or lyrics in a place that is highly visible, as an additional reminder of the positive in your life. If you use a portable musical device, it may be tempting to record your voice and play it back when you need to hear its message, but there is nothing to compare with experiencing the internal vibrations of your own voice, even if you are subvocalizing. Utilize the present tense, and repeat your affirmation with intention, purpose, and passion to enhance the impact.

Challenge your "whatifs" and negative thinking by using some of the techniques described above. Cultivate awareness of your thoughts and emotions, and show yourself compassion. Do something for yourself every day. Make time to enjoy some pleasant activity, even if it is taking a deep breath, watching the clouds, or listening to your favorite music. If you keep a journal, write about something you are grateful for.

Know that these resources are available to you when you need them most, and be sure that you are not becoming overwhelmed with possibilities, right now, as you read these various suggestions. If you are, remind yourself to do just one thing.

Existential Preparation

One existential definition of anxiety is, "a dizziness of freedom…In anxiety there is the selfish infinity of possibility, which does not tempt like a choice but ensnaringly disquiets with its sweet anxiousness" (Kierkegaard, trans. 1980, p. 61). When you prepare to meet your companion, do you experience this dizziness of overwhelming thoughts or an overabundance of choices? As you prepare existentially to meet your companion, you may notice that your own choices in daily life accurately predict how you feel and think. In *Doorway to the Soul*, Ron Scolastico (1997) suggests that a life of freedom and openness is possible when you make choices out of love and kindness, as opposed to fear and ego. He offers the following self-assessment exercise as a first step in connecting to the meaning of your life and accessing your soul:

> *Lovingly observe your daily experience in order to become aware of the choices that you have made that day.*
>
> Observing the choices you have made opens the possibility of making new choices.

1. How have I been living today?
2. What have been the primary focal points of my thinking, feeling, and choosing?
3. *To what have I given my precious time and energy?* (p. 100–101).

Mindy is a music therapist who took this exercise to heart, and found that she was living in fear of not being prepared to meet her companions. Mindy obsessed over her musical readiness, spending an inordinate amount of time practicing the guitar and learning new songs. In her mind, she often counted the musical genres that she did not know and made lists of musical titles that she had not played. After completing this self-assessment, it became obvious to her that it was not possible for her to ever learn all of the musical repertoire that she might be asked to play at any given time. Mindy realized that her presence during sessions was compromised by her thoughts of inadequacy, and that many of her daily choices were fueled by fear. She saw that she needed to own her talent as singer and guitarist. She made a choice to practice self-acceptance in place of guitar, and initiated daily meditation, mainly as an opportunity to slow her overactive mind and express gratitude for her talents. She still practiced her musical skills, but she was vigilant regarding her intentions. She checked in with her feelings to see if she was experiencing the joy of learning a new piece or doing this out of pure duty. As long as she was clear as to her purpose, she maintained ample self-esteem, as well as a calmer demeanor. Over time, Mindy began to silence her powerful inner critic and modeled the sort of acceptance that she hoped her companions would feel. She developed a healthier identity as a music therapist through assessing her abilities and limitations realistically and making choices that would nurture, rather than restrict, her self-concept.

This account highlights how Mindy approached self-actualization through self-inquiry. Another way to undertake the existential journey is through phenomenological analysis. The subjective experience of making meaning of one's work and one's life is key to this process. Like other existential approaches, phenomenology values the individual's own perspectives and point of view, and delves deeply into personal interpretations of experience.

Be Prepared

Michele Forinash and David Gonzalez (1989) offer "A Phenomenological Perspective of Music Therapy," adapted from Lawrence Ferrara's phenomenological analysis of music (1984), as a means to absorb the essence of music therapy. The following are some guidelines for this personal exploration, based on their ideas. If you are ready to dig a bit deeper into the existential depths of your identity, you are invited to investigate your relationship to music therapy in this phenomenological exercise. To process more effectively, be sure to share your responses with a trusted friend, counselor, or therapist.

Craft your response to any or all of these prompts:

1. **Your background**: a musical autobiography, including music that has significance to you or is associated with important stages of your life or life experience
2. **Your history**: evolution of your process of becoming a music therapist
3. **Syntax**: analysis of the music that you love, including any common themes in the musical elements or lyrics
4. **Sound as such**: analysis of the qualities of the sounds and music that you create as a musician and your psychological and emotional responses to this music
5. **Semantic**: meaning of the music that you relate to most and the meaning of music therapy
6. **Ontology**: your essence or life experience as it is expressed in your work or identity as a music therapist
7. **Metacritical evaluation**: summary or most significant aspects of your responses above and their overall meaning.

Are the choices you are making daily based on the values you described above? As Mindy discovered, self-awareness is what preparation is all about.

Spiritual Preparation

To be prepared spiritually, you do not necessarily have to be religious or believe in God. For the purposes of this book, spiritual preparation means that you are in touch with something great and awesome that is beyond everyday existence. Michael Singer (2007) informs us:

> Ultimately, the word "beyond" captures the true meaning of spirituality. In its most basic sense, going beyond means going past where you are. It means not staying in your current state. When you constantly go beyond yourself, there are no more limitations. There are no more boundaries. Limitations and boundaries only exist at the places where you stop going beyond (p. 119).

Spiritual growth allows for this exploration. It may start with an experience that you are unable to understand or describe fully. It may evolve through your sense of mystery or when you experience coincidence that is outside of your usual expectations. As a music therapist, you encounter the beauty of music and the miracle of life in your daily work. Some consider this experience to be spiritual. Even if you haven't thought much about the power behind these experiences, you probably appreciate their transcendence.

It is easy to get caught up in the demands of living each day and lose sight of the exceptional that is happening in every moment. You may be facing personal challenges at home, such as caring for children and parents, or ill loved ones, in addition to providing music therapy for many companions who are suffering. With these constraints, do you give yourself the space to contemplate the awe and splendor of your sacred work?

In his book, *Awe*, Paul Pearsall (2007) writes:

Awe makes us feel powerless and insignificant yet at the same time also strongly empowered, because we feel we've been uniquely blessed by being given a brief challenging glimpse of a deeper significance to life that we may never understand but must keep trying. It's as if the universe has given us a special privilege—that it sees us as worthy and deserving enough to trust us with a look at its secret, whatever that may be. Awe is when life grants us the chance to think differently and deeper about itself, so that we are not left squandering its gift by languishing it away. Being in awe can make a real mess of our lives by disrupting our certainty about ourselves and the world, but it also enlivens and invigorates our living and can change how we decide to live…With the fuller, deeper awareness and total engagement with all of life that awe brings, the highs are higher, the lows lower, and the sadness will be as deep as the moments of rapture are profound (p. xix).

In choosing a path as a music therapist, you have chosen to be with others who are in pain and whose future is uncertain. Archetypes of suffering and reminders of the brevity and impermanence of life reside in your workplace. Are you able to truly be there alongside your companions? In *The Wisdom of No Escape*, Pema Chödrön (1991) says that we humans avoid pain and seek comfort. Yet we can live more fully and joyfully when we are open and curious to the bitter and sweet in each day. She tells the story of the Navajo, who "teach their children every morning when the sun comes up, it's a brand new sun. It's born each morning, it lives for the duration of one day, and in the evening it passes on, never to return again" (p. 26). There is great wisdom in this tradition, for it teaches the blessing of greeting each day with an appreciation for every precious moment.

As you meet your companion and concentrate on being aware of this precious moment, you may feel ready to offer your talent and your presence, but how will you bond empathically, as Sam did with Debra? Can you allow yourself to relate to the pain, anxiety, or distress so that you can truly bond with your companion? Some music therapists frame their therapeutic relationship such that companions become their muses. This special relationship deeply connects therapist and companion in an imaginative, inspired, and authentic place where mind, body, and spirit meet.

Be Prepared

Every music therapist needs a muse. Who or what is the source of your inspiration? How can you bring this resource into your session? Are you equipped to allow your companion to be your muse?

Take some time to contemplate your relationship with your companions, and think back to a moment of change. It does not have to be transcendent or profound, but it might be. It could be an instant of humor, a smile, a tear, or song. Journal about the gifts that you brought your companions in this moment. Then write about the gifts that you received.

Musical Preparation

Musical preparation is the one area of our journey as music therapists that may be most familiar of all. You have studied and practiced to earn your music therapy credential, so you probably feel prepared musically. But, as you pursue your career as music therapist, your relationship to music is bound to change. If your principal instrument is cumbersome, you may not always have it handy. If your instrument of choice is brass, it may not be feasible to play it in the confines of a shared hospital room or infusion cubicle. If you are an aficionado of a specific musical genre, you will not necessarily find many kindred spirits in your companions. When you are unable to express your own musical needs in your sessions, it is easy to lose sight of the reason you entered this field. You might feel less fulfilled or less confident that you are offering the highest caliber of music for your companion.

In an experiment run by my students at Berklee College of Music, we surveyed more than 500 college students with varying levels of musical training, including music majors who had extensive musical backgrounds. We asked them to complete the Brief Music in Mood Regulation Scale (Saarikallio, 2012), and found an indirect relationship between the number of years of musical training and the frequency of using music as an emotion self-regulation tool. The longer students had spent learning music, the less they used music functionally in their lives to affect their moods. We thought it unfortunate and ironic that so many highly trained music students whose passion brought them to music school failed to appreciate the impact of the medium that inspired them.

Take time to contemplate your musical self, and find yourself a muse. Unveil your instrument, your operatic voice, or some musical channel that may have been closed. Bring more music into your life, and bring more life to your music.

Be Prepared

Does creating music bring you joy? Are you playing the instruments that you love most or singing when you can? Do you take time to listen to your favorite music, not just as background sound while you are multitasking or biding time? Do you listen deeply to the effect that music has on you?

Set aside time to perform, sing, or compose some music that you love. You can also simply listen to a recording (of you or your favorite musician). Savor the qualities of this music by:

* noticing the memories that it elicits
* following your moods as the music flows along
* being mindful of what is happening in your mind, body, and soul.

Then put yourself in the position of companion, rather than therapist.

What music or music experiences would you prescribe for yourself? Is it time to join a chorus or band? Would you like to study your instrument again or learn a new one? Are you feeding your musical needs in continuing education? Are you attending concerts or using your talent to stage musical events? Make a plan to have music play a role in adding more flow and peak experiences to your life.

Your Journey

You can examine each level of your being. You can perform a phenomenological analysis of your past journey, and look at your daily choices. You can work your mind and body, or overwork them both. Hopefully, you have discovered sources of inspiration and gifts that you have received and given along the way. As you step into your clinical session with your companion, put your whole self in. Shake it all about, loosen up, and enjoy the prospect of a new session or a new companion.

7

Stepping into the Journey with Your Companion

In the Introduction to his master's thesis, Sam philosophized about how the therapeutic process is both personal and interpersonal:

> What I love about being a therapist is that it's a field where I get paid to grow myself. Every client that walks into my office offers something different for me to develop a relationship with. As I'm able to form myself in new ways in response to the client, that expansion is what holds the possibility of change for the client as well. And so for the therapy to be effective, we have to be in it together. We have to both be penetrated by each other and thus we have to change and grow together. If I'm not willing to participate in that process, to be just as transformed as the client, then it doesn't leave much room for the client to change either (Samuel Hanser, 2009, pp. 2–3).

Now that you have tuned into your personal journey, you are ready to step into the session and learn how you and your companion can accompany each other on a course to wellness.

© The Editor(s) (if applicable) and The Author(s) 2016
S.B. Hanser, *Integrative Health through Music Therapy*,
DOI 10.1057/978-1-137-38477-5_7

Orchestrating Your Arrival

Being Present

No matter what your philosophical inclination, regardless of your training or approach, being present is a significant, perhaps the most significant, element of being a therapist. Before introducing the music, the technique, or yourself, you must be immersed in the moment, self-aware, open, and accessible to your companion. Cultivating presence is a lifelong process that enhances your effectiveness as a therapist and contributes to your own wellbeing and self-actualization. It may also be referred to as mindfulness, a philosophy birthed in ancient India and fine-tuned in Buddhism. To be present requires an alignment of mind, body, and spirit, and is, thus, a hallmark of integrative health.

Psychotherapist Elana Rosenbaum was diagnosed with non-Hodgkin's lymphoma. In *Here For Now: Living Well with Cancer through Mindfulness*, Rosenbaum (2005) tells a story of being visited by two important people in her life when she was critically ill with pneumonia, after a stem cell transplant:

> I remember them entering the room, gazing at me, recognizing my stillness and simply sitting down. It seemed they brought peace with them. They were not afraid. They felt no need to talk to me, cheer me up, or give me anything material. Instead, they sat and meditated. I felt held. I knew I was safe. All was well. Surrender brought peace and with it all the freedom I ever wished to have... I believe that I survived because I surrendered and let myself sink deep down into the quiet space I felt as I looked out at the sky. Breath by breath, I let myself be breathed. I sunk deeper down into the bed, into each slow, labored breath, and relaxed (p. 113–114).

This is a powerful testament to the influence of presence in Rosenbaum's recovery. She took what she needed from her friends' visit—their breathing tempi, their peaceful demeanors, their deep intentions. The visitors said nothing, did nothing, and fixed nothing. But they each must have been grounded and centered in a way that allowed them to exude peace and be fully present for her, even though they must have been sad and fearful to see their friend in such a state. They sat and meditated, and Elana breathed.

In *Therapeutic Presence*, Shari Geller and Leslie Greenberg (2011) define what it means to be present in a therapeutic relationship:

> Therapeutic presence is the state of having one's whole self in the encounter with a client while being completely in the moment on a multiplicity of levels—physically, emotionally, cognitively, and spiritually. Therapeutic presence involves being in contact with one's integrated and healthy self, while being open and receptive to what is poignant in the moment and immersed in it, with a larger sense of spaciousness and expansion of awareness and perception. This grounded, immersed, and expanded awareness occurs with the intention of being with and for the client in service of his or her healing process. The inner receptive state involves a complete openness to the client's multidimensional internal world, including bodily and verbal expression, as well as openness to the therapist's own bodily experience of the moment in order to access the knowledge, professional skill, and wisdom embodied within. Being fully present then allows for an attuned responsiveness that is based on a kinesthetic and emotional sensing of the other's affect and experience as well as one's own intuition and skill and the relationship between them. The therapist's presence and consequent in-the-moment physical, emotional, and cognitive awareness are a reflection of the client's multilevel expression and act as a receptor and a guide for the process of therapy.
>
> Presence practice provides therapists a way to release the residue of taking in the client's pain and experience. From this perspective, the commitment to presence can help therapists maintain energy and positive flow of experience to prevent burnout. By feeling in contact with their own vitality, therapists can maintain a sense of health and inner connection, including greater well-being, decreased burnout, greater self-care, improved interpersonal relationships, decreased anxiety and heightened vitality (p. 7).

Geller and Greenberg unpack many themes that you can explore in your own life and work as you tune into your physical, emotional, cognitive, and spiritual needs, as outlined in Chap. 6. These authors refer to the embodied experience of knowing yourself and your abilities, and being aware of how this knowledge facilitates the attunement, or alignment, that is possible with another person. This insight may be viewed as part of the therapeutic relationship or alliance, the choice of terms depending upon your philosophy of therapy, but it is interesting that they use the musical term *attunement* to identify this connective resonance.

The word *attunement* means to "bring into a harmonious or responsive relationship" (*The American Heritage˚ Dictionary of the English Language, 4th Edition*, Houghton Mifflin, 2009). The word itself underscores the tweaking, twisting, and turning that are inherent in tuning an instrument. Because you are a music therapist, while you are getting acquainted, you and your companion are attuning to the music as you attune to each other. Through your mutual musical engagement, you tune into the melodic, harmonic, and rhythmic elements, as well as the images, memories, and references that are evoked for each of you. Subtly, the nervous system aligns with the music. Palpably, the body responds when the tone, tempo, and timbre gradually ascend to a climax, or decelerate to peaceful silence. Part of the wonder of music is its ability to soar into frenzy, or suspend into consonance and harmony. Being mindful of where the music is taking you and your companion helps you awaken your mind, body, and spirit, and become a better music therapist.

Geller and Greenberg speak of "presence practice" as a technique for learning how to attune, and they differentiate between mindfulness and therapeutic presence. Practicing mindfulness fosters the therapeutic relationship. When you are mindful of your own thoughts, feelings, sensations, and behaviors, you are practicing openness and receptivity, and you are becoming fully present.

Jon Kabat-Zinn (1994) states:

> Mindfulness means paying attention in a particular way: on purpose, in the present moment, and nonjudgmentally. This kind of attention nurtures greater awareness, clarity, and acceptance of present-moment reality. It wakes us up to the fact that our lives unfold only in moments. If we are not fully present for many of those moments, we may not only miss what is most valuable in our lives but also fail to realize the richness and the depth of our possibilities for growth and transformation (p. 3).

Kabat-Zinn warns that this practice is not rehearsal; it does not make perfect. "Rather we are inviting ourselves to interface with this moment in full awareness, with the intention to embody as best we can an orientation of calmness, mindfulness, and equanimity right here and right now" (p. 22). The process of reaching this state of awareness can be as simple as feeling the breath as it enters and exits our bodies. When the mind wanders, you focus on the breath. When the emotions commandeer attention, you focus on the breath. When the body signals that something is wrong, you focus on the breath. It is remarkable that such a straightforward exercise can elicit massive shifts in our state of being. In his book, *Focus: The Hidden Driver of Excellence*, Daniel Goleman (2013) says that when emotions hijack our wellbeing, we can recover by absorbing ourselves in focused activity. But we must be mindful that this requires a certain type of attention:

> Restoration occurs when we switch from effortful attention, where the mind needs to suppress distractions, to letting go and allowing our attention to be captured by whatever presents itself. But only certain kinds of... focus act to restore energy for focused attention. Surfing the Web, playing video games, or answering email does not (p. 56).
>
> The key is an immersive experience, one where attention can be total but largely passive. This starts to happen when we gently arouse the sensory systems, which quiet down those for effortful focus. Anything we can get enjoyably lost in will do it.
>
> Total positive absorption shuts off the inner voice, that running dialogue with ourselves that goes on even during our quiet moments. That's a main effect of virtually every contemplative practice that keeps your mind focused on a neutral target like your breath or a mantra (p. 57).

Goleman is making a persuasive case not just for the benefits of focusing attention but also for immersing in an absorbing experience. The reverie of a music therapy experience certainly meets this criterion. In that state, amidst beautiful music, your presence is able to work its magic. With a highly focused attention and a release of extraneous thoughts and influences, you can arrive fully present to the awe of the moment, a unique time that will never recur. Amidst pain, suffering, or uncertainty, you can learn to balance this focused attention with the process of letting go. Kabat-Zinn (1994) says, "You can't stop the waves, but you can learn to surf" (p. 30). In the process, music helps us stay afloat.

Being Compassionate

A key element within the supportive environment of the therapeutic relationship and attunement is compassion, or "*tsewa*" in the Tibetan language. The Dalai Lama XIV (2000) believes that compassion is necessary for human survival and for the wellbeing of all sentient beings. In *tsewa*, you are removing the ego, generating empathy, and establishing a deep kinship with all living beings. The Dalai Lama says: "The practice of compassion is at the heart of the entire path" (p. 101). "It is on the basis of your interactions with others that you can attain the highest spiritual realizations" (p. 103). Russell Razzaque (2014) agrees, in *Breaking Down Is Waking Up: Can Psychological Suffering Be a Spiritual Gateway?*

> The more we connect and share with others, the more we recognize our commonality—both the positives and the negatives—and the more we do this, the more we see ourselves in them and, indeed in all there is. That's where we realize that being compassionate was the very purpose of our existence in the first place. Put simply, it's how you find yourself again (p. 245).

Compassion for your companions and self-compassion comingle in the moment. It may appear paradoxical to go inward and reach outwards toward another at the same time. But Angeles Arrien (2010) provides insights for enhancing this type of relational presence, in *The Four-Fold Way: Walking the Paths of Warrior, Teacher, Healer and Visionary.* She presents the shamanic traditions of indigenous cultures through the inner archetypes that every individual possesses:

1. The Way of the Warrior is to show up. You can choose to be fully present.

2. The Way of the Teacher is to practice nonattachment to outcome and to be open to whatever unfolds.
3. The Way of the Healer is to pay attention. Focusing on authentic things that carry meaning from the heart is this way.
4. The Way of the Visionary is to tell the truth. A nonjudgmental attitude can engender intuition and inner vision.

This advice is consistent with many of the approaches of ancient healing, and offers guidelines to practice compassion. These ways call upon your innate abilities, invoking your natural, authentic way of being.
Sam also defined compassion:

> Compassion is what results when you see an "other" as your Self. It is what allows an other to see his or her Self through you. Ultimately, all relationships are but a path toward realizing the one true Self (Samuel Hanser, 2010, p. 32).

Bracketing

It is time to check in. Are you overwhelmed with instructions? Are you frustrated by all those "non-instructions" to allow, let go, and let be? Breathe. It is time to bracket. "Bracketing" means to put a feeling aside temporarily and get on with what you are doing. It is a phenomenological term that refers to the process of suspending previous knowledge and objects of inquiry in order to attend to and describe, rather than explain, that experience (Forinash & Gonzalez, 1989). It is a useful technique for the music therapist who has conceptualized a treatment plan that was created over hours of mental and musical preparation.

As tempting as it is for your mind to focus on your music therapy interventions, you know that it is most essential to be fully present first with your companion. Your plan may be on your mind, but you will need to lose your attachment to it. Bracketing your plan and all that went into it enables you to focus on your therapeutic presence, free yourself of assumptions and expectations, and attend to what is transpiring in the moment. The plan will unfold and its essence will be realized most effectively when you attune to the experience of being with your companion.

It is helpful to give yourself space, as you learned during your spiritual preparation in Chap. 6, to witness and deliberate on the profound nature of connection, and set an intention for your session.

Setting an Intention

An intention is a purpose, hope, or aim for your session. As opposed to a goal, objective, or endpoint, your intention holds a wish that has meaning for you and/or your companion. It may contain something you personally need in order to create a healing environment, for example, "My heart is open to whatever unfolds," "I am centered and calm," "May I be present," or "I shall bring a sense of peace into the room." It may be about your companion, for example, "My companion will have a moment of healing," "Music will soothe my companion," or "May my companion come to a state of acceptance."

Setting an intention primes your brain to get ready for something special. It is much like an internal motivator to remind you to look out for signs of this thought coming to fruition as the session progresses. Articulating your intention helps you gain clarity about what to notice, what to carry with you, and what you have to offer. When your intention becomes internalized and a part of who you are, it will guide you through the session. Once you have orchestrated your arrival, you are prepared to enter the room and meet your companion.

Entering

Sam's words center me when I take my first steps on the journey with my companion:

> Your destination is this moment NOW along the journey. So arrive fully. Let yourself be HERE. Accept it, allow it. And witness the wonderment of creation all about you... If you are willing to receive, you will hear. And what is it that speaks? Your Self. When you can recognize your Self that is the All, then you shall have awakened to your true being (Samuel Hanser, 2010, p. 38).

Welcoming

As you walk across the threshold to meet your companion, you are carrying an aura of compassion and healing. When you arrive, do so only when you are ready to be fully present. Then hold your intention to serve this person. You are serving and nourishing your companion with a "meal" of music.

Introduce yourself with inflection so that the sound of your name offers your companion a sample of the song that you will sing and the music that you will make. Offer plenty of time and space for responses. In every encounter, I introduce myself a little differently, to respect the uniqueness and individuality of every relationship. Here are some of the things I might say. You can select, mix, match, and adapt these alternatives to suit your personal style:

"Hello, I am Suzanne. I'm your music therapist. Your body (and its condition) is (are) in good hands with your medical team. I'm here to (one or more of the following):

- take care of the rest of you
- bring out the healthy you
- help you find your healthy and creative self
- be with you and bring you music
- help you orchestrate your story
- show you ways that music can help you relax, restore, and cope with some of your symptoms
- share music that meets your needs, for example, helps you get some rest, focuses your attention away from your pain, provides a creative outlet to express what is going on with you, offers a medium to learn about your healthy self, releases your inner musician, and so on."

A conversation may introduce a brief assessment of the companion's musical history. Ask questions, such as:
- Do you like music?
- Do you listen to music?
- When you listen, what does music do for you?
- Are you a musician? A singer? Have you ever played any instruments?

Explore your companion's answers with interest. Introduce music therapy in your own way, but be sure to describe how music can aid your companion, and clarify what your companion can hope to gain from experiencing music therapy. Apply your natural curiosity to assess how formal or informal that assessment can be. Use statements or questions, such as:

- I can show you how to use music to help you heal.
- We might explore how music makes you feel.
- What do you think music can do for you? Is there something that you would really like to do musically? Have you always wanted to sing or play an instrument?
- Is there some music that absolutely sends you?
- What are some of your favorite songs or music?
- Do you have a favorite singer, musician, songwriter, or group?

Guiding questions show your interest in your companion. You can introduce music at any time, so that your companion has a sample of what you do. Follow up with any of the following, along with demonstrations, if appropriate:

"Music therapy might help you:

- relax
- focus on the positive and creative forces within you
- bring out the musician inside you
- identify inner calm
- use your creative energy or find your creative healing energy
- learn coping strategies using your own special music
- move through your pain
- restore your energy
- recover
- find your creative self—I'll bet you didn't think you would develop your talent in this hospital!
- learn not just to get through this, but really LIVE through this
- make your day more musical and less anxious
- tap into your hidden talents
- make your hospital stay a creative retreat
- identify your own resources for healing
- give you an experience of awe"

You might give more specific examples:

- I can teach you how to focus on music to relieve your pain.
- We can sing some of your favorite songs, and you might forget some of your symptoms.
- I would like to play some music for you and take your mind far away from the hospital.

Hopefully, you have your own special way of introducing yourself and what you do. When you display your musical instruments that will, literally, accompany the journey, offer them as the precious gifts that they represent. Present them as if on a tray of shiny silver in a ceremonial healing banquet. Uncover your offerings with great care. As this ritual unfolds, bring your awareness to your companion and your intention. Then check in with your emotions and reactions. Breathe. Offer your presence and compassion. Bracket those thoughts and plans that you don't need just yet.

You can decide when to start the music versus have a conversation about music. In most cases, I like to introduce myself through music. I particularly enjoy playing the Native American flute to set a tranquil mood and reinforce my intention. I ask my companion just to listen and notice any effects. Playing the flute resets my own parasympathetic nervous system on a course to relaxation. The deep intake of breath and the lengthy, extended exhalation into the flute naturally signal soothing parasympathetic activity. The musical illustration gives my companion a flavor of music therapy to come, and we can talk about the influence that it had on mind, body, or spirit.

Many of my colleagues prefer to begin with a stringed instrument, a guitar or harp, or their own voices to initiate a musical conversation. Use your intuition and your growing connection with your companion to gauge how to apply music at this stage.

Actively Listening

Listen actively. That means using your whole body to respond to your companion's words and affect. Your body language and facial cues are authentic communicators of support and interest, and naturally engender trust and openness. Your eye contact, gestures, and facial affect are capable of encouraging your companion to say more or less, to get excited or relax, and to respond or just be. Your demeanor in this period of getting acquainted will contribute to your attunement.

When your companion speaks, listen for words that communicate underlying emotions. Restate the exact words to acknowledge that you have been listening and then reinforce the depth of that feeling, such as, "I see that you're nervous about this procedure," "Yes, you're afraid you'll need surgery," or "It is so overwhelming to be faced with all these decisions." Venture an educated guess about the feelings that may lie underneath or beyond your companion's words, such as, "That must be frightening," "That sounds like a lonely place to be," "Do you feel sad about being hospitalized?" or "It is so frustrating to wait so long for these lab results." These are not just your conjectures. Rather, your response will emanate from the verbal and nonverbal cues you receive from your companion and will reflect your potential interpretations. Whether your companion agrees with or refutes your understanding, your comments can provide a springboard for conversation about those unspoken feelings. When your friendly conversation turns inward towards the unstated, it becomes an exchange of confidences between intimates and bonds your relationship at a more profound level.

Gentle, probing questions show your interest and concern, and lead the way to a more formal assessment of your companion's needs and background. Concentrate on the emotional elements, as opposed to the content. For example, you might say, "It has to be difficult to be bedridden all day," instead of saying, "When will they let you out of bed?" Or, you may ask, "What are your concerns about having this diagnosis?" instead of "What is your diagnosis?"

Bring awareness to the rhythm of your conversation, and conform to your companion's tempo. If appropriate, gradually slow down a frenetic interaction or speed up a lethargic one, gently guiding the flow. Your intonation will provide important cues to your intention. With your companion's help, identify some of the presenting problems that you can address through music therapy. Modify your initial intention as you hear more from your companion. Address each of the levels of awareness, as you discuss physical, emotional, mental, existential, and spiritual needs.

You might frame the conversation around some of the issues and techniques you began to apply to yourself in Chap. 6.

Enhancing Comfort

Physical comfort is an important prerequisite. Is your companion in a comfortable position in the bed or chair? Are you comfortable? Are you leaning over the hospital bed and twisting your body in order to maintain eye contact with your companion? Ask your companion what you can do to make him or her more at ease. Find a more natural position for your own body. Is there natural lighting in the room, and would your companion like you to open shades?

A healing environment must provide the smells, sounds, sights, and tastes of home, or provide peace, wherever possible. Due to restrictive diets and potential allergies to different smells, it may not be feasible to provide new sensual offerings to our companions. But you can consider other changes in the immediate environment to create a pleasant sensory experience. If there are family or friends visiting, they are excellent sources for collecting sounds and signs of home. Let them be proxies for informing you of your companion's tastes and wishes, particularly musically and artistically. If there are greeting cards or photos of loved ones, make sure they are positioned or mounted where they can be seen clearly by your companion.

Whether or not there are objects and images of personal significance, your presence and your music are innately capable of bathing your companion in comfort and beauty.

Retreating

Changing your routine by taking time for yourself can be a transformative experience. When I visited southern India, I chose to stay at an ashram and live rather primitively while engaging in a spiritual retreat. I elected confinement to a simpler life without electronic distractions and duties to my family and community. I chose this opportunity to be me and see me without all the frills and makeup. I sought this time for greater self-awareness and contemplation. Far from the customary environmental contingencies and responsibilities, I created a space for self-reflection in pursuit of personal meaning. For me, the requirements were openness, silence, and faith that this experience would guide me in directions that I needed to travel.

Moving my body halfway around the world, I saw the sun set when dawn brightened my New England home, and my body's clock chimed a wake-up call when everyone was fast asleep in India. This alone made me physically weaker and psychologically more vulnerable. In this unfamiliar place, it was difficult to know where I would be safe, where I could find things I needed, and whom to trust. The day after several of us arrived at the ashram, one man left for home, unable to cope with the uncertainties and personal discomforts. I prevailed, feeling as though this vulnerability contributed to my openness to a new way of thinking about my life and my lifestyle. This nascent environment was where I started writing this book.

When our companions enter the hospital, that backward LATIPSOH world, they are confined by illness. They have not chosen this retreat. The ambiance, with its concomitant pain and suffering, offers a schedule that is prescribed and artificial, with interruptions for treatments and examinations. The tests are often true tests of endurance, like puncturing delicate skin to examine the blood flowing in the invisible rivers of the veins and arteries. Other extractions of bodily fluids can be even more invasive and painful, as are many treatments that will be endured. This prison has an undetermined term. Bed rails protect from falls, but also constrict any movement beyond the bars. Tubes line the track for healing medicines and removal of toxins, but also tie our companions to the bed. Rest and recuperation may be antithetical to the medical regimes, but necessary for healing to take place. It is up to us music therapists to transform the institution of the hospital into the retreat center of the ashram, where one comes not only for healing, but for insight. We can create a healing environment for our companions, with our companions, whether hospitalized or at home, with space for spiritual development as well as physical recovery.

The sounds must vary between music and silence. I benefited from the many hours of silence to allow myself to feel truly peaceful. There is a famous quote by Debussy: "Music is the silence between the notes." Interestingly, there is a great deal of brain activity in the silence that precedes a musical phrase, in anticipation of the music. Of course, you will recall that the silence after OM is believed to be a significant part of connecting the chanter with the Divine. Silence occurs when we halt the influx of auditory stimuli to which we can never close our ears. Although there is no true silence (we can always hear our own inner workings), there are times when we need to stop the music, come to rest, and listen deeply. We music therapists must be as adept at honoring silence as we are in respecting the music that we offer.

Whatever our companions' religious beliefs, faith is a critical aspect of the healing process. Faith in the physician and medical team, faith in the treatments being offered, and faith that there will be movement in the physical state of being over time, all contribute to healing. Experimentation on the placebo effect (placebo is Latin for "I will please") confirms the healing properties of a treatment that holds promise for cure or amelioration. When one believes in the positive impact of a therapy or medication, its influence will likely be greater than otherwise expected. Trust in the music therapist to provide beneficial experiences, and confidence in music as a therapeutic tool, will boost the impact of music therapy. As you allow your companions to sample many musical gifts, your mutual engagement is capable of fostering the attunement and union that result in trust. This musical alliance is particularly valuable in setting the stage for special rituals and ceremonies that accompany landmarks in the healing journey.

Creating Rituals and Ceremonies

Chödrön (1991) writes, "Genuine, heartfelt ritual helps us reconnect with power and vision as well as with the sadness and pain of the human condition. When the power and vision come together, there's some sense of doing things properly for their own sake" (p. 78). Rituals are performed for their symbolic value and empower a person to rediscover and connect, whether it is to the Divine in ancient observances or modern religion, or to the sacredness of every moment and human action. Healing rituals have been practiced by our ancestors and contemporary healers alike. Ceremonies bring people together in community to acknowledge and show reverence to life transitions, milestones, and special occasions. Music therapists have the opportunity to design and enhance rituals and ceremonies that commemorate stages of healing and bring meaning to the experience of illness or wellness.

As you start out on this journey with your companion, you might wish to establish a ritual for both of you as something that you practice together whenever you meet. This may take the form of a welcoming song to signal the start of your sessions. It may be a musical improvisation that represents the bond of attunement between you. It may be as simple as clearing a space for music therapy, or as complex as creating a soundscape for healing. Whatever you choose, your music and your presence will reinforce an intention for music therapy.

As portable music devices are wiring people to their music, your companions, especially younger ones, are probably accustomed to hearing recorded music whenever they wish to plug in. Providing your live music establishes a very different atmosphere. With the vibrations of sound, intimacy of a shared musical experience, and individualization of music in real time, our companions have what may be a rare opportunity to feel sounds and interact with them as they desire. Within this context, your live music has an acoustic advantage that literally brings your companions closer to the source of its creation, all within the safe container of the therapeutic relationship. You customize these musical experiences to the companion's preferences and change it to accommodate evolving needs. Throughout the generations, active music-making has enhanced rituals and ceremonies significantly.

In *Rituals of Healing: Using Imagery for Health and Wellness,* Jeanne Achterberg, Barbara Dossey, and Leslie Kolkmeier (1994) provide a formula for creating a healing ritual:

• Select a goal, problem, or disease.
• Start the ritual with preparation and intention (meditation, relaxation, or focus on the breath).

- Suggest images for the following:

  - problem or disease
  - inner healing resources (faith, strength, optimism)
  - external healing resources (love, family, support systems)

- Complete the ritual with images of wellbeing or desirable state of mind, body, and soul.

Music therapists integrate music into rituals to help generate these images and set a peaceful mood. The musical elements may include:

- predictable rhythms to provide the heartbeat of the music
- simple, flowing melody to accompany gentle guidance
- harmony with just a few surprises as you bring up the problem, and with resolution at the solution
- slow tempo for relaxation
- soft dynamics for a peaceful experience
- steady ostinato, or repeated ground bass line, for a sense of constancy and grounding
- variations and embellishments, like a trill to emulate bird calls, to bring the external world of nature inside
- selective dissonances and musical suspensions to represent a problem that resolves into consonance, to represent the path to wellbeing
- reharmonization of traditional arrangements, such as deceptive cadences and other unexpected harmonies to represent questions and answers, and add movement or surprise to the music.

Here are two simple rituals for my companions, Kate and Martin. Please adapt for your needs, as you see fit.

Kate's Ritual. Kate commences her chemotherapy with a blessing over the bag of medications that will be infused into her body. To prepare the ritual, Kate's nurse and I begin in silence, and place our hands over the liquid. We whisper, "May this medicine flow and bring swift healing," repeating the phrase louder and louder. Then we sing the first stanza of the Beatles' "Let It Be." Kate says, "When we do this, I feel protected and loved. It gives me confidence in my treatment."

Martin's Ritual. Martin is preparing for surgery. I ask him to close his eyes and picture a complete recovery. Martin says, "I am smiling and pain-free." I ask about his inner resources, and he responds, "a healthy heart." I ask if there is anything that he needs to let go of, and he says, "Tension." Martin agrees to try a short, guided meditation. He sits comfortably, and I strum the guitar in between the following phrases:

Take a deep breath and inhale life-affirming breath. Exhale anything you don't need right now. If you find that you are feeling tense, gently move that part of your body and breathe into it. Bring life-affirming breath to any points of tension with your inhalation, and let go of tension as you exhale.

(*I observe Martin moving his neck and shoulders, so I guide him to breathe into each part of his upper body.*)

Breathe deeply and easily, along with the music.

(*The musical interlude imitates waves of tension and release, as I strum eighth notes during inhalation, and quarter notes for the exhalation and release.*)

Focus your attention on your breath, and as you breathe in, say to yourself, "My healthy heart," and as you breathe out, say to yourself, "is beating strong."

(*We continue for five repetitions.*)

Go back to focusing on your breath, and breathe with the music.

(*I begin adding variations of themes and reharmonizing the chords to develop and extend the music in interesting ways.*)

If you notice any worries or thoughts that you don't need right now, recognize them and let them go, without judgment. Let them go as you exhale. Inhale life-affirming breath.

(*I simplify the music here, and play while checking in to ensure that Martin looks relaxed.*)

Now picture yourself the morning of your surgery. You are smiling and confident.

(*The music gains momentum by becoming louder, slightly faster, and more rhythmic.*)

Your heart is strong. You feel some anxiety, but you focus on your breath. You inhale confidence. You exhale anything you don't need. You feel more and more confident and calm. Try that now. As you inhale, think "confidence;" as you exhale, think "Let go and be calm." You sleep as your surgeon does what he does so well. The surgery goes very smoothly. You wake up smiling and with some pain, but confident that you will experience only the amount of pain that you can handle. Your heart is healthy. Recovery is swift.

(*I slow the music down and gradually come to silence.*)
How do you feel, Martin?

Assessing

You have observed and listened to your companion throughout the session. In addition to the conversations you have had, you were able to observe responses to your music, and follow up with questions about what your companion was experiencing internally. This has informed your overall assessment of needs and will help you develop a plan to address them. In *Manage Your Stress and Pain through Music*, Dr. Susan Mandel and I (Hanser & Mandel, 2010) provide some guidelines for assessment of stress and pain, complaints that are common in the medical setting.

The stress assessment asks companions to describe their stress. They explain where they tend to feel tension in their bodies and what they are thinking when they experience stress. They rate their overall stress and body tension, so that they can monitor changes under varying conditions and notate their responses in a log. The pain assessment requires them to describe the nature of their pain, rate its strength, examine factors that affect any fluctuations in pain, and detail conditions that increase or ease the perception of pain. When you understand your companions' perspectives and experiences, you will be able to more finely tune your intervention to help them. Be sure to record the specific words used by your companions to describe their viewpoints, so that you can affirm these, when you develop your customized plan. Using their words reinforces the unity between you, and can strengthen your alliance.

You may wish to use a visual analogue scale (VAS) to assess the current status of your companions. The VAS is straightforward, speedy to administer, and can provide a pre-test and post-test for evaluating change and growth during the course of music therapy. Here is a simple one that I designed at Dana-Farber Cancer Institute in Boston. When I print this assessment, the line is exactly 10 cm long, and I can easily measure the distance from its start to the marks made by companions, to compare their responses before and after a session (see Fig. 7.1).

This scale assesses four clinical outcomes: tension/relaxation, comfort, happiness, and pain, but you can substitute any factors that are important to your companion. Consider including: anxiety/relaxation, agitation/peace, fulfillment, balance, acceptance, hope, spiritual weakness/strength, or any other goals.

Keeping the Music Alive

When you leave your companions, think about how they can access music in your absence. You may or may not be able to lend them musical instruments, but if they have access to a music listening device, you can help them create playlists so that they can manage their moods and potentially their symptoms. *Manage Your Stress and Pain through Music* provides a music listening log (see Fig. 7.2) to help you prepare these playlists for your companions. The suggested playlists include:

- attention-focusing music for pain management
- energizing music for depression or isolation
- relaxing music for anxiety reduction
- sleep-inducing music for deep relaxation
- spiritual music for peak experiences and flow

I like to interview my companions about the music that they loved playing, singing, or listening to throughout their lives—from childhood through adolescence into adulthood—at important milestones or events, as well as during their daily activities. Then I sort their favorites into the playlist categories above. Alternatively, you can use these classifications to outline your interview and then develop the playlists. If you are not able to devote the required time to this task, you could ask your companions for their top 10 or 12 favorite songs or pieces of music. Simply learning about music preferences teaches you a great deal about your companions and focuses them on significant memories, relationships, and values that this music elicits. Rather than talking about their physical conditions, illnesses, and treatments, identifying favorite songs gets them to talk about who they are and what it is important to them. Music therapist and physician Dr. Maria Hernandez burns these playlists onto a personalized CD that she gives to the participants in our research at Boston Medical Center. Her companions conceive the title and suggest design elements for the CD label. Their creations are legacies of their identities and serve to elevate their moods when they are in need. CD titles are as diverse as the people who created them. Here are a few:

- "Sorrowful Songs for Sleep"
- "Relieve"
- "Eight" (for eight hospital admissions)
- "The Zebra Effect" (he felt like a zebra because nobody could diagnose his malady easily)
- "The Pancreas Collection" (yes, he was admitted for pancreatitis)
- "Bacha Salsa"
- "Mom's Music"
- "Mi Musica Alegre" (she loved to dance)

Going Home

At the close of our session, I try to summarize what I learned about my companion's needs, wishes, and musical interests. I make sure that we are in agreement about our intentions and plans, and we determine the time of our next encounter. I like to end every session with music as a way of saying farewell. The music is the choice of my companion, and when I don't know this particular music, my companion is usually a willing teacher.

The next challenge is exiting the room. We have undoubtedly formed bonds, so I will need to form boundaries before moving to my next companion or to my family at home. Every therapist has a distinctive way of

ANSWER <u>BEFORE</u> (<u>AFTER</u>) THE SESSION

<u>Directions</u>

Put a mark on the line at the point that best describes how you feel right now.

1. **Extremely
   Tense**   **Extremely
                                               Relaxed**

   _____

2. **Extremely
   Uncomfortable**   **Extremely
                                               Comfortable**

   _____

3. **Extremely
   Unhappy**   **Extremely
                                               Happy**

   _____

4. **In Extreme
   Pain**   **Not In
                                               Pain**

   _____

Fig. 7.1 Visual analogue scale

taking this protective stance that allows us to preserve energy and build up a new supply quickly. My way is to perform a little ritual of my own when I cross the threshold once again. If I am not carrying too many instruments, I back out of the room, keeping my gaze on my companion

Music Listening Log

Rating Scale

Date: _____

0   1   2   3   4   5

0 = None   5 = Most

Playlists (categories)
A. *Attention focusing*
B. *Energizing*
C. *Relaxing*
D. *Sleep inducing*
E. *Spiritual*
F. *Other* _____
G. *Leftovers*

Favorite Music Selections:

- Music with happy memories

                                          Rate Relaxation   Rate Enjoyment   Playlist

Childhood _____   _____   _____   _____

Teenage years _____   _____   _____   _____

Television, movies, concerts _____   _____   _____   _____

Relationships _____   _____   _____   _____

Milestones, celebrations _____   _____   _____   _____

Vacations _____   _____   _____   _____

Religious or spiritual occasions _____   _____   _____   _____

- Recent listening _____   _____   _____   _____

                                          _____   _____   _____

Match Your Music

	Playlist		Playlist
Good morning	_____	*Painful encounters*	_____
Off to work	_____	*Bedtime*	_____
Household chores	_____	*Weekends*	_____
Time to unwind	_____	*Travel*	_____
Stressful moments	_____	*Other*	_____

Fig. 7.2 Music listening log (Reprinted with permission from Figure 4.8, page 37, Hanser, S.B., & Mandel, S.E. (2010). *Manage Your Stress and Pain Through Music.* Boston, MA: Berklee Press)

for as long as I can. It is the same ritual I perform after prayers at the Western Wall in Jerusalem, when I continue to face the wall, walking backwards until I am no longer surrounded by those who are praying and meditating. It is a demonstration of my respect for the sacred. Then I take a deep life-affirming breath, and just as Sam would have me do, I focus on "this moment NOW along the journey. So (I) arrive fully. (I) let (my)self be HERE. Accept it; allow it. And witness the wonderment of creation all about (me) (Samuel Hanser, 2010, p. 38)."

8

Orienting to the Journey: The Mythic Way

In his writings, Sam Hanser refers to truth as the destination for the journey through life. Sam warns of the fear that leads us away from the path home:

> I wish you many blessings on your journey… There are many paths to the truth but the truth is One. And you must walk your own path for only yours can lead you to this truth. Ultimately, we are all on our way home. In the meantime, it helps to keep in mind that the relative realm holds relative truths—these are constantly changing. In the realm of the absolute, however, there is absolute truth—this is eternal. We occupy both, so both are relevant. Just remember, you will encounter many relative realms on your journey, but you can never leave the realm of the absolute.
>
> When in doubt, the truth is self-evident. If it must be explained and justified and argued away, then it is not truth. Only fear works through logic and dependency, while the truth needs no defense. Always, as has been said, the truth will set you free (Samuel Hanser, 2010, p. 1).

© The Editor(s) (if applicable) and The Author(s) 2016
S.B. Hanser, *Integrative Health through Music Therapy*,
DOI 10.1057/978-1-137-38477-5_8

Sam would say that to contact the absolute realm, you must be absolutely present. This is difficult when you or your companions are in pain and experiencing suffering in the present moment. But pain exists in the relative realm. It moves, morphs, and changes. It has a journey of its own. It is by paying attention to the way that the pain is changing that you can gain insights about how you can reduce the suffering around it. As music therapists, we can remain present with our companions' pain, and shake it up or gently guide it with our music.

When faced with a chronic or terminal illness, the truth may be hard to bear. Fear leads us to a dark place that obstructs our view of the absolute truth. The medical vernacular may confuse us. We can become separated from the safe and familiar places, and people we know and love. The truth lies along our path, but it can be obscured by the veil of pain and suffering. The journey from illness to wellness twists and zigzags, and it is easy to get lost at any of the mileposts on the way.

The idea of taking a journey is symbolic, metaphoric, archetypical, and representative of living life with its many vicissitudes. The multiple meanings of "journey" are at the core of this book. Moment to moment, we travel in different directions through time and space. Similarly, the journey from illness to wellness is multidimensional and unique for every individual. This chapter and the next introduce six people who have embarked on this path, some of whom used music or music therapy and some who did not. Their insights are instrumental to understanding how music therapy can enlighten our companions to the awe of the journey.

Joseph Campbell's mythic journey of the hero (Campbell, 2008) parallels the challenges and rewards in our companions' travels through the medical system. Campbell's hero is an archetype for the individual who resides in the ordinary world of the common day but is called into the unknown, a place of supernatural wonder. The themes of this journey are as omnipresent in ancient rituals and modern dramas as they are in stages of psychological growth. I offer an interpretation of the steps of the Hero's Journey as they relate to the road from illness to wellness.

Campbell's Mythic Hero	Companion with Music Therapist
1. Hero becomes uneasy in the common day world	Companion finds a sign or symptom
2. Hero is called into the supernatural world	Companion knows something is wrong, but the cause or meaning is mysterious
3. Hero is fearful and becomes a victim	Companion is fearful, and ignores the signs, becoming a victim
4. Guide, mentor, or supernatural aide appears	Music therapist appears and gives the companion the gift of music
5. Hero crosses the threshold	Companion enters the medical center or into the unknown and goes inward
6. Hero undergoes an initiation of trials, for example, dragons to be slain; finds allies and enemies	Companion undergoes painful and unpleasant medical procedures; is stripped of dignity; finds people who hurt and people who help
7. Hero meets Goddess, who shows unconditional love	Music therapist returns and offers unconditional regard; reminds companion of the gift of music that can transform the experience of illness
8. Hero confronts death or fear of abandonment	Companion confronts death or loss
9. Hero learns the sustaining power of an imperishable energy	Companion learns the sustaining power of music and love
10. Hero leaves the world of the supernatural	Companion leaves the medical center
11. Hero is tested again	Companion experiences challenges after recovery or returning home
12. Hero returns home or continues the journey with the gift of the elixir	Companion returns home or continues with gifts of music and love

The steps along the journey from illness to wellness are analogous to the mythic hero's epic adventures. Both are fraught with uncertainty and fear, imbued with power and wonder, and enhanced by insight and love. Although everyone's path is distinctive, many individuals who are ill will encounter similar milestones. In this chapter, we see how Sally's and Helen's journeys follow the hero's ways.

First Signs and Symptoms

Sally's Journey

I was in for an annual checkup, and my doctor noticed that my white blood cell count was off. I went to the hematologist referred by my doctor and that's when I learned that I had something in the spectrum of leukemia or lymphoma. I was stunned: "Is that what you are saying, that I have either leukemia or lymphoma?" I asked several times. She recommended a bone biopsy and CAT scan (computerized axial tomography, an x-ray that reveals cross-sectional images). I never thought that I could have cancer. From that appointment on, I was just trying to keep my head together and trying not to go down the road that this is the end of my life. Nothing was clear. I was trying to not spin into the future. My life shrank to the day-to-day stuff, but there was a sense of my conscious mind having tunnel vision and not wanting to see anything beyond the necessary things every day. This felt like a safer place to be than what I would have been going to—what things might be. All of my energy was trying to keep balance, keep going, and that felt harder than terror.

I was focused on the day-to-day, and my sister was worrying about me. One of the things that my sister did was to check in with me every day, and I told my sister that made things worse. "These calls—I can't deal with them every day," I said.

The CAT scan was first. I was conscious of being really scared because I was going to find out if "they" were in the lymph nodes or not. I was terrified because I felt that I was entering the medical system, and this was the beginning of something, and it might be lymphoma, and I was scared to death. Another part of me was intellectually interested in the CAT scan process, what was going on in my body, what they were showing. When the technician said, "It's going to feel like you are peeing," that was really interesting. There was a curiosity on one side and a terror on the other.

When I said my world shrank, I realized afterwards that I was numbed out. I had the bone biopsy a few days later. The physician explained that it wouldn't be painful and would take about 20 minutes. So she is doing the procedure, and she says that I am about to faint. I guess that I wasn't as relaxed as I thought. When I went back for the bone biopsy results, the doctor said, "It can be anything from reaction to a virus to leukemia," and I'm thinking, "Okay, I am entering the cancer system." I then saw a hematologist along with the physician. They went through the results, translating them into layman's terms: "This result is in the normal range. There is nothing to worry about."

There was such relief, but my sister and I didn't want to look elated in front of the other cancer patients. That was the end of being in the medical system. I realized that I hadn't felt my body in a while. I needed a break and really went underground. I needed time off to re-enter the world.

The Road Traveled

Sally's shock over the possibility of having lymphoma or leukemia made her retreat into a gloomy place inside herself, where she could avoid the frightening external possibilities. Fear made her a victim of the uncertainty of her future, and she was unable to feel anything. Fortunately, Sally only wandered a short way into the pit of medical tests before she was able to return home free of concern. Even then, re-entry was difficult. The doctors' final pronouncement rendered the entire journey meaningless. She took the first three steps of the Hero's Journey, from the doctor's office with its mysterious and shocking news, to the unreal province of a potential cancer patient, to the obscure place of numbness, never allowing herself to meet her guide. She could not reach out to a friend or ask for help throughout her ordeal. I wonder if music therapy could have given her comfort, lulled her to sleep, or contained her fears in a supportive, loving way. I wonder if she could have immersed herself in the music deeply enough to emerge transcendent, as Joseph Campbell would predict.

The Road Beyond

When you encounter the "dis-ease" of problematic signs or symptoms, your response can be fraught with panic, agitation, or numbness, as it was for Sally. Whether you are experiencing lethargy or achiness, pain or immobility, you need to identify what it means in order to find its source and alleviate the problem. But fear of the unknown throws off our rhythm, our stamina, and our wellbeing.

Today, anyone can go online and investigate what is wrong with them. A symptom is any subjective factor that you identify. A sign is more objective and can be observed by someone else, like Sally's medical report. One particular website requires entering your symptoms and pointing to their location on the schematic of a human body. Upon completion, it spews out a list of potential medical conditions. I tried it and described some minor discomfort that I had been having. After I answered all relevant questions, it listed kidney stone, tick bite, or spinal stenosis, among other varied and threatening conditions. I wasn't worried about my pang of pain before, but after getting the information I was seeking, I sure was!

Encountering these first signs and symptoms can signal danger, threat of major impairment, fear of a debilitating condition, or any number of psychological panic reactions. Of course, the condition may be quite temporary and benign, or it can be the first sign of something quite severe and life threatening. Because most people discover worrisome symptoms at home during the course of their daily lives, they usually do not have immediate access to expert opinions. Even with the benefit of medical expertise, as in Sally's case and with my experience online, the signs can be inconclusive and misleading. If the symptoms are severe, you might call an emergency number or find transport to the nearest emergency room. These circumstances alone can be extremely stressful, to put it mildly.

A few months ago, while eating dinner at home, my husband felt faint and turned ashen. I called 911, and the fire company sent their crew immediately. Sirens blasted through the neighborhood, and a team of firefighters in full garb started pushing our furniture aside as I frantically threw the dishes out of the way. A gurney rolled through our front door, and more furniture was upended. An IV was started, and my husband was wheeled out to the ambulance. After a wild ride to the local hospital, the emergency room assistant required paperwork and explanations that made me feel incompetent, as I couldn't answer all of the questions about my husband's medications and medical history. The medical team was unable to diagnose the cause of his near fainting. However, we were relieved that they did rule out the most severe causes. We were extremely grateful to these emergency responders and the seriousness with which they approached his case. However, it was the ensuing trauma of entering the emergency system that raised his blood pressure and heart rate, not his underlying condition. His heart proved to be in perfectly fine condition, but the psychological sequelae strongly affected his functioning and wellbeing.

These sorts of crises occur at times when people need help coping with their internal worries as well as the external environment. But before they access the team of healthcare professionals that includes a music therapist, they are on their own. Once within the healthcare system, our companions can benefit from techniques that they can employ the next time they encounter concerns or symptoms. They need to be reminded that acknowledging fear is important, as is being patient and kind to one's self, while sensing worrisome cues that something is wrong. Being reactive when we feel under threat may be instinctive, but more adaptive responses can stall the exacerbation of symptoms or signs that are due to anxiety. Our companions may not be able to control symptoms directly, but they can learn to manage their nervousness and fear, and to ameliorate some of their symptoms. You can teach your companions how to call upon their inner resources as well as music therapy interventions for dealing with the fear of the unknown.

There are many self-help books on coping with stress and fear. Drs. Arthur Barsky and Emily Deans wrote one, called *Stop Being Your Symptoms and Start Being Yourself: A 6-Week Mind-Body Program to Ease Your Chronic Symptoms* (2006). These two physicians present a positive approach to thinking about your symptoms. They suggest taking control of your health, shifting the focus from symptoms to yourself, rethinking your symptoms, changing your life situation, undoing the damage of unproductive behaviors, brightening your mood, and learning coping strategies. Music therapists build on these techniques to remind our companions that they are not their symptoms, but rather whole persons and creative change agents who can take charge of their wellbeing.

By focusing on the breath, your companions can get in touch with their internal rhythms and bring awareness to both the regularities and irregularities of their natural breathing rhythms. They can learn to "tune in" and attune to the healthy aspects of their being by listening to music that they love, while noticing their innate responses. The associations and memories that come to mind, the visual images that are elicited, and the changes in mood are indicative of the positive psychophysiological changes that are possible when engaged in music activities. One of the self-directed music therapy techniques useful at this stage is music-facilitated breathing. Your companions can experiment with a variety of musical stimuli and self-assess the influence of these pieces on their breathing, their moods, and their overall wellbeing.

Music that is meaningful and significant can change your companion's state of mind and body almost immediately. While engaged with music, you and your companions will be able to observe the specific impact of each musical experience, and select those activities or pieces to affect desirable change. Following a musical path together provides an opening into the internal world of your companion and a way to initiate a psychotherapeutic relationship and process that can illuminate the nature of your companion's fears and hopes.

Diagnosis

Helen's Journey

I was born with the "Sick Cell" and my mom said that I had a crisis when I was six months old and when I was four years old. I needed to be in the hospital often, and there were certain things that I couldn't do because it would trigger getting sick. My friends didn't know what was going on with me. One time, I got sick at school and they had to call the ambulance, and the whole, entire school was looking at this poor girl going in an ambulance to the hospital. So when I went back to school, they were asking, "What happened to you? What's wrong with you?" and I was so embarrassed.

I always avoided talking about it, because for people that didn't know what sickle cell was, they thought it was contagious. Often, my immune system was compromised, so anything in the air could get me really sick. They had me on reverse precautions, which meant that I had to cover myself completely with a mask, hat, gloves, everything. So, once when I got into an elevator, the people who were inside saw me, and they all moved to the other side of the elevator. You could see in their faces the fear of getting it.

I was always behind, having to be in the hospital. I actually finished my high school years at home because I got so sick that I couldn't go back to school. But I was strong enough to be at my graduation. I started college and I got really sick and had to stop. I mean, sickle cell has been tough, but on the other hand, it's not stopping me from doing the things that I like.

When my daughter was three years old, I got extremely sick. Nobody here could care for her, and I was in the hospital. A baby needs mom, and I couldn't provide for her. When she came to visit, she would cry, "I don't want to go. I want to stay with mommy. I want mommy." I'm in pain with a disease that is causing pain, but then I am in emotional distress because my child is crying, and she wants to stay with me.

When I start to get sick, I think, "Oh my God, I don't even want to think about it," and I start doing more work or trying to distract my brain by doing something else. This time around in the hospital, my coping skill was having music therapy. When I am by myself, all there is, is pain, pain, pain. I can only think about all the problems that I have. But when I have a distraction, and I have the piano, which is awesome; it allows me to cope. I use all these coping strategies that my music therapist taught me—the breathing, the images. I am more relaxed, the pain is not as severe, and it works!

I have learned how strong I can be and how to have more faith in God. I learned that life is difficult and not everything that I want can happen. I don't think I have enough time. So, I want to try everything. I'm not afraid to try. Because, I'm like, "Wait, if I don't try, I might not have another chance." It's kind of heavy, because I don't know for sure. But in my mind, I am thinking I might die sooner, so I better try all this and gain a lot of knowledge in life, because I might not be here tomorrow, you know?

The Road Traveled

To her high school friends, and strangers who feared her surgical mask as an indicator of a contagious disease, Helen became defined by her diagnosis. But Helen has prevailed, graduated from high school, married, had a daughter, and kept a good job. The travails have been enormous, but she was guided by the love of her family and her faith in God. One of her strongest allies was the music therapist who taught her how to be a musician and how to use music to help her cope with pain, whether in the hospital or at home. Helen's experience with Dr. Maria Hernandez, her music therapist, provided her with a new identity as a pianist. Dr Hernandez taught Helen some familiar tunes on the keyboard, then added a bass note or two to provide a bit of challenge. Helen practiced for hours. This motivated her to move past her pain and play music she never thought could emanate from her own fingers. Helen's journey started as a baby, but never did she succumb to that third step in the Hero's Journey of becoming a victim of a cruel, chronic disease. She was continually tested in her hospitalizations, but crossed each threshold with hope and spiritual strength, thanks to the support of her mother, husband, and music therapist.

The Road Beyond

When your companion's medical condition is labeled with a diagnosis, the fear and uncertainty surrounding the meaning of initial signs and symptoms are generally relieved. A diagnosis brings some answers, sometimes eagerly awaited and sometimes dreaded. The diagnosis will map the rest of the journey, at least the next steps and a prognosis. When there is an easily treatable condition, the report may be better than expected, and the response is, most often, gratitude. When, however, the diagnosis is more serious, it can result in a psychological and existential emergency. The diagnosis of a chronic or untreatable disease will obviously affect the future in significant ways, and our companions may struggle to find a course of action. Finding meaning in the experience may come to the forefront in the companion's life. In the case of a condition that has treatment options, these will have to be weighed and considered. The diagnosis offers an indication of what will be required. As your companion integrates this new knowledge about treatment, it may become easier to communicate and reach out for help.

Your music therapy strategies can mirror this process by engaging your companions in group music therapy, or facilitating their participation in musical ensembles or choirs, where they may attain support from others and the encouragement to ask for what they need. Group members have the opportunity to show empathy and compassion through their shared musical experiences. On the other hand, a person can choose to go "solo" at this time, and listen to music to go deeply inward. Analyzing the lyrics of a song is another technique to examine feelings and emotions that are surfacing at this time. Toning and singing offer dynamic and rich methods of expression to communicate a reaction to the diagnosis, while also helping to bring homeostasis to the nervous system as it responds to the imbalance in the person's health. Now that your companion is more knowledgeable of what is wrong physically, and a medical regimen is devised, a more comprehensive music therapy treatment plan may be developed. Based on your companion's musical background and preferences, and their responses in your initial assessment and welcoming session, a stress/peace management technique may be personalized. Along the way, each companion develops a musical identity, as differentiated from the diagnostic label they are given.

When victimhood results from unknown or feared consequences of initial symptoms or a diagnosis, your companions are thrust into step 3 of the Hero's Journey. There is no doubt that receiving an unwelcome diagnosis is a life-changing event. Here is a brief excerpt from Elana Rosenbaum's book (2005), describing her response to the diagnosis of non-Hodgkin's lymphoma:

> My diagnosis forced me to confront habits that kept me from being well. It forced me to pay attention and really notice what helped me stay well and what I needed to let go or change. Caring for myself properly meant I really had to listen to my body and nurture myself, mind and body. I needed to maintain an open, steady heart and forgive myself if I strayed. I also needed to be able to accept support. My intention and commitment NOT to SUFFER became paramount in my ability to cope with the rapidity of change that the diagnosis of cancer wrought in my life (p. 14).

Rosenbaum found a path through her journey by being mindful of her process. She went inward to listen and outward for support. She found coping strategies in writing and art that enabled her to cope with this serious diagnosis.

> I wrote to sort out my feelings and restore a sense of calm and quiet to the home inside of me. Sometimes the pictures (I drew) reflected silent screams

of anguish or wild lows of frustration so deeply embedded in mind and body that only color and form could represent them. Writing and drawing allowed my internal states to come out and be released (p. 14).

Elana Rosenbaum interpreted the meaning of her diagnosis through words and images. Later she called upon her external resources to create a healing ritual amongst a circle of family and friends. She was able to set a new intention for reaching inward and outward to discover inner and external resources. Elana told me about a ritual that she created, prior to her stem cell transplant:

> I invited neighbors, good friends, and acquaintances. I asked everyone to bring some musical instruments, and to lead us in some chants and songs. I just remember lots of drums and people beating.
> Then David, my husband, went into the middle of the circle, chanting, "Heal, Elana, heal, heal, heal." More than anything, I remember my husband and the music, and the beat of the drums, as he was really saying, "Let her live." I'll never forget the feeling of my husband and all these people physically, emotionally, spiritually just wishing me well (personal communication, 2014).

It is not necessary to face a challenging diagnosis alone. Mentors and allies abound if we look in their direction or seek them out. Support systems and groups, community agencies, and other helping hands are available in many communities. However, some individuals are reticent to reach out and ask for help. When they do not proceed to step 4 of the Hero's Journey, and encounter a guide or mentor, they can remain frightened, helpless victims.

In their seminal text, *Stress, Appraisal, and Coping*, Richard Lazarus and Susan Folkman (1984) point out that coping is not necessarily a natural, reflexive process. The manner in which people cope is dependent upon their ongoing and continuous evaluations of events as they unfold, their preparedness to deal with stressful events, and their confidence in being able to handle them. As our companions learn about their diagnoses, they may engage in problem-focused coping in order to make the best decisions regarding treatment options. They may use meaning-focused coping to find a higher purpose behind their medical conditions. Russell Razzaque (2014) describes what tends to occur when someone is faced with physical pain or psychological depression:

> (R)arely do we sit with the pain we are feeling when something doesn't go our way (as is often the case)—paying attention to the experience in our body—and giving it some space and time. Instead we go into avoidance mode. We keep ourselves busy, we think, we act, we talk, we eat, we work, and we do whatever we can to zone out. Engaging in those activities is almost a form of anaesthesia. But this itself then generates more stress and makes us more unhappy. (pp. 133–134)

The Power of Myth is a series of interviews of Joseph Campbell by Bill Moyers that was published in 1988 after Campbell's death. In the chapter titled, "The Journey Inward," Campbell asserts: "(A)t the bottom of the abyss comes the voice of salvation. The black moment is the moment when the real message of transformation is going to come. At the darkest moment comes the light" (p. 39).

If you can only summon the courage to enter the abyss, you may experience transcendence. This is where emotion-focused coping can be the elixir. It is the coping mechanism that helps to regulate the emotions associated with stress and distress, and seeks to bring homeostasis to the delicate balance of the nervous system. One specific method is called emotional-approach coping, which attempts to engage the person in exploring the meaning of emotions through expressing and processing them, rather than just soothing or releasing them. Of course, this technique is the basis for many interventions, such the Bonny Method of Guided Imagery and Music (BMGIM) and other existential or transpersonal approaches to music therapy. According to the Association for Imagery and Music,

> The Bonny Method of Guided Imagery and Music is characterized by the use of specially sequenced western classical music designed to stimulate and sustain a dynamic unfolding of imagery experiences. Sessions in this one-to-one modality are conducted by facilitators who are formally trained in The Bonny Method of GIM.

In an extended session of up to two hours, you and your facilitator discuss your current life situation, set goals for your work together, and establish a focus for the session. After following a guided relaxation, you then turn your attention to listening to the selected music, allowing it to become a vehicle for exploring deeper states of consciousness. You verbalize to the facilitator the images, feelings, sensations, memories, and other awarenesses evoked by the music. The imaginal realm provides a rich milieu for personal insight. Your facilitator interacts verbally with you to help you develop and expand your imagery experiences. At the close of the music, your facilitator assists your return from the deepened state and reinforces the insights you have gleaned from the exploration.

Your music and imagery experiences are reflections of you and are unique to your personal relationships, feelings, and personality. You may have glimpses of transpersonal inspiration which both challenge and nurture your sense of who you are and who you can become. Your creativity may be awakened. You may gain new perspectives on your life issues and may feel empowered to work with them with renewed energy (http://ami-bonnymethod.org).

This sounds like just the prescription you need to prepare for treatment, the next stage of the journey.

9

The Journey from Illness to Wellness

Sam's master's thesis describes the journey with his client, Debra. He recounts one of the sessions in which he used acupressure and reflexology:

A silence and a stillness entered the room while I was doing this. It was as if the warring that had been going on inside of Debra found detente, a moment of peace. I have come to believe that as we grow into full embodiment, we summon grace. And as I watched and felt Debra descend more fully into her body, what I experienced in the room was grace. It was grace that was making an offering to Debra and not through our doing as much as by the quality of our being. It was through an experience of embodied presence that grace was filling the room.

While on the one hand it is true to say that I was doing something to Debra, the power of this physical contact came from finding peace and stillness within my own body and then making that peace available to her. Our systems entered into what neurobiologists call "limbic resonance" as though the stillness in me was a tuning fork entraining her resonance into that peace as well. This peace is what invited Debra's presence into her body. And that presence is what summoned the grace that we were experiencing.

© The Editor(s) (if applicable) and The Author(s) 2016
S.B. Hanser, *Integrative Health through Music Therapy*,
DOI 10.1057/978-1-137-38477-5_9

That is the essence of what somatic psychotherapy is about for me: growing into our bodies and receiving the experience of grace. I don't believe you can make grace happen but I do believe by showing up completely and fully within the body we open ourselves to be receptive to an experience of grace. And that grace is what does the healing. After a full year of being tortured by a continuous migraine Debra had her first experience of relief from pain after that session (Samuel Hanser, 2009, pp. 6–7).

Medicine is not an exact science. Spontaneous remissions occur, and cures accrue from unexpected sources. We cannot always know the cause and effect or the reason that the same treatment may work for some but not others. Research evidence informs us of efficacy with the probability of some error, but there are always exceptions. Integrative health encourages us to remain open to the possibilities of interventions that contribute to a comprehensive treatment plan. Let's look at the unfolding journeys of some companions as they progress from treatment to wellness.

Treatment

Shula's Journey

This past summer, I underwent my fourth abdominal operation. As soon as the anesthesia wore off, I developed a healthy appetite and began to eat foods I liked. From my previous experiences, all of this seemed normal. After a few days, however, I lost my appetite and began to feel extremely nauseous. Ultimately, I vomited a very large quantity of clear, green liquid that turned out to be bile. For the doctors, my having vomited bile was a clear indicator that I had developed an ileus, a type of bowel obstruction that results when peristalsis stops.

The nurses attached me to an IV pole that would deliver fluids and medications. I also had a urinary catheter inserted. I wore electrically operated "boots" through which air was pumped and released continuously in order to prevent a thrombosis in my legs that could occur from lying in bed. A nasogastric (NG) tube had to stay in me. In the meantime, I could neither eat nor drink—not even ice chips, not even a sucking candy. Thus, for the indefinite future, I more or less had to lie in bed and could not move much.

While the NG tube ultimately remained in me for 10 days, time stretched before me without boundaries. As I tried to get comfortable in the bed, making myself ready to do nothing for an indefinite period, I began to feel distress—almost panic. I did not have the energy to read a book or even listen to music. I felt stuck with myself and miserably watched the clock hands move very slowly.

One night, when a nurse, Lateesha, came into my room, we immediately recognized each other from one of my previous hospitalizations. She said she remembered me because I had told her a story—the fairy tale of the Princess and the Pea. I lay in bed with my empty stomach, raging thirst, NG tube, IV line, urinary catheter, brand new permanent ileostomy (opening in the wall of the abdomen), two abdominal drains, an oozing incision and plugged-in space boots, thinking about the Princess and the Pea. And then, a kind of miracle occurred.

All of a sudden my mind became occupied. "How did the story of the Princess and the Pea actually go?" I asked myself. "Maybe I should create the book myself and put the story in my own words, adding simple pictures. Maybe I should make a copy for Amalia, my granddaughter, too. How would I actually make the book?" I lay there having these creative thoughts and the time flew by. Creative thinking lifted me out of the here-and-now into the then-and-there. I was actually happy. I fell asleep.

The next day, I lay in bed and decided to create a kind of greeting card to send to all the people who had sent me notes and flowers, telling them I had gotten out of the hospital. The whole project was in my head. I would take a photo of the hospital bed without me in it and announce that I had gotten out. Then I thought I should fashion the card after a birth announcement, except the exiting human would be me rather than a newborn baby. So, within 12 hours or so, I had had two experiences of intense, satisfying creativity.

What are the implications of my story? Of recognizing that creativity can lift a person out of the time/space and even the pain and fear dimensions of confinement. For me, the implications became profound recently when I learned that I have to have yet another surgery. But now that I have studied the experience of operation #4, I decided to act on what I've learned. I have planned a creative activity to undertake while in the hospital. It's very demanding. I want to teach myself how to chant in Hebrew the Torah portion titled "Shlach Lecha," which is read every year around my birthday. I have never chanted Torah, but I have always wanted to learn how to do it.

The Road Traveled

Shula endured step 5 of the Hero's Journey, as she entered confinement for an unknown duration and crossed the threshold of medical intervention once again. In step 6, she bore the trials of hunger, thirst, immobility, and discomfort. The hero's Goddess in step 7, the smiling Lateesha arrived, as Shula was contemplating her fate. The story they had shared inspired Shula to find a creative solution that not only helped her survive her long and lonely confinement but could also reconfigure her concerns about subsequent surgery. She slayed her metaphoric dragons by concentrating on the design of a book and greeting card that required all the creative thinking that she could muster. These activities demanded just the right amount of skill and challenge to create an experience of flow. Shula chose a complex mental task of her own creation and employed innate abilities that did not require any physical effort to access her inner healer. Subsequently, Shula virtually replaced her worries with details of a new proposal to learn to chant a Torah portion, an unmet goal in her life. This creative and demanding task, similar to Helen's introduction to piano transformed her hospitalization into a highly motivating learning experience.

It is notable that Shula claimed she "did not have the energy ... to listen to music." Her external world was filled with pumps, tubes, and gadgets that controlled her every movement and provided her sustenance. Perhaps Shula could not conceive of taking in another piece of external stimuli or sensation such as reading a book or listening to music. It is curious to imagine how her experience would have been different if a music therapist were available on her unit to guide her with presence and musical presents.

The Road Beyond

When your companions' conditions necessitate aggressive therapies, the treatment may be more painful or unpleasant than the initial manifestation of the disease. Sometimes the treatment plan includes surgery or other invasive procedures. Dealing with a surgical operation or the challenging symptoms and side effects of treatments such as chemotherapy requires courage. Like Shula's Lateesha, a loving and caring figure will enable the hero, or companion, to move through the next challenge. Like this archetypal figure, music therapist Peggy Huddleston eagerly steps into the role of guide and mentor in her efforts to help surgical patients transform their experiences surrounding invasive medical operations.

In her book, *Prepare for Surgery, Heal Faster*, Peggy Huddleston (2012) suggests several techniques to prepare our companions for difficult medical procedures and surgery, as well as help them heal afterwards. Huddleston is the mentor/goddess in steps 3 and 7 of the Hero's Journey. Many of her techniques involve loving affirmations, guided visualizations, and creative ways to relax and focus on the positive. Here is an example of one of Huddleston's successful cases. About to undergo shoulder surgery, Nancy is trying to come up with healing images:

> She recounted that a good friend, a renowned surgeon, had explained that her shoulder's torn rotator cuff probably looked like frayed ropes. He described how her surgeon would be reattaching these frayed ropes, her tendons, to her shoulder bone. Nancy didn't like the image of "frayed ropes." She said, "I've been around enough boats to know it's impossible to pull old ropes together into a strong one."
>
> To get a more positive image, she called her surgeon's resident and asked him to describe her operation. Nancy said, "Instead of frayed ropes, he talked about securing my strong, pink biceps tendons to my shoulder bone"… When she noticed worries about her operation popping into her mind, she replaced the worries with pictures of her healed shoulder (Huddleston, 2012, p. X).

Nancy had learned how to achieve deep relaxation by practicing in the weeks before her operation. Post-surgery, Huddleston led Nancy through another exercise:

> When she [Nancy] was deeply relaxed, I said, "Let an image of your shoulder appear … Ask it: What comforting feeling do you want me to give you?" Nancy answered, "It wants a feeling of softness and protection."
>
> I responded, "Ask: How many times a day do you want me to give you this feeling?" Nancy said, "It wants it for 10 seconds, whenever I think

about my shoulder, and three times a day for five minutes when I am very relaxed."

As we continued talking, Nancy broke in, "I just did it. I gave it that feeling. I'm being softer and more protective of my shoulder whenever I shift my position."

For two weeks, whenever she thought about her shoulder, Nancy gave it feelings of "softness and protection" for 10 seconds. In addition, three times a day she scheduled the five-minute healing sessions ... Other times in the day when she worried about her shoulder, she switched her worries to images of healing for one minute. By repeating the imagery, she created a pervasive healing theme that reverberated throughout her consciousness (Huddleston, 2012, p. X).

Imagery like Nancy's can be extremely effective in coping with the fears associated with an upcoming surgical procedure. Accompanying images and affirmations with uplifting or soothing music is a powerful addition to this process. Your companion's playlists will offer potential musical accompaniments to the experience of surgery.

The American Cancer Society (ACS) informs consumers about what to expect if chemotherapy is the prescribed treatment. The ACS website states:

Research has shown that chemo can impact the thinking functions of the brain (known as cognitive functioning) for up to 10 years after treatment. Some of the brain's activities that are affected are concentration, memory, comprehension (understanding), and reasoning ... Chemo can bring major changes to your life. It can affect your overall health, threaten your sense of well-being, disrupt your daily routines, and put a strain on your relationships. It's normal and understandable for you and your family to feel sad, scared, anxious, angry, or depressed (http://www.cancer.org/treatment).

Almost every system of the body is affected by the toxins in the chemotherapy cocktail, and every individual's response is distinctive, but it is possible to reframe these treatments into opportunities to focus on their life-giving powers and life beyond the infusion unit. *Blessings for the Journey: A Jewish Healing Guide for Women with Cancer* (Mayyim Hayyim

Sixth Day Group, 2009) is a spiritual sourcebook that I co-authored with a team of gifted women. While investigating creative solutions for coping with chemotherapy and radiation, we came upon some resources that express this positive approach. Kaethe Weingarten's "Treatment Dedication Project" asks people who have cancer to dedicate each treatment to a person, project, charity, or organization that is doing good in the world. Another creative idea is having loved ones collect news about proactive people or community projects that are making the world better. These stories can be read while being infused, taking the person outside of personal fears and discomfort by providing a broader perspective on what is possible.

Of course, there are more creative modalities that facilitate focusing outside of the discomfort of treatment and fear for the future. During treatment, a sterile medical environment can be transformed into one with exquisite music, art, and movement. Music therapy strategies for pain management include both passive audioanalgesia (listening to sounds and music) and guided imagery, and when feasible, more active techniques such as singing, playing instruments, and movement/dance. You and your companions can identify pieces of music that magnetize attention in order to compete with the perception of pain. Chanting affirmations is another positive coping strategy. Composing a personal jingle offers an intention that your companion repeats in order to redirect attention to the healing that will take place with successful treatment.

In my clinical work and research at Dana-Farber Cancer Institute, I developed a music therapy program to help women with metastatic breast cancer. As part of our research protocol, my fellow music therapist Lorrie Kubicek or I offered three individual sessions, concurrent with chemotherapy. In the first, we played live music for our companions, asking nothing of them except for an idea of how they liked the music or what they wished for us to play. We used guitar, keyboard, Native American flute, dulcimer, and/or lyre, as well as our voices. We took cues from our companions and played improvised as well as precomposed music.

In the second session, we started with any music that our companions desired and then invited them to play along with us. We improvised together, offering simple percussion if they did not have previous experience on any of our other musical instruments. The rain stick was a favorite, as our companions realized that they could summon the sounds of nature right into the infusion unit. Hand chimes were also popular, due to the resonance they produced, especially within the steel and glass acoustic environment. Melodic instruments tuned to the pentatonic, like the lyre or xylophone, provided consonance no matter what notes were played at any one time. Ukulele and dulcimer, tuned to a major chord, enabled untrained musicians to play lovely harmonies. We created new pieces of music together and recorded those that our companions liked most.

In the third session, we invited our companions to write a song with us. Some wrote a song about a loved one; others wrote to a loved one. A few wrote about the experience of music therapy, and one wrote a musical "thank you" to the staff. Recordings of these songs proved to be living legacies to give loved ones as a precious reminder of the meaning of their relationships.

We found that heart rate, relaxation, comfort, and happiness improved when compared from pre- to post-sessions. One woman told me, "I never thought I would have fun, and look forward to coming for chemotherapy." Another companion, Barbara, had to have her blood drawn, something she always dreaded. This time, she found herself singing to herself. For the first time, the blood flowed easily and she hardly knew that the vein had been punctured. She was incredulous at how unaware she was of the procedure while her attention was focused on singing. She expressed gratitude at having found a way to successfully overcome pain and anxiety associated with blood draws. Barbara taught me an important lesson: Those inner healers can be very creative when it comes to applying the music therapy techniques they learn.

What If There Is No More Treatment?

Garrison's Journey

It was December 12th when I was feeling something in my stomach, and I ended up in the emergency room because of the pain. We did a CAT scan, and the physician said, "I am really shocked. You have a huge tumor, and you will have surgery, and it has metastasized to your liver." I was there by myself. "I am really sorry," he said. "You should tell your family."

You're in the ER alone. They put some tubes in you. It's very dark and you think about all the people in your life and the people you have responsibility for, and it's just dark thoughts—because you don't really expect that kind of diagnosis. At that moment, this is the beginning of an unknown journey. I determined, at that moment, that this was a new challenge, and we always say we don't know what our strengths are until we need them.

People say to me, "I don't know how you are doing it. I would want to kill myself." What's the alternative? Do you lose hope or despair? I choose hope and choose life and make the adjustments that I have to make. We can find that inner strength, like a universal bank account that you haven't had to withdraw until you need it. If I feel like it's something that's being done to me, then I remove the power to overcome it. If I look at this as something that was done to me, I ask, "Why me?"—those aren't the kinds of questions that bring answers that help. This is my mission to show the highest life condition. What can challenging this illness achieve?

I am a musician, and I couldn't play for a whole year. Then I was asked to play a gig with a band at the huge auditorium. I hit the distortion on the amplifier, and I played this solo that I couldn't believe. There was a standing ovation, and it was clear to me that the music could help me to transcend my physical body. I wasn't playing chord changes. Maybe something channeled. The next week, this group asked me to play with them again. I wasn't sure I could do this. I hadn't been playing in such a long time, and we never played before together. We played, and it was just like having a conversation, and you just listen and follow the moment. It led to the next moment. The music carried everyone to this moment where there was no longer a roof. After that, I realized that I cannot stop playing music. It is a strong vibration and powerful healing force. In the beginning, music was a healing art. That began my healing process.

I was listening to "A Love Supreme" by John Coltrane. When I heard the music, there was spirit there, and I began to cry. I asked this presence to help me find my path. Once you begin to see the fundamental aspect of our connections to each other, we can perceive things that others don't notice. If you are playing music from an intellectual standpoint, you can play well. Only if you can reach beyond this can you achieve something more. If we begin to perceive this, and find our own path, we can find ourselves.

Music is unsurpassed in the vastness of spirit.

The Road Traveled

With his humility and his humanity, Garrison teaches us about music with the conviction of a mystic. After a yearlong hiatus in music performances, he was able to access his higher Self when he reconvened with the spirit of music. In the process, Garrison discovered both his inner music and his inner healer. He took hope and life along on his journey, and this enabled him to reach a state of self-transcendence. Garrison is the hero who is repeatedly tested and is unafraid of the mysteries of life and death. The impenetrable power of music guides his steps.

The Road Beyond

Sometimes there is no treatment or no further medical intervention indicated. For some, grueling diagnostic workups continue, only to leave behind a diagnosis of exclusion, like fibromyalgia, or a failure to produce a definitive diagnosis. Other diagnoses are for untreatable diseases, and palliative care is the best that medicine can do. Will our companions require short-term treatment for physical discomfort? Is the most significant issue related to anxiety or other psychological concomitants? Are there coping strategies that can be implemented for our companions when they are in pain or in need? As music therapists, we are equipped to handle the psychosocial and spiritual needs of our companions for whom medical treatment is unavailable. Whether the intention is to bring acceptance of a challenging diagnosis or preparation for the end of life, we can help people write songs to communicate how they are experiencing these challenging conditions, improvise with them to offer a mode of expression for their internal processes, or soothe them through playing and singing beautiful music for and with them.

In his fascinating book, *They Can't Find Anything Wrong! Seven Keys to Understanding, Treating, and Healing Stress Illness*, Dr. David Clarke (2007) presents cases from a variety of his patients who have undiagnosed conditions that he boldly claims are actually "stress illnesses." Here he presents Ellen:

Ellen has lost all hope. In her late 40s, a mother of two daughters, Ellen introduced herself by looking up from her hospital bed and saying wearily, "Don't waste your time with me, Doctor. They've been trying to diagnose me for fifteen years and my tests are always normal ... They can't find anything wrong!" Evaluated by over a dozen specialists and sixty separate hospital stays at a prestigious university medical center had failed to uncover the cause of her debilitating symptoms or give her any relief. Fortunately, and much to Ellen's surprise, a little over an hour later I was able to cure her illness.

... Stress caused Ellen's symptoms, just as it causes a variety of symptoms in millions of patients today. Physicians use many terms for this condition, but I call it, simply, "stress illness" (pp. 16–18).

This is dramatic evidence of how treating stress can not only result in better psychological outcomes, but also significant changes in health. While it is important to exercise caution in making claims about the impact of music-facilitated coping strategies, it is certain that some music therapy strategies can be extremely effective in relieving stress, thus potentially influencing health significantly. There is solid evidence to support these claims.

Resilience and Recovery

Arthur's Journey

I worked out a lot in high school, and I started feeling really groggy. I thought I had the flu—I was just so tired. Over about a month, I lost a lot of weight. I had this large lymph node in my groin. It got to the point that I couldn't walk. I would get spiking fevers, feel really hot and sweaty, and had really bad back pain.

I was diagnosed with anaplastic lymphoma, which is a condition where your cells get enlarged, and they can grow really fast. When I got the diagnosis, it was honestly a relief because I already felt as if I may have been dying. Chemotherapy was a time when I lost my hair and more weight. Fortunately, I never threw up which was really great. But, I think, mentally, it put a lot of wear and tear on me. I would fall into depression very easily for about two years. I don't know if it was the hormones or the treatment, but I kind of think it was both.

During treatment, I played a lot of music, and I think that's one of the things that helped me forget how I was feeling physically. Music was a really big part of my treatment, because while I was growing up, I always wanted to help people in one way or another. I thought, "There are other people here, and people who are helping me. I want to give back. I want them to hear my music." I thought music was the way that I could let them know, "Thank you for everything you're doing for me."

During my illness, I did a lot of songwriting. This was a way that I could reflect upon myself, a way that I could connect with others. It was just a really big moment when I realized what music was about for me. When I had learned about music therapy, it sparked something, but I didn't look into it right away. Then I got sick, and everything aligned. It was like, "This is my purpose. This is what I'm supposed to do in life: help people through music, and give them a better quality of life through the music that we can make together."

A lot of my treatment took place over the summer, and I came back to high school a month after classes had begun. I was really excited to go back. But it wasn't what I thought it was going to be. I started realizing my life is just so much different than all these others because of the things I've seen, the things I've been through, and the things that I'm thinking and still thinking. There were two other students who were diagnosed with cancer around the same time as me. They were a couple of years younger, and that summer they had passed away. It was almost this sense of guilt hanging over my head that I was the one who survived, and they didn't. I wanted to be happy because I was back here at school. But it was really hard because I was experiencing these people and life and school in such a different way than I had before. All these kids were talking about things that I just couldn't relate to, because everything in my life just became so much, I guess you could say, deeper. They were really concerned about, "What car are my parents going to get me? Who am I going to prom with?" Those are all great things, and they're important in life, I guess, but to me, at that point in my life, they weren't important.

When I was sick, I played so much music, and that was a very positive experience for me. The doctors even said to me many times, "I think your recovery was pretty quick because you were capable of keeping an optimistic side to life." Being healthy beyond physical health is everything, because if you're not mentally there, you can't be physically there. It all ties in together: the mind, the body, the spirit, and the immune system. Cancer made me realize that any time you are not capable of doing anything in life to your full capability, you feel limited. I think, because of cancer, I've learned how to be empathetic with that.

The Road Traveled

Arthur is now on his way to becoming a music therapist. His resilience, in response to the many tests on his journey, is a testament to both his character and his willingness to tread inward, to access the meaning of his cancer and his future. He met every criteria for resilience that the American Psychological Association has set out, as we learned in Chap. 2, for example, positivity, acceptance, self-discovery, hopefulness, and optimism. But he went even further, using his musical talent as a language to communicate his inner process, while he navigated through the external symptoms, diagnosis, treatment, recovery, and return home. Like the hero, Arthur was unafraid to tread into this territory, and his strong altruism no doubt also contributed to his recovery. Arthur's chosen career path will benefit a new generation of companions whom he will guide through music therapy.

The Road Beyond

During the period of recovery, our companions may take stock of where they are. This can be a time for understanding the meaning of the journey taken and considering what lies on the road ahead. Your companions have the opportunity to accept new identities as they venture inward and outward to uncover the significance of this experience. They may only be able to see the scars and losses associated with their medical conditions. Or they may consider themselves survivors, resilient warriors, or simply individuals transformed by the process. Fortunately, music provides a creative vocabulary for this exploration.

Resilience is the amazing ability that Arthur showed in rebounding strongly and giving back to others. Joan Haase et al. (2014) found that there are a number of protective factors that enhance an individual's resilience in illness. These include: family functioning, courageous coping, hope-derived meaning, social integration, and spiritual perspective. On the other hand, illness-related distress and defensive coping are factors that threaten psychological adjustment and resilience. Devised to assess these resources and risks, the Resilience in Illness Model (RIM) has been used to measure outcomes of music therapy. In research by Sheri Robb and her co-investigators (2014), therapeutic music videos were developed by adolescents or young adults who were undergoing hematopoietic stem cell transplants in eight Children's Oncology Group sites across the USA. The main purposes of this intervention were to provide predictability through structured music experiences, autonomy by offering musical choices, relationship-building with the music therapist, and meaning-making through expressing important values in their music videos. Results demonstrated immediate, significant improvement in courageous coping. After 100 days, there was significant improvement in social integration and family environment. This music therapy intervention was effective as a positive coping technique for young people with a high-risk cancer, and shows great promise for other applications.

While your companions are recovering from an illness, surgery, or injury, the process of regaining their previous level of healthy functioning is known as rehabilitation. Traditional methods of rehabilitation include physical, occupational, speech/language, and other allied health therapies, including music therapy. Music therapy is an appropriate adjunctive treatment to other forms of rehabilitation, as it can maximize compliance with medical regimens and improve quality of life. Often, rehabilitation is required to maintain functioning and prevent further damage or recurrence. In cardiology cases, a healthy lifestyle and reduction of stress support better health outcomes. Music therapy has been shown to reduce blood pressure and contribute to short-term changes in reported stress and anxiety in individuals who enrolled in cardiac rehabilitation programs (Mandel, Hanser, Secic & Davis, 2007). Neurologic music therapy (NMT) stands out as an effective means of treating various neurologic conditions and is supported by an impressive body of literature (Thaut, 2005).

Rehabilitation also provides services that emphasize the new habits and skills that may be necessary to maintain good health and prevent recurrence or damage. Scheier et al. (1989) studied 51 men who were undergoing coronary bypass surgery. They examined the way the men coped and recovered, observing them from pre-surgery to six months afterwards. They were interested in looking at their positive thinking, which they termed, "dispositional optimism." Remarkably, this factor was predictive of a faster rate of postsurgical physical recovery, use of problem-solving coping strategies as opposed to denial, return to normalization of activities, and enhanced quality of life, when compared with those who were pessimistic.

Recovery may entail a time to hibernate, to replenish energy and renew perspective. It can be a time for displaying gratitude for reaching this milestone on the journey and for the gift of recovery. What better way is there to show gratitude than to compose a song for loved ones, caregivers, support system members, and others, just like the women who participated in our cancer research did? Songwriting is an effective music therapy technique that can include original writing or even just the substitution of lyrics from a favorite song for personally relevant and meaningful ones. At their most expressive, words and music are potent ingredients for a tonic of emotions that express recovery and wellness. Improvising through music, likewise, gives your companions the opportunity to explore the sentiments that have accompanied them through the progression of illness, recovery, and re-entry into a person who is well. Performance of original or precomposed music can allow your companions to present their healthy selves to their community at this critical time.

Acceptance and Peace

Karl's Journey

Do you want to know how I heard I was dying? This is no word of lie, this is how it went down:

They put this thing in my neck, called a swan, with a sensor that goes down into the chambers of the heart, so they can sense the pressure inside the heart and that tells a big story. So I am lying on the bed, and not 20 or 25 minutes later, this doctor and about eight other people came in my room—filed into my room, rapid fire—boom, boom, and stood there staring at me.

The doctor came in last, and he sat on the edge of the chair near the bed, and he said, "We got the results of your test. There are four stages of congestive heart disease, with '1' being the best and easiest to treat, and '4' being the final and end, and untreatable. You're a '4.' So your alternatives are transplant, or artificial heart, or we'll fix you up on the best meds we can, and we can send you home. I'll give you 6 to 12 months." That was it.

That was it. I lay in that bed thinking, "I came in here fine. I came in here okay, and now I am getting all these bullets flying at my head. All of a sudden, I am told, "You're gonna die." So where I was then was in a really bad spot, and I didn't know what it was. I didn't realize I was depressed. I thought I was just in a bad mood. They wanted me to go transplant—and they wanted an answer now. Keep me there, throw an artificial heart in, if they have to, and then do the transplant. You know what's funny, when I thought transplant, I knew immediately that I wouldn't come off that table. I knew I wouldn't survive it. So I said, "I can't do this now."

There are a lot of medicines for different diseases, but to open your mind and be open to other types of therapy, like music therapy, is important. I think that multiplies the effects of any kind of drug, and in many ways, it's more beneficial because you do it yourself—it's in your own mind—it's not something artificial. Every chance I get, I sit on the porch, feeling the breeze, just listening to the birds, and absolutely loving life.

If I can enjoy another year—wow—that would be amazing. But at some point, my heart is going to say, "Okay, you had about enough." I'll slow down and get sluggish, and, like the old soldier, I will just fade away. I know what's coming. I've accepted it. I intend to write a thank-you letter that I want read at my funeral—to all my friends, all my family, all the people whom I care about. Every day I open my eyes, I thank God for giving me another day to enjoy (quoted with permission from Dr Kathleen Howland).

The Road Traveled

Karl inspires all of us to find a way to practice gratitude and find peace. The Hero's Journey does not end with confrontation of death. No, the hero faces mortality and learns that there is more to life than what the physical body experiences. This is certainly Karl's path. The hero leaves the supernatural world and is tested once more. The hero prevails and is able to return home with acceptance of whatever may come.

The Road Beyond

Our companions meet death or the loss of functioning, and it can threaten everything they know. Or, as it was with Karl, they learn that love and beauty live on. Often, they must attack new adversaries, or spiritual challenges, before they can find their way home or journey onward. Some use this opportunity to realize a new creative self—to learn a new musical instrument, like Helen; to sing a new song, like Barbara; or just to make more room for experiencing the beautiful in life, like Karl. By engaging with music that elicits a sense of awe or optimal flow, it is possible for your companion, as listener or performer, to appreciate a profound sense of peace. With your help, your companions can enhance their highest potential through active participation in music and the arts. This process can also aid in maintaining optimism and wellness, even when the body is failing.

Sometimes, music expresses something that defies rational analysis. Some, like Garrison, refer to this impact as deeply spiritual. Others merely take it in, knowing that they need not understand it to appreciate the unique mind-body-spirit trio that is integrated in a musical experience. Sometimes listening to music brings tears to people's eyes; some music makes them nostalgic; some music is so beautiful that words cannot describe the experience.

When they engage in musical experiences, your companions learn that they are capable of creating something uniquely reflective of who they are. Performing music that they always wanted to play or sing can be an awesome achievement. Writing an original song can "express the inexpressible," as Aldous Huxley claimed. Singing a song full of personal meaning brings another dimension to the lyrics and makes them vibrate with full intention and immensity. We all have an ability to create. By awakening our musical selves, we launch our greatest abilities and capabilities, and discover our highest human potential.

As we move toward optimal health and/or wellness of our whole being, the accompanying musical journey enables us to be the best that we can be. When we begin to realize the immensity of our hidden creativity and talents, and attend to the magnificent musical parts of ourselves, we stride into our full potential. The absolute realm opens before us, giving meaning to our experience and spreading light over our existence.

Part III

Pathways through the Journey

There is a vision for music therapy: It is to comfort and awaken, bring peace, help people cope, and find their musical selves. In Part III, I offer a sampling of music therapy techniques designed to evoke these transformative potentials. I hope that you will adapt these ideas and add your own in-the-moment inspirations to make this vision possible for you and your companions. As you consider the pathways on the journey, there will be techniques that are straightforward and methods that seem esoteric or abstract. Take those that suit you and your companion, and trust your judgment.

10

The Way to Comfort

During his time as an undergraduate student at Parsons The New School of Design, Sam created a graphic piece, called "Words Meditation." Charged words, including, "sickness, fear, pain, confusion, and separation," as well as "love, faith, gratitude, joy, and healings" cover the entire picture. Juxtaposed over them is a shadowy image of Sam, meditating in lotus position, wrapped in a red and yellow hue, representing the saffron robes of the monks and the fire of human existence. His balanced stance virtually displays the comfort that he always felt when he meditated, even among the angst of black-on-white verbiage that screams discomfort. Sam was comfortable breathing and chanting on his meditation cushion. Is it possible to bring this sensation of comfort to your companions amidst their pain and suffering?

The Meaning of Comfort

Comfort usually refers to being free of pain or constraint. But it is possible to feel comfort, or to be comforted, when in dire straits. Many people associate comfort with a feeling of being with loved ones, at home,

© The Editor(s) (if applicable) and The Author(s) 2016
S.B. Hanser, *Integrative Health through Music Therapy*,
DOI 10.1057/978-1-137-38477-5_10

or in close physical contact with something fuzzy or someone cuddly. Unfortunately, those things may have to be given up when our companions are put to bed in the hospital. However, the safe and soothing container of musical experience and your caring presence is quite capable of producing a strong sense of comfort.

When I call music therapy a container, I am using the metaphor to represent a space that is safely bounded, with sufficient room to swim around freely and discover new things but small enough to feel protected within its enclosure. The predictable beginning and ending of a piece of music, along with its rhythmic, melodic, and harmonic rules and regulations, help create this symbolic container. The container can be a bubble of life and splendor inside a very scary place, especially when filled with stunning live sounds, which are jostled around to unearth enchanting music in real time by an empathetic therapist.

In your companions' hospital room, you may not be able to provide the comforts of home, love, or family, but you can unite your companion in deep intimacy with music. You can help your companion release the feelings that underlie the experience of being ill, and you can teach your companion how to self-soothe. The vibrations of your live music can actually penetrate the organs—to your core and your companion's—an intimacy seldom enjoyed. I liken this inner massage to the experience of an expectant mother. Musical vibrations buzz the innards with a resonant hum. Can they summon the unborn spirit?

Comforting

What does comforting your companion mean to you? If it is holding or embracing, can you use your music to provide a solid, yet soothing, symbolic hug? If it is being with the familiar, do you know which music is associated with the safety of home or the affection of loved ones? When your companions are open to receiving, it is relatively easy to find out what they need. A simple assessment of their musical preferences, associations, and memories provide the ingredients to mix with your therapeutic presence.

More important, what does comforting mean to your companion? Sally wanted to be left alone. She was not ill, but quickly became a patient, numbed by the fear of having cancer. She could not bring herself to solicit acts of comfort. Shula was so overwhelmed that she could not conceive of having any further sensory stimulation. She had to create her own sense of flow through her creative thought processes. What appears as resistance may be indicative of fear, or simply a need for silence and solitude. It can be difficult to distinguish between the two, as was the case with Mary.

Mary was hospitalized, due to complications of metastatic lung cancer. She was severely depressed and spent much of the day looking at the blank wall opposite her bed. She was unresponsive to the social worker's questions about how she was managing at home, and refused involvement in any of the services offered to her. Expecting resistance, I began playing soft music on my guitar at the entrance to her hospital room. After a few minutes, Mary looked right at me, smiled, and asked if I knew "Amazing Grace." I crossed the threshold and began singing softly. Mary closed her eyes and fell asleep.

Although not every person responds so quickly to music, Mary allowed me to open the door of communication so that she could sample music therapy. Our few sessions hatched a plan to involve her in the choir at her neighboring church, thus enabling her community to encircle her in comfort.

Breathing into Comfort

The comfort of a deep breath is usually within our power. Yet breathing is an essential involuntary act, so we do it without paying attention to its impact. When we learn to discipline the breath, however, we have access to thousands of years of yogic wisdom to instruct us in the techniques of *pranayama*. As one of the limbs of the Yoga Sutras of Patanjali, *pranayama* provides ways to focus attention and discipline the mind through manipulating and witnessing our life-affirming breath.

Whoever can swallow the breath
like the tortoise
or pull the breath in and circulate it
like the tiger
or guide and refine the breath
like the dragon,
shall live a long and healthy life.
—Master Ge Heng, alchemist and immortal, second-century China
(Jahnke, 1997, p. 83)

The methods of *pranayama* are being translated into modern practices that are accessible and effective. With its concomitant lowering of heart rate, blood pressure, and oxygen consumption, the deep breathing and other techniques of breath control have the potential to reset the autonomic nervous system. It decreases metabolic activity and enhances parasympathetic involvement, while practitioners report enhanced states of alertness and invigoration (Jerath et al., 2006).

There is an impressive body of research to support powerful outcomes of the practice of *pranayama* for people with various medical conditions. For instance, in an investigation of individuals who have chronic obstructive pulmonary disease (COPD), Katiyar and Bihari (2006) found that the practice of *pranayama* improved lung function, as well as depression and anxiety. Those who practiced these techniques regularly reported feelings of hope, locus of control, self-esteem, and independence. In another study by Dabhade et al. (2012), individuals with heart arrhythmia benefitted from *pranayama*.

I like to begin introducing my companions to breathing practices by requesting that they notice their breathing. Is it slow or fast, deep or shallow, regular or irregular? Unlike other visceral functions, such as cardiovascular activity or digestion, the breath can be voluntarily regulated. I demonstrate how breath is intimately related to emotion. With a powerful snort, I show them how I breathe when I am angry. With a luxurious exhalation, I show them how I breathe when I think about love. With a gasp, I demonstrate surprise. Then I may share how deep breathing can help us relax and how focusing on the breath can calm a busy mind.

I ask them to bring their attention to their own breathing, and notice the tempo and rhythm of the breath. This focus is a key component to *pranayama* and a good start to any breathing practice. I might have them practice a popular yogic breathing exercise known as the three-part breath. This involves filling the abdomen, then ribcage, and finally bringing air up into the collarbone. I suggest a pause and then an exhalation that empties the system downward through the body. A few deep breaths can quickly activate the calming parasympathetic nervous system.

Next I introduce some simple suggestions for sustaining slow, even breathing. The renowned Buddhist master Thich Nhat Hanh offers wonderful guidance for this practice. In one of his many treatises, *Peace Is Every Breath* (2011), he provides some simple thoughts to evoke deep, life-affirming breaths. I use these as scripts to guide breathing exercises:

Breathing in, I feel my breath coming into my belly and chest.
Breathing out, I feel my breath flowing out of my belly and chest.

Breathing in, I am aware of my entire body.
Breathing out, I smile to my entire body.

Breathing in, I'm aware of some pains or tensions in my body.
Breathing out, I release all the pains and tensions in my body.

Breathing in, I feel well.
Breathing out, I feel at ease (p. 19).

Breathing in, I see myself as a flower.
Breathing out, I feel fresh.

Breathing in, I see myself as a mountain.
Breathing out, I feel stable and solid (p. 40).

Breathing in, I know anger is manifesting in me.
Breathing out, I'm taking good care of this energy of anger in me (p. 106).

Hearing the Bell
Listen, listen,
This wonderful sound
Brings me back
To my true home (p. 133).

I like to add intonation to these lines so that they become beautiful songs. As I sing the incantations, the tones rise as I sing, "Breathing in " and the tones descend as I sing, "Breathing out."

Next I improvise musically with various sounds and instruments while my companion notes any changes in breathing tempo or rhythm. The simple realizations that there is a connection between these techniques and changes in breathing, and that breathing more deeply can induce a more relaxed state, are insights demonstrating that your companions have some relaxation techniques at their disposal.

Pranayama provides a wide variety of breathing techniques to induce different states, but I find that the power of these techniques lies in their simplicity. While it is important to provide our companions with options, I usually find that the most basic techniques are most easily integrated into daily practice and provide comfort without requiring a person to master a specific methodology.

Comforting the Body

Another essential ancient practice is massage. The impact of touch is obvious when we reach out to hold someone's hand or make contact with a "High five!" Of course, our companions may be seriously deprived of touch, especially when they are confined to their beds. How close you come to your companion and the use of your touch is something you will have to evaluate, as everyone has a different sense of personal space and desire or aversion to touch.

Massage therapy is an evidence-based practice that is offered in many centers for integrative medicine. Music therapy and massage therapy are excellent partners, and most massage therapists use music to enhance the individual's experience. Because music therapists are adept at identifying the most potentially soothing music for their companions, collaboration can maximize our companions' satisfaction, and perhaps best meet their needs. You might suggest selections from your companions' "relaxing music" playlists to accompany their massages.

Even the use of the hands held over the body has been used as an integrative intervention. The practice of therapeutic touch is the "intentional and compassionate use of universal energy" that entails passing the hands over the body's energy field, from about 2 to 6 in. away. In the integrative medical environment, it is often practiced by nurses, and entails a five-stage process, much like music therapy:

1. centering
2. assessing energy flow and blockage
3. intervention of clearing or unruffling the flow of energy throughout the body
4. re-evaluation by balancing or rebalancing the energy to congested parts of the body
5. closure.

The Therapeutic Touch International Association credentials qualified practitioners and teachers, and trainings and mentors can be found around the world. If you are interested, you can benefit from this training (http://therapeutic-touch.org).

Reiki is relatively modern, having been established in 1922. Although there is little research evidence to support its claims, Reiki has become popular in the West as a form of bodywork that entails the practitioner transferring "universal life energy" to the companion in order to "restore harmony to the biofield, increase the client's energy to heal, and balance the body's subtle energies" (Koopsen and Young, 2009, p. 74). While the science is lacking, you may very well encounter energy healers who practice these therapies in the integrative setting.

Facial Massage

In *Manage Your Stress and Pain through Music* (2010), Susan Mandel and I include several techniques for relaxing the body, one of which is a gentle, facial massage. As I sit behind a piano keyboard, I ask my companions to let the music cue their fingers' soft strokes around their faces. I often play Bach's Prelude #1 from the *Well-Tempered Clavier* to accompany small, circular movements around the cheeks, mandible, and temples, penetrating the facial muscles just enough to smooth out spots that are tight or taut. The C major key and open arpeggios imply the tender touch that I recommend my companions use for working out tension in their faces. Deeper kneading on the neck and a bit of a pinch on the nose round off this method of self-massage. Find your companion's most beloved music or choose from the relaxing music playlist to accompany this technique.

Progressive Muscle Relaxation

Progressive Muscle Relaxation (PMR) is a popular and effective form of relaxation training, pioneered by physician Edmund Jacobson (1938) and now used in cognitive-behavioral interventions, like biofeedback techniques, systematic desensitization for fears and phobias, and many other stress management strategies. PMR involves tightening and releasing the muscles in various parts of the body, one by one. When working with people who are ill, I often skip the instruction to squeeze or constrict the muscles and go right to the relaxation.

Roger Jahnke (1997) offers such a variant of PMR, much like the "body scan" of mindfulness-based stress reduction. Accompany these instructions with your companion's favorite relaxing or sleep-inducing music:

Allow the breath to be full and relaxed, not urgent. Deeply relax and visualize each of the body parts relaxing or filling up with healing energies. Visualize the parts that you are addressing glowing radiantly with vitality. On each inhalation bring your attention to the next area of the body. On the exhalation relax the area and silently affirm the following to yourself:

Now my feet and toes are relaxed.
Now my calves up to my knees are deeply relaxed.
Now my thighs are completely relaxed.
Now my buttocks are completely relaxed.

Now my hands and fingers are completely relaxed.
Now my arms are fully relaxed.
Now the muscles and organs in my pelvis are relaxed.
Now the muscles and organs in my abdomen are deeply relaxed.
Now my chest is completely relaxed.
Now my back is relaxed.
Now my shoulders are relaxed.
Now my neck is fully relaxed.
Now my face and jaw are relaxed.
Now my eyes are deeply relaxed.
Now my temples and forehead are relaxed.
Now my scalp is relaxed.
Now my head is totally relaxed (p. 105).

Drummassage

Group drumming, drum circles, and drum massages are community-based techniques used by music therapists and others, often to instill a sense of unity and bring sensation to one's internal rhythms. Christine Stevens (2012) and Kalani Das (2011) provide texts that describe these methods in detail. *Drummassage* is a relaxation technique developed by Berklee College of Music Professor Steve Wilkes, whereby a group of drummers surround a passive listener in an aural bath of drums. One leader begins a slow, regular beat and the others follow with their drums, providing little embellishment. The low frequencies and quiet, repetitive rhythms, reminiscent of tribal ceremonies, are designed to induce a relaxation response. In a pilot research experiment to test its impact, Tessa Kaslewicz (2014) asked participants to rate their responses pre- and post-treatment on a visual analogue scale. Every one of the 23 participants of Drummassage found the experience relaxing and peaceful, and also reported a sense of physical loosening. All agreed that it was transformative. Comments included:

"I felt like I was lucid dreaming."
"Chilllll"
"Followed the sound and breath, and let go of intrusive thoughts."

"I get energy from the big drum. The small drum—that's my spirit. It's like someone is walking on my body. When you stop, I feel a flowing atmosphere."

"All my internal chatter just stopped."

These responses display the ability of Drummassage to focus thoughts, redirect energy, and induce an altered state of consciousness. While this technique may not be acoustically practical or conducive to use in a medical setting, encircling your companion with deeply resonant and primal sounds that vibrate the body is capable of providing an internal sense of comfort. When your companion is in pain, it may be deeply soothing to feel the body vibrating along with the drums. To enhance the impact, ask family members or friends to play the drums along with you to help create an aura of loving energy.

Comforting Imagery

As described in Chap. 8, The Bonny Method of Guided Imagery and Music (BMGIM) is a powerful methodology for an inward journey to healing. There are three levels of training required to qualify as a certified practitioner, and you can learn more about how to facilitate guided imagery and music through the Association for Music and Imagery (AMI) at: http://ami-bonnymethod.org/. If you are not trained in this approach, however, you can still use music to arouse images in the eyes of your companions' minds.

There are many sources for enhancing imagery. First of all, listening to music that has positive associations and memories will often elicit imagery all by itself. Pieces of music that were composed with nature in mind, including Respighi's *Pines of Rome* and *Fountains of Rome*, Saint-Saëns' *Carnival of the Animals*, and Beethoven's *Pastoral Symphony*, were inspired by beautiful or happy scenes. These images can bring one far away from the sick bed and into a place of splendor. Other program or programmatic music, such as Mussorgsky's *Pictures at an Exhibition*, Strauss' *Til Eulenspiegel's Merry Pranks*, and Rimsky-Korsakov's *Scheherazade*, was written to follow stories and visions. This music is particularly likely to evoke visual images. For some people, the music immediately prompts a vivid picture or story. Yet others are not predisposed to visual imagery and may think that something is wrong with them if they cannot find their imaginations conjuring up clear depictions. Of course, this is far from the case, as every person experiences music through his or her own lens. Some people's bodies are more responsive to music than their minds, some the reverse, and everyone benefits from music therapy in their own distinctive ways.

Belleruth Naparstek is a psychotherapist who uses imagery quite extensively in her practice. In *Your Sixth Sense: Unlocking the Power of Your Intuition*, Naperstek (1997) talks about a woman who wanted to create some personal imagery to help her cope with a cancer diagnosis. She had been using the image of "big, gentle polar bears surrounding and looking after her, and of being gently held in a soft, white, furry bear's lap" (p. 4). When Belleruth heard this description, her intuition led her to a "very clear image of a great big guy bear, standing upright, forelegs crossed over his chest, looking very powerful, aggressively protective, and very male—in other words, a huge Daddy Bear" (p. 5). When Belleruth suggested this male image, the woman became quite animated. She sought out this sort of protection, but the males in her life were unreliable and even destructive. The invention of a bear as a trustworthy protective totem allowed her to bring this important symbol into her life and also into her healing.

The breathing visualization that I prepared for Martin, as he was preparing for surgery (see Chap. 7), was another form of imagery designed to bring on a sense of comfort. To create your own imagery script, keep the following in mind:

- Start with instructions on finding a comfortable position.
- Ask the listener to focus on the breath and to practice some deep breaths or three-part breathing.
- Slowly invite the companion to imagine a journey to a wonderful place or describe one yourself, based on a setting that he or she knows and loves. You might retell a story that your companion has shared with you. You can create a set of healing images or a poem about gratitude. Embellish your words with specific targets that bring out all of

the senses, such as the smells of the forest, tastes of those home-baked cookies, temperature of the air, the light, environmental sounds, wind on the skin, colors of nature, and animals nearby. Most of all, involve your companion in the decisions, wording, and descriptions for this experience.

- Observe your companion's reactions to your reading, and adjust your pacing accordingly. If your companion appears to tire or become fidgety, suggest taking a few breaths, or prepare to bring the guidance to a close.
- Slowly suggest returning from this imagined place, and ask your companion to generate more energy in the body by moving fingers and toes, and gradually, other parts.
- Bring the music to a close and spend some moments in silence.
- Ask your companion to open their eyes and come back, feeling the comfort of this place or story.

Comforting the Mind

Meditation

Imagery exercises such as this are often considered forms of guided meditation. Indeed, meditation has been defined in numerous ways throughout history and applied in almost every religion. Some meditation practices attempt to empty the mind in silence; others summon the Divine while chanting mantras; still others focus on a meaningful object, word, or image. Currently, modern Western iterations and adaptations include mindfulness-based stress reduction, emotional self-regulation techniques, chanting affirmations, single-focused attention, lovingkindness intentions, drumming, guided imagery and music, and a wide variety of other techniques. There is considerable evidence of the efficacy of many types of meditation in managing anxiety and depression, as well as ameliorating physical symptoms related to stress. The research literature supports its applications in medical settings (Arias et al., 2006; Fortney & Taylor, 2010), citing particular impact for autoimmune and neoplastic illnesses, epilepsy, and anxiety disorders.

Mantra

The ancient yogic mantra is one of the most basic meditation techniques, in which one repeats a word or phrase to engage the mind and calm the mood. Chapter 6 gave examples of some simple affirmations that you can repeat or sing to prepare yourself for music therapy. Our companions, too, can soothe themselves by chanting, singing, or subvocalizing mantras or affirmations. The Buddhist *metta* and loving kindness meditations are longer mantras that you learned in Chap. 6: "May you be free of danger. May you have mental happiness. May you have physical happiness. May you have ease of well-being." These intentions can be offered for all sentient beings next: "May all sentient beings be free of danger," etc. Finally, the companion chants, "May I be free of danger. May I have mental happiness. May I have physical happiness. May I have ease of well-being."

One way to chant is to take a deep, three-part breath and repeat, aloud or silently, the word or phrase. While the words, "heal," "love," or "peace" can be very comforting, they are connected with a long history of associations. For instance, when one's love life has been complicated by multiple relationships, the word "love" may unearth conflicts as well as joys. It may be more useful to chant in a foreign language. With a different tongue, the brain is not connecting the word with that large network of memories, some of which may not be helpful toward the goal of wellness. So a fresh, new word, like "shima," meaning "love" in the language of Hopi Native Americans, has a lovely, novel taste in the mouth. Sanskrit mantras are also said to carry the vibrations of the world's beginnings in their utterance, and every language carries its own unique heritage and intonation. Find words that carry significance and connect your companions to their cultures or new worlds.

By setting important word(s) or mantras to music, our companions will devote more brain activity to the musical chant and thus become fully absorbed. We music therapists can assist our companions in creating a personal jingle. Just keep it simple, positive, and active. Examples include: "I am healing," "I am coping the best I can," "I can rest and recover," "I feel myself getting better," "I am grateful to be in good hands," or "My heart is beating strong." The accompanying melody might be a simple scale, a phrase from a familiar song, or a theme from a comforting piece of music. Be sure to resolve the musical phrase to the tonic or modal center. As these are only samples to generate ideas, help your companion devise a personal, meaningful one that affirms a believable, realistic, and positive attitude or intention.

Comforting Sounds

Listening

You learned about nāda yoga in Chap. 5. Nāda yoga is really the science of listening, as the wisdom to be well resides in our inner music, or *anahata*. Help your companion find this *anahata* by listening for the sounds from within the body. When environmental sounds or internal thoughts invade this quiet contemplation, you can urge your companion to "let it be" or "let it go," and resume attending to one's own inner sounds. If this is too abstract an assignment (and it is, for many), suggest finding the inner rhythm. The breath or the pulse can be a guidepost for this rhythm, and the companion can then play this rhythm on a drum or other percussion instrument to give it a voice. You can then improvise music to further develop this intimate musical encounter.

Toning

Toning is a form of energy healing that uses vocalization to cause internal vibrations that are said to help the body surrender and release tension. In their book, *Toning: The Creative Power of the Voice*, Laurel Elizabeth Keyes and Don Campbell (2008) provide instructions on the process:

> Stand erect, with feet several inches apart. Stretch both arms high and let them drop back, shoulders swinging on the spine as a cross bar rests on top of a T, in perfect balance.
> The eyes must be closed. Begin to look inward, and feel.
> Let the torso ride on the pelvic region and imagine the hipbones as protruding level auto headlights ... Standing erect should cause no strain but

give an easy, relaxed feeling. Let the body sway like a flower on its stalk in a breeze.

Relax the jaws so that the teeth are slightly parted. Let sound come up from it, not down upon it from the mind, but up from your feet. Let the body groan. It may be only an audible deep sigh but it is a feeling of release of emptying out, or resting. Encourage it to be vocal. Always start with low groans.

Let the body groan as long as it likes and with abandon … Whatever happens, do not let the mind influence it. Make the mind obedient, be still …

The session may last ten minutes or an hour, but when the body feels cleansed a sigh is released and you know that the body-voice is satisfied (pp. 50–51).

Like other forms of energy healing, toning has little or no research to support its claims. However, this is a popular technique in sound healing literature, and many of its practitioners find that this visceral release changes the way they feel.

Comforting Songs

Songwriters compose a great many songs that are intended to move the listener and singer. In an emotionally effective song, the messages that reside within the lyrics are strengthened by the use of musical techniques to support the comforting intent of the lyric, such as the yearning of suspended cadences and extended resolutions to the tonic chord. To induce a sense of comfort in most listeners, the musical elements should be predictable or systematic.

In *Sweet Anticipation: Music and the Psychology of Expectation*, David Huron (2006) describes how music and musical expectations, in particular, affect the emotions:

Expectations provoke emotional responses. The evolutionary purpose of emotions is to act as motivational amplifiers that encourage behaviors presumed to be adaptive while discouraging behaviors presumed to be maladaptive. There are no neutral emotions.

Expectations that prove to be correct represent successful mental functioning. Successful predictions are rewarded by the brain. Successful expectations evoke positive feelings which we may then mistakenly attribute to the outcome itself, a phenomenon known as misattribution. As a result, we tend to prefer a predicted outcome. In addition, if we repeatedly make successful predictions for a given outcome, then the predicted outcome can itself evoke positive feelings through classical conditioning.

An example of the prediction effect in music can be found in the phenomenon of tonality. Once a tonal context is established, listeners tend to experience some pitches as more pleasant or preferable than others. Once a metrical context is established listeners tend to experience events that occur at the most expected moments to be more pleasant or preferable to other states.

Although expected events are generally preferred, highly predictable environments can lead to reduced attention and lowered arousal—often leading to sleepiness. This tendency can be counteracted to some extent by using energetic sounds or other sounds that have an innate tendency to increase arousal. Unsuccessful expectations evoke a form of mental punishment, typically in the form of stress. Failures of expectation provide important information that helps brains select between competing mental representations for events. Mental representations that prove to be poor future predictors atrophy (p. 361).

This description makes intuitive sense and reminds us of the importance of providing predictable patterns in the music we offer to comfort our companions. Huron also suggests that not every passage need be "peaceful," as the effect of resolution can be even greater when it follows tension:

A lengthy dissonant passage is likely to lead listeners to expect further dissonant sonorities. If the music shifts toward a more consonant texture, then the resulting contrast will tend to evoke a pleasing effect that can be greater than experiencing only the consonant passage (p. 22).

I have been collecting lists of songs that exude themes of comfort, and with the assistance of the music therapy students at Berklee College of Music, I am continually updating my repertoire of contemporary offerings. Figure 10.1 is a list of favorites that have been reported to have a comforting effect.

SONGS OF COMFORT

59th Street Bridge Song (Feelin' Groovy) Simon and Garfunkel	
Amazing Grace	Traditional
Ben	Michael Jackson
Brave	Sara Bareilles
Bridge Over Troubled Water	Simon and Garfunkel
Circle of Life	from Disney's *Lion King*
Defying Gravity	from *Wicked*
Don't Carry It All	The Decemberists
Don't Worry, Be Happy	Bobby McFerrin
Everybody's Talkin' at Me	Harry Nilsson
Feelin' Good	Nina Simone
Give Me Love	George Harrison
Hard Times Come Again No More	James Taylor and Yo Yo Ma
Heal the World	Michael Jackson
Heavenly Day	Patty Griffin
Jubilee	Mary Chapin Carpenter
Keep on the Sunny Side	A.P. Carter
Let It Be	The Beatles
Let It Go	from Disney's *Frozen*
Life Here Is Gold	Thomas Dybdahl
Life Is Wonderful	Jason Mraz
My Favorite Things	from *The Sound of Music*
One Love	Bob Marley
Place to Be	Nick Drake
Smile	Nat King Cole
Thank God I'm a Country Boy	John Denver
We'll Meet Again	Vera Lynn
You've Got a Friend	James Taylor
Shake It Off	Taylor Swift
Slumber My Darling	Alison Krauss
Stand By Me	Ben E. King
There Can Be Miracles	Mariah Carey/Whitney Houston
Things Can Only Get Better	Dream
This Must Be the Place	Shawn Colvin
Truckin'	The Grateful Dead
When the Red, Red Robin	Bing Crosby & Peggy Lee
You Can Never Hold Back Spring	Tom Waits
You Are Loved (Don't Give Up)	Josh Groban
You'll Never Walk Alone	from *Carousel*
You've Got a Friend	James Taylor

Fig. 10.1   Songs of comfort

Singing

In the foreword to Baker and Wigram's (2005) book, *Songwriting: Methods, Techniques, and Clinical Applications for Music Therapy Clinicians, Educators, and Students,* Even Ruud states:

From childhood on, we all relate to songs and songwriting in a personal way. Children improvise with their voices, create mock versions of familiar songs, and engage in a host of changing forms of identifications with songs and singers on their way to adulthood. The song text often provides an early experience of how to symbolically represent the world, and of how we can use metaphors to understand the meaning of what is happening to us (p. 9).

Thus, singing songs is a visceral and fundamental expression of our identities. During vulnerable times, songs of comfort and familiarity may be able to evoke the familiar and change mood instantly. Bailey (1984) used comforting songs in her music therapy sessions with cancer patients and their families. She explains:

Through songs, they can communicate their problems, their past or present unsatisfied needs or desires, their happiness, their loneliness. They can be reminded of sad or happy times which may provide further insight into present problems or which may take them away from their immediate discomforts. Through singing or listening to songs, they can learn or teach, can experience or reexperience events and feelings, can auditorially touch and be touched (p. 6).

Bailey's musical interventions allowed individuals to take in what they needed from the songs, without needing to "do" anything, as singing along is optional. The singing required little besides openness to experiencing the music and noticing its impact.

Surgeon and musician Dr. Patravoot Vatanasapt designed a group singing program to enhance the rehabilitation of those who have undergone laryngectomies. I was privileged to address Dr. Vatanasapt and his colleagues at Khon Kaen Medical Center in Thailand, in 2012, and witness this truly integrative approach. The singing techniques incorporated rhythmic vocal projection and whole-body eurhythmics to enhance breathing, swallowing, and speech, post-surgery. It appeared that the anxieties associated with speaking were alleviated as the group of singers swayed in time with the music. Vatanasapt and his colleagues reported 75% success rate in esophageal speech training for those who participated (Vatanasapt, Vatanasapt, Laohasiriwong, & Prathanee, 2014).

Lullabies

How do we recreate those first healing songs, the lullabies that Ted Gioia (2006) analyzes in *Healing Songs*? In her book *Essential Musical Intelligence*, Louise Montello (2002) suggests a powerful exercise to try with your companion:

> Begin by accessing an image of yourself rocking a tiny infant in your arms. Let all of your senses engage with this image. Feel the soft, grainy texture of the cotton baby blanket next to your skin. Smell the clean, pure scent of your innocent little baby. Feel the waves of your heartbeat as you rock your baby in sync with the universal pulse. Feel the vibration of unconditional love as it wells up from the heart to your throat and then out through your loving voice and arms. When you feel ready, listen for the words to your lullaby. They may come to you in a stream of consciousness or as a rhyme. You might want to work with rhythm first. Use a rain stick, Tibetan bell bowl, ocean drum, or shaker to create a soothing rhythm. Take all the time you need. You will know when you are finished, as the music will feel effortless and natural to perform. If you play an instrument, you might want to accompany yourself or play a solo section after you have sung the first verse or two (p. 100).

Perhaps we all seek the comfort of a mother's lullaby when we are afraid, in pain, or in unfamiliar places. Indeed, the lullaby, chant, meditation, breathing, imagery, singing, listening, toning, and other methods presented here are intended to comfort by taking us within our Selves to tune into the realms of inner healing. Just like Sam, we all have a place of comfort inside us. Trust your intuition to know how to take your companion there. Count on science to inform you of the most potentially efficacious strategies, based on what we know about mind-body connections, the impact of ancient methodologies, and the wisdom of holistic, integrative health.

11

The Way to Awaken

The sun is made up of rays of light. It is its rays of light—no more, no less. To me, God is like the sun and each soul, a ray of light … You are one of the rays of God's light. We all are. The rays are the sun as the sun is its rays. There is no distinction. Just so, we are a part of God as God is a part of us. (There's really only one of us.) All mystical schools provide practices that lead us toward the realization of this identity, and quite accurately, it is called enlightenment. Enlightenment simply means that you are living as your soul in all its shining glory. It is by no means the end. It is simply the rebirth of your conscious creation. So step into the Sun-self. Own your light. And keep beaming (Samuel Hanser, p. 6).

The Meaning of Awakening

This chapter is about awakening and enlightening, and how to light up like the sun, even while experiencing the darkest possible moments. In his book, *A Lamp in the Darkness: Illuminating the Path through Difficult Times*, author Jack Kornfield (2011) offers advice to awaken "the one who knows:"

© The Editor(s) (if applicable) and The Author(s) 2016
S.B. Hanser, *Integrative Health through Music Therapy*,
DOI 10.1057/978-1-137-38477-5_11

If you pay careful attention in the midst of your crises, you will begin to sense a witnessing consciousness, a wise presence inside of you that could be called "the one who knows" … Even in the toughest times of illness and loss, in your deepest depressions and griefs, underneath even your most catastrophic challenges and fear, the one who knows in you remains calm and clear. It already accepts whatever is going on … And it knows long before we do that the end of our suffering begins when we turn to face our suffering and embrace its truth and healing wisdom (pp. 5–6).

Kornfield goes on to say that for this awakening to occur, one must live in the present. The message of yogis, mystics, and psychotherapists is: Be present with a compassionate heart, and you will find everything you need. Music therapist Louise Montello (2005) promises:

Through awakening your essential musical intelligence (EMI), and using it as a bridge to connect the higher reality (intuitive wisdom) with the earth plane (sensory and ego-based thoughts, feelings, and memories) you can literally create heaven on earth and manifest balance and harmony in your life (p. 87).

So let's get started on the road to awakening.

Pillars of Awakening

These teachers make it sound so simple, yet under the shadow of pain and suffering, the way to awaken may not be apparent. Ron Scolastico (1997) asserts that there are four pillars of growth to help us move through challenges and awaken inner wisdom. The first pillar is the openness to trust in yourself. The second is the knowledge that you create negativity, and that all negative thinking and emotions are temporary. Because these thoughts and emotions can change, they cannot cause permanent damage. The third is understanding that all living and sentient beings are related. The fourth pillar is a spiritual belief that we are surrounded by love and goodness. We just need to stop, look, and listen.

As a music therapist, I believe that we can help our companions through these pillars of growth by showing them how our music-infused strategies elicit positive thinking and feelings through the universal and inexplicable beauty of music. When our companions show openness to these musical experiences, they demonstrate their trust in us and the music. The next step is to trust themselves and to know that they have what they need to heal. Scolastico suggests a mantra, "I may feel temporarily unworthy, but I am permanently a magnificent being!" This can be made very powerful when you give spontaneous expression to these words as lyrics set to music.

Awakening the Breath

The breath stirs the elixir that we carry with us. It can comfort us, and it can also wake us up. Here are some breathing techniques from the yogic traditions:

In Chap. 10, you learned a three-part deep breathing for eliciting a sense of comfort. After your companion has mastered this relaxing exercise, try a new technique. If you double the length of the exhalations in relation to the inhalations, you feed the nervous system and activate the parasympathetic nervous system, quieting the body and the mind. Rhythmic accompaniment has the advantage of providing a timekeeper, so you won't have to count or keep track of the time. With your favorite melodic instrument, play the first four steps of an ascending major scale (C, D, E, F) at a comfortable, slow tempo (find a pace that is comfortable for your companion, or start with ♩ = 72) while you instruct your companion to inhale (I use my ascending hand to signal the in-breath). For the exhalation, start the descending scale from the fifth tone, and repeat each note twice (G, G, F, F, E, E, D, D) in the same tempo, so that it requires twice the time to complete. Start the ascending sequence again, and continue for a few rounds until you end with a deep, cleansing breath on the final C.

Alternate nostril breathing (*nadi shodhana*) requires more concentration, as it involves coordinating the actions to close off one nostril alternately with the other. This technique is designed to balance the autonomic nervous system and the two sides of the brain. It is implemented as follows:

- Hold your right hand at the end of the nose, and raise the thumb and ring finger, letting the index and middle fingers relax. These two fingers will be used to close the two nostrils. As you inhale and exhale with different nostrils, take twice as much time to exhale as inhale. Pause briefly between inhalations and exhalations.
- Close the left nostril with your ring finger and inhale through the right nostril.
- Close the right nostril with your thumb and exhale through the left nostril.
- Inhale through the left nostril.
- Close the left nostril and exhale through the right nostril.
- Inhale through the right nostril, then close the right nostril and exhale, then inhale through the left nostril.
- Continue repeating the cycle just a few times.
- Let the hands rest and breathe deeply.
- Notice how you feel.

Rhythmic music that suits your companion offers cues to coordinate the exercise. I start out simply, using one low and one high tone, the low one for inhalation and the high one for exhalation. I play four low tones for the inhalation, pause briefly, and play eight high tones for the exhalation. You may be tempted to get creative with your accompaniment, but remember that the purpose of the music is to facilitate your companion's slow, relaxed, breathing tempo by prompting the initiation and duration of the breath with a steady beat.

Awakening the Body

Awakening the body does not require gymnastics. It may only require awareness.

Focusing

Gendlin (1982) identifies the bodily felt sense in his book, *Focusing*. The felt sense is the awareness of the body's response to thoughts, actions, events, and emotions. When Gendlin wrote the first edition of *Focusing*, he was informing the evolving field of somatic psychotherapy, the career path that Sam was taking when his life was taken from him. Somatic therapies work through the body to bring awareness to issues. The body never lies—it is a true representation of experience. Focusing involves attending to the subtle shifts and changes that the body goes through, noticing areas that might be stuck and labeling the sensations with a word or phrase. Insights may arrive after your companion listens to the body. But do not attempt this if your companion is in significant pain or distress. Also be sure that you have already established a trusting relationship. Here is a script that I have adapted from *Focusing*:

- **Relax the body.** Pay attention to the place inside your body where you tend to feel things. Ask yourself, "How is my life going? What is the main thing for me right now?" Sense the response from your body. When there is a concern or worry, do not go inside it. Stand back and say, "Yes, that is there. I can feel that." Create a space between you and that sensation. Then ask the questions again. Sense whatever comes.
- **Feel the felt sense.** From the body's responses to the questions, choose one. Do not go inside it. Stand back from it. Pay attention to the place in your body where you usually feel things, and in there you can get a sense of what that "main thing" feels like. Let yourself feel an unclear sensation of what all of that feels like.
- **Sense its quality.** Let a word, phrase, or image surface from the quality of this unclear felt sense. It could be a juicy adjective, a descriptive phrase, or a picture. Stay with the felt sense until you have a word, phrase, or image that describes it very well.
- **Alternate.** Feel that felt sense again, and then focus on the word, phrase, or image. Listen to your body's response as you alternate between the felt sense and the word or phrase. How is your body reacting to the fit? Is there resonance between them? Notice changes in the felt sense, as you think of the word(s) or image. Continue to alternate until the word(s) or images seem to fit the felt sense really well.
- **Ask.** Ask yourself, "What is it about this main thing that creates this quality or resonates with the word(s) or image?" Sense that quality

again and ask, "What is in this sense?" Stay with this sensation until there is a shift or release.

- **Receive**. Receive whatever it is that comes from that shift or release. Be friendly toward the experience. Notice again what the body feels.
- **Add music**. (Music therapist: Prepare excerpts of music of different tempi and temperament. Play the first example.) Notice any changes in your body's felt sense. (Play a second example.) Notice any new changes in your body's felt sense. Be friendly toward the experience.

Amy Weintraub (2012) suggests an adaptation of focusing in *Yoga Skills for Therapists: Effective Practices for Mood Management*. Ask your companion to lie down in a comfortable position, and read the following:

> Back of the body heavy, sinking into the earth like a stone in sand. Legs heavy and sinking. Spine, back of the head, arms, heavy and sinking. From this earthbound density, a lightness begins to arise. Body light and floating. Front of the body, light and shining. Breath flowing through the front of the body—face, chest, abdomen, pelvis, tops of the legs. Front of the body light and floating, whole body light and floating above the floor (bed). Body light and floating like a cloud.
>
> Feel the heaviness in the body and the lightness in the body simultaneously. Body heavy and light … Notice an area of discomfort in your body. Perhaps an unpleasant tightness or numbness. Allow the breath to join the area of discomfort without trying to change anything … Breathe into the area of discomfort.
>
> Is there an area of comfort in the body? … Go back and forth between the area of discomfort in the body and the area of comfort in the body. Take two long breaths into the area of discomfort and feel the emotion, if there is one, associated with that discomfort. Take two long breaths into the area of comfort, and feel the emotion if there is one associated with the pleasant feeling in the body (pp. 171–172).

It is the attention to and exploration of the subtleties of the felt sense that provide much of the value. Note that I have admonished you to avoid this technique when your companion is in considerable pain for a few reasons. First, if your companion has a short hospital stay, you may not have had the time to strengthen your relationship and you may not have the opportunity in the future to continue working through the felt sense. Secondly, your role may be more supportive in nature, as opposed to insight-oriented. Third, your goal may be to focus attention away from the body and onto comforting images or pleasant memories. However you choose to adapt this technique, orchestration of the instructions, for example, thick chords in the low register for "heaviness," and twinkling trills for "lightness," adds depth to the experience.

Pema Chödrön (2013) believes in the power of concentrating on the body's sensations, even in the midst of substantial pain. In her lecture, *When Pain Is the Doorway: Awakening in the Most Difficult Circumstances*, she urges:

> Stay with the felt sense of the pain. It is not going to stay that way. Everything is always in flux and moving. Emotions and thoughts keep moving and changing. Keep going back to the feeling—the bodily felt sense—come back to the rawness of the experience. It will teach you something … If you get beneath the feelings, you are entering into a dynamic flow of going deeper into the understanding of the underlying feelings— the layers that feed the propensity. All of it is fluid … It is open and dynamic and shifting, and if you give it your attention, you can bring insights into it.
>
> What you're feeling is in process—it is in motion, evolving. It feels monolithic and a huge problem, but if you come to know it intimately, you will find that it is fluid, and it can open right up into a huge mind and huge heart. It's your potential rather than your huge, shameful obstacle.

This intense investigation of pain is appropriate only when your companion is seeking this sort of growth, and you are in a strong therapeutic relationship in which you have appropriate supervision and support. When the conditions are right, accompanying your companion on this journey through pain can be transformative, perhaps for both of you.

Movement to Music

When hooked up to IVs and catheters, fear of disturbing or inadvertently removing a tube is likely to result in muscle tension that can exacerbate discomfort and pain. Gentle movement to music may be the right prescription for loosening up the muscles and lightening up the mood. Before beginning movements, however, be sure to check with nursing staff about the mobility and physical limitations of your companions. You will need to garner approval from medical staff and customize this technique with your companion's needs and restrictions in mind.

Start with improvised music or selections from your companion's relaxing playlist that are slow and that flow. Let the music signal fine movements for the fingers, toes, or unrestrained and mobile parts of the body. Demonstrate some lighthearted swaying, soft twists or turns, and easy stretches. Then return to the music, and ask your companion to notice the impact of these slight movements on tension. Repeat or carefully extend those that feel good. If there are no obstructions or contraindications, introduce a dance with the hands or fingers and toes. Let the music decelerate and come to an end.

Yoga and Music

The *asanas* (postures) of yoga regulate the body in order to regulate the mind. While it is not feasible to introduce the postures and stretches of a traditional yoga class, it may be possible to adapt some of the simpler asanas designed to manage stress (always with the advice of nursing staff or physician order), such as stretching out the arms or gently tilting the head, while adding musical accompaniment, of course. The *mudras* (gestures of the hands and fingers) are used in tantric ceremonies and classical Indian dances, but they may also provide a mode of expression for your companions. Amy Weintraub (2012) suggests:

> Invite your client (companion) to put her right hand on her heart, as though she is pledging allegiance to her heart. This may be enough, or you might suggest that she place her left hand on top, linking her thumbs in a hand gesture called Eagle Mudra.
>
> Add imagery by inviting her to bring into her heart's mind a soothing, serene image, or her inner resource—a place where she can imagine feeling calm and serene. (I avoid using the word *safe*, as the mind, especially in someone who has a history of trauma, may immediately resist—"There is no safe place for me in the world!") (p. 35).

If your companion appears restful and content, you might like to conclude with some beautiful music, while lovingly releasing the Eagle Mudra.

Drumming

In *Music Medicine: The Science and Spirit of Healing Yourself with Sound*, Christine Stevens (2012) provides a plethora of activities for using sound and music to awaken or soothe. She is particularly adept at using drums therapeutically. Stevens says, "The magnetic pull to the drum breaks through resistance and the barriers that block our own healing journey. Rhythm turns off the mind and calls to the body's primary intuition" (p. 42). She is reassuring about drum technique:

> As a tool of wellness, one the most significant aspects of drum medicine is in the primary spiritual teaching of the drum: if you think too much, you'll screw up. This is true for any natural body movement—if you think about every step as you walk, you will trip. Drumming is the ultimate "be here now" strategy, a deactivation of the mind's wandering into the past or future. You must be in the moment; otherwise, your playing will suffer. The drumbeat calls your mind to the "now" moment just like the metronome calls the body to walk to the beat. We entrain our minds to the beat of now, and drumming becomes an active meditation (p. 43).

Obviously, in a hospital or setting where the acoustics are bright, the strong resonance of drums may be disturbing to others. However, the ocean drum, rain sticks, and shakers may substitute, particularly if the goal of drumming is to reinforce the heartbeat or emphasize the moment. So when you can, drum. Drum your heart out. Just be sure that neighboring companions aren't sleeping.

Imagery to Awaken

In *Relaxation Revolution*, Herbert Benson and William Proctor (2010) recommend a visualization that awakens the healthy companion:

Sit quietly with your eyes closed and picture what it was like to be free of the disease or symptom that you are experiencing … If you can't recall a time when you were symptom free, just visualize what you think or imagine it would be like to move about without the pain … Picture yourself engaging in any physical act that you would like to be able to do without pain or other symptoms. You might see yourself throwing a ball, swinging a tennis racket, gardening, playing some pickup basketball, or kicking a soccer ball with a child or grandchild. Your choice of mental picture should be personal; select an activity that you enjoy doing but have found you can't do because of your symptoms.

The main idea … is to identify your particular symptom or disease, but then to see yourself completely healed of that symptom or disease… Hold these dynamic inner images in your mind for 8 to 10 minutes and play with them in your imagination. Construct a kind of mental motion picture where you are the healthy central character … After the 8- to 10-minute period, continue to sit quietly for about a minute with your eyes closed, but this time, allow "regular" thoughts to reenter your mind. Then open your eyes and continue sitting quietly for about another minute (p. 100).

While reminders of the whole and healthy self may help your companion think positively, they can also evoke a sense of loss, particularly with a serious, chronic, or degenerative condition. As with all of these scripts, you will choose those that fit your companions' needs, and adapt them to personal interests and issues. Debrief after guiding your companions to a different place, and ensure that they are in a good place.

Davis, Eshelman, and McKay (1995) suggest engaging the fingers in mudra-like circles, while imagining several pleasant events. Known as the five-finger exercise, and adapted by music therapists at University Hospitals of Cleveland, this version is also part of the music therapy protocol at Boston Medical Center. Be sure to individualize the instructions based on your companion's capabilities and interests. This entire exercise can be accompanied by playlist selections, or you can improvise music in between these prompts. Just be sure to leave plenty of time to experience each prompt:

Touch your thumb to your index finger. As you do so, go back to a time when your body felt healthy fatigue, when you had just engaged in an exhilarating physical activity. You might imagine that you had just played tennis, jogged, etc.

Touch your thumb to your middle finger. As you do so, go back to a time when you had a good experience.

Touch your thumb to your ring finger. As you do so, go back to the nicest compliment you have ever received. Try to really accept it now. By accepting it, you are showing your high regard for the person who said it. You are really paying him or her a compliment in return.

Touch your thumb to your little finger. As you do so, go back to the most beautiful place you have ever been. Dwell there for a while (adapted from Five-finger exercise on p. 82–83).

Sometimes, a companion does not want to recall exhilarating activity because of infirmity; sometimes, finding a good experience is challenging because of depression; authentically accepting a compliment is difficult for some; and identifying a beautiful place may evoke a sense of loss because that place is far away. However, I have never yet encountered a person who could not find, out of the four possibilities, at least one pleasant image or memory. Not only might your companions enjoy a relaxing respite, but their responses can open up an opportunity to talk about who they are outside of the medical setting, offering a glimpse of their personalities and history.

Awakening the Mind

Daju Suzanne Friedman (2014) was a Chinese medicine professor and practitioner of medical qigong. When diagnosed with cancer, she applied *Rinzai Zen* teachings to her own life, and wrote *Zen Cancer Wisdom: Tips for Making Each Day Better*. Friedman offers advice for those with cancer, but her wisdom applies to people with any serious condition:

> You may find that you hate this cancer, or you may come to embrace it. This is your path, your journey. Regardless of your view of it or how you got here, you are now on a path you likely didn't expect to find yourself on. Will you take it on mindfully or mindlessly?

You may not end up as the same person you were before cancer came along. Many of us grow from the experience. It is hard to face something like cancer without having one's perspective changed. I feel wiser from living with cancer—though I'd have rather just seen the movie. The path has been filled with many obstacles, and sometimes even with gifts. I've tried my best to pay attention to each step, lest the learning pass me by (p. 165).

Friedman offers a technique to stimulate the insights that she herself gained from examining a daily *kōan*—the Zen story, question, paradox, narrative, or poem designed for contemplation:

Use this very moment to take a brief inventory of your life as it is right now. It is perfectly fine and acceptable to acknowledge the difficulties and challenges you've faced since your diagnosis.

For this exercise however, find something positive that you've come to learn, experience, understand, or appreciate since you've been walking the cancer path. My bet is that there is at least one positive shift in your life that has resulted from the challenge of cancer.

Here's your kōan for today: If you call cancer an obstacle, it is like putting frost on top of snow. If you don't call cancer an obstacle, then you are trying to smell a flower by cutting off your nose. So what will you call it? (p. 167)

Friedman also used a special technique to awaken her creativity:

My own outlet is the art of shakuhachi—the Japanese bamboo flute. The shakuhachi is difficult to play, and I don't necessarily always achieve a peaceful feeling or lose myself in the flow of practice. Nonetheless, because it is so difficult, playing it requires my full concentration and focus. I must be careful to get the tilt of the flute just right, to place my fingers in the proper positions for each note, and to blow in a way that creates the proper sound for each note, all while trying to read the music (in Japanese) correctly.

When I play the shakuhachi, there is no room left in my brain for thinking about anything other than exactly what I am doing at that very moment. This level of concentration naturally clears my mind. I couldn't even entertain stressful thoughts or get swallowed up in emotional drama if I wanted to! As an added bonus, the calm feeling and focused awareness I get from playing remains with me long after I put the flute down.

My mentor in Chinese medicine always told his anxious and worried patients to cultivate a hobby that required the use of their hands. A ridiculously large portion of your brain is dedicated to the movement of your first fingers and thumbs. Apparently it takes a lot of brainpower to be prehensile. Take advantage of this biological reality!

What does your wordless self-expression look like? Get your creative juices flowing in a way that involves your body and mind. When the mind and body move and flow freely, so do your emotions. No magic words required! (p. 149)

Friedman's approach is a recipe for flow.

Waking Up

Sometimes, awakening just means waking up.

Calming and Waking from Medically Induced Sleep

Our companions who are anesthetized wake after surgery or procedures under the influence of strong medication. They may be disoriented and incoherent, or they may be in pain. Waking up to familiar music can make a significant difference, not only in their psychological states of mind but also their physical vital signs. Imagine hearing favorite songs or melodies even before your eyes are open. As a result, the shock of recovery room lights, bandages, restraints, appendages, and tubes is muffled with tender music.

To prepare your companion, ask the nursing and medical team if they will allow earphones to be worn during surgery or a medical procedure. In addition to the playlists you may have already prepared, interview your companion about favorite songs that are familiar and that carry particularly positive memories and calming associations. Select the most appropriate pre-surgery intervention for your companion by consulting the techniques in Chap. 10 for comfort, such as comforting the body, comforting the mind, and comforting images. Provide music from the comforting music playlist as you implement this strategy. Work with the medical team to develop a feasible plan for music listening immediately before and during the procedure. For IV insertion or other painful operations, ask if one of the team can activate the attention-getting playlist at this time, and coach your companion in some pain-relieving strategies (to be described in Chap. 13). Request that the anesthesiologist or nurse assigned to your companion activate the new favorites playlist before wheeling your companion into the recovery room.

Music therapy techniques for surgery and painful procedures are supported by experimental research. There are several randomized controlled trials of music-based and music therapy interventions that document impressive outcomes, including: diminished anxiety pre-surgery (Augustin & Hains, 1996); immune function and hormonal changes as evidenced by cortisol levels and lymphocytes pre- and peri-surgery (Leardi et al., 2007); and positive changes in pain, blood pressure, heart rate, and use of oral analgesics post-operatively (Tse, Chan, & Benzie, 2005). In their systematic review of music-facilitated procedural support research, Olivia Yinger and Lori Gooding (2015) reveal that about half of the studies resulted in impact on anxiety, and approximately one third of the studies reported pain reduction. There was a wide range of strategies used, from simply listening to music to active engagement in music therapy activities.

Awakening through Music Listening

Montello (2005) says:

> Listening to music is a natural way to develop concentration. The sensual, emotionally evocative quality of certain kinds of music brings the decidedly mental practices of concentration to a feeling level, thus integrating head and heart. It is at this point of integration that the potential for deep healing lies (p. 69).

For our companions, listening to the music that is personally meaningful may itself be enlightening. While there are many music therapy techniques that can accompany listening, the power of hearing beautiful music should never be underestimated.

Lyric Analysis

To delve further into your companion's perspectives on life, it is interesting to probe into the reasons that a certain piece of music is so appealing. The lyrics of a special song typically have messages that mirror personal philosophy or life experience. Thus, they reveal much about our companions and naturally open conversations about private issues that otherwise might require considerable time and trust to generate. Lyric analysis is a common music therapy technique whereby client and music therapist examine the words to a song and relate them to the person's life situation, emotional state, and other circumstances (Silverman, 2009). It is easy to implement with anyone interested in talking. Sometimes our companions suggest the songs, and sometimes music therapists present music that carries particular themes, like comfort, hope, and gratitude. The conversation may begin with general questions about our companion's interest in or history with this music; it may focus on certain lines that convey emotions or issues underlying pain or distress; or it may relate to the companion's wishes and dreams. Regardless of specific content, discussing the musical and lyric content of pieces is a convenient springboard to dive into our companions' inner worlds, and has been known to awaken insights. See Fig. 11.1 for a list of songs with themes of hope that might be well-suited to lyric analysis.

Awakening Energy

Humming

While some of our companions are reticent to sing, everyone can hum. In *The Healing Power of the Human Voice*, James D'Angelo (2000) has formulated a humming ritual for the "Mmmm" sound that concludes "Om" and "Amen," and initiates the delicious "Mm-Mm-good!" utterance. Humming is another activity designed to vibrate and bring awareness to each area of the body.

SONGS OF HOPE

Angel	Sarah McLachlan
Ain't No Mountain High Enough	Marvin Gaye & Tammi Terrell
Blackbird	The Beatles
Brave	Sara Bareilles
Don't Stop	Fleetwood Mac
Don't Stop Believin'	Journey
Don't Worry, Be Happy	Bobby McFerrin
Don't You Worry 'bout a Thing	Stevie Wonder
Eyes on the Prize	The Emmaus Group Singers
Give Me Love	George Harrison
Go the Distance	from Disney's *Hercules*
Hakuna Matata	from Disney's *Lion King*
Have It All	Jeremy Kay
Heal the World	Michael Jackson
Here Comes the Sun	The Beatles
I Believe I Can Fly	R. Kelly
Imagine	John Lennon
It's a Good Day	Peggy Lee
It's My Life	Bon Jovi
Man in the Mirror	Michael Jackson
Lean on Me	Bill Withers
Let the Good Times Roll	B.B. King
Let's Face the Music and Dance	Ella Fitzgerald
Let It Go	from Disney's *Frozen*
Lovely Day	Bill Withers
On the Sunny Side of the Street	Billie Holiday
One Love	Bob Marley
Roar	Katy Perry
Silver Lining	Kacey Musgraves
Singin' in the Rain	Gene Kelly
So Small	Carrie Underwood
Somewhere Over the Rainbow	Judy Garland
That's Life	Frank Sinatra
Three Little Birds	Bob Marley
Tubthumping	Chumbawumba
Uptight (Everything's Alright)	Stevie Wonder
When I Get Where I'm Going	Dolly Parton
You Can Make It If You Try	Sly and the Family Stone
You Get What You Give	New Radicals
You Gotta Be	Des'ree

Fig. 11.1   Songs of hope

To allow the natural sound of MMM to do its best work, draw in a slow, deep breath and try different tones from high to low to see which one resonates your head region most vibrantly. Essentially the MMM is a nasalization of vocal sound ... The object is to vibrate the MMM first in the head region and then allow it to seep down into the upper chest.

Make the sound strong, buzzy, and bright by putting a smile on your face. To hear the sound in its full resonance place the index fingers lightly over your ears with the rest of your hand embracing your face ... Have gaps between the hummings where you will breathe normally and observe what happens. Then take in another slow, deep breath just before emitting the next prolonged MMM sounding. And so on (p. 83).

Singing Bowls

Singing bowls are part of traditional healing practices in Tibet. These bowls are made of magnificent brass or quartz to resonate deeply when a mallet or "ringing stick" strikes the bowl. The soft suede of the mallet can be drawn around the circular rim of the bowl to create harmonic overtones. The bowls are used to signal the start and end of meditation and to resonate the various chakras of the body. In *How to Heal with Singing Bowls*, Suren Shrestha (2009) shares a rationale for use:

Everyone has a vibration that is a signature of their health and wellbeing. You could think of it as a natural result of the processes that run our physical bodies as well as our mental, emotional, and subtle bodies. Similar to a musical instrument that can fall out of tune through use, our bodies can also fall out of vibrational harmony and potentially develop illness. Stress and negativity create blockages of a healthy flow of energy, showing up in the energy field around our body as lower energy disturbances at first, and later as illness in our physical body.

Sound and vibration can be used to re-tune us to health and one of the most powerful modalities for this is the use of Tibetan singing bowls. When there is a deep relaxation through soothing, resonant sound, the body is affected on a cellular level, opening up the flow of energy to move back toward vibrational alignment with health. Sound can help us shift our energy frequency from lower to higher, removing the lower frequencies of emotions such as fear, anger, and resentment ... (p. 13).

Not every medical center will welcome a set of singing bowls into the sterile environment, and not every companion will be open to being vibrated with them. However, when feasible, and without making any claims regarding their healing value, singing bowls can create a novel experience to remember.

Perhaps more accessible, but also lacking in scientific verification, are the tuning forks used by John Beaulieu (2010). His approach entails "BioSonic Repatterning" through tuning forks, based on the Fibonacci and Pythagorean scales. Beaulieu discovered his methodology when he entered an anechoic chamber where he could hear the sounds created inside his own body. He began to use tuning forks to "tune" the imbalances in his internal sounds and went on to study ancient sound healing methods to integrate into his own. Intuitively, his approach started with the deep listening that nāda yoga requires and has evolved to include vibrational exercises associated with the five elements.

Chanting Through the Chakras

Chapter 4 introduced the wheels of energy that permeate our bodies, known as chakras. Judging from the upsurge in the number of books on the topic, the study of chakras, sometimes called *chakrology*, has been increasing in popularity. Each approach presents a new slant on ancient philosophy, a different set of syllables to chant, a variant of the musical tones to bring resonance to a particular chakra, or another promise of bringing balance and harmony to life. But because there is neither scientific evidence to support its outcomes nor research comparing one practice over another, it is difficult to recommend a single approach. Thus, the art of chanting through the chakras is controversial in medical circles. Nevertheless, the vibrations of chant to awaken energy can be recognized and felt viscerally. This process has helped many to sense and intuit how energy can get stuck at key locations in the body and how it might flow more easily. Here I share a practice I adapted from Anodea Judith (1987), using the *Bija* (seed) mantras that are derived from the Sanskrit. This narration includes many elements of the chakras, so as always, feel free to edit, adapt, and personalize for your companion.

- Sit comfortably, with a straight spine and fairly equal weight on the left and right sides of your body.
- Take some deep, cleansing breaths, allowing the air to enter the belly, then rib cage, then up to the clavicle. Pause briefly and exhale, emptying the breath through the rib cage and then the belly.
- Imagine the root chakra, representing the earth, at the tailbone at the base of your spine. Sit like a mountain, gathering strength from the earth. Fill that area with the color red, and chant the syllable *Lam* on the lowest note you can chant. Then affirm your strength by silently repeating, "I have everything I need to heal."
- Imagine the second chakra, representing the element of water, at the sacral area below the naval. Fill the belly with the color orange, and chant the syllable *Vam* on a note that is a little higher and that vibrates this part of the body. Then affirm, "My body is flowing with healing liquid."
- Imagine the third chakra, representing fire, in the solar plexus, between the naval and the heart. Fill this central area with the color yellow, and chant the syllable *Ram* on a note a bit higher that vibrates this part of your body. Affirm, "I have the fire and strength to heal."
- Imagine the fourth chakra, representing air, in the heart. Fill the heart with the color green, and chant the syllable *Yam* (sounds like *Yum*) on a note that opens your heart and feels wonderful. Affirm, "My heart is open."
- Imagine the fifth chakra, representing sound, in the throat. Fill the throat with the color blue, and chant the syllable *Ham* on a note that feels natural to sing. Affirm, "I speak the truth."
- Imagine the sixth chakra, representing light, at the point between your eyebrows where a third eye might be found. Fill the third eye with the color violet, and chant the syllable *Om* on a comfortable note that is a little higher. Affirm, "I can see clearly."
- Imagine the seventh chakra, representing ether or the cosmos, at the crown of the head. Fill the crown with the color white and sit in silence. Affirm, "Grace is with me."

Montello (2002) suggests following up with music listening. You can identify a piece of 20 to 30 minutes from your companion's relaxing music playlist for this exercise:

> Bring your awareness to the outer rims of your ears and feel the music expand your listening and take you where you need to go. Next focus on the pulse of the music as it resonates in your heart center. You might even be able to feel the beating of your heart as you breathe in and out through your heart chakra along with the pulse of the music. Choose your favorite of the two techniques and stay with it for the duration of the exercise. If distracting thoughts or feelings emerge, do not give them any energy. Gently bring your focus back to the music. When the music is over, rest in the quiet stillness of the moment and allow it to expand for as long as you are comfortable. You may end your meditation with an affirmation for healing, abundance, or anything that brings greater peace and joy into your life and the lives of all sentient beings (p. 95).

Awakening Songs

Chanting and Singing

In the foreword to Baird Hersey's book, *The Practice of Nada Yoga* (2014), Krishna Das extols the value of chant and song:

> The whole idea of chant is to release ourselves from the obsessive thinking that holds us prisoner. It is not only to be focused on what we are experiencing in that moment. It is to simply chant and allow the practice to work on us.
>
> When people sing and really get into it, they are disappearing. They are enjoying. They're not enjoying that they are enjoying. They are just enjoying. They have left that meta-judgmental thing behind. So when they stop singing, that silence just mushrooms out and blossoms immediately because of the absence of ego-centeredness in the room. That's what sound does (p. xi).

Power Songs

In Chap. 7, Angeles Arrien's (2010) *Four-Fold Way* revealed archetypes that are carried within everyone. Arrien described the Way of the Visionary as truth-telling. To access this visionary archetype, she suggests:

> Singing power songs is a valuable tool. Some native traditions say that one way to stay connected to the Great Spirit is to "sing for your life." In Africa it is said that "If you can talk, you can sing; if you can walk, you can dance." Oceanic societies believe that if you want to know how to tell the truth, begin to sing. These ancient societies have long realized that singing is a healing resource (p. 85).

The power song is also contemporary. Christine Stevens (2012) says that when she asked people about their power songs, they responded with selections such as "I Will Survive," "We Are the Champions," and "I Believe I Can Fly." Here are her instructions for awakening your power song or your companion's:

> Think of which songs have boosted your spirit, caused you to dance, or spoken a message that rings true in your heart … Take an inventory of powerful songs in your life. Power songs often appear in difficult and transitional times in our lives. Choose one power song that has meaning for your life right now …
>
> Make it a regular practice to consciously listen to or sing along with your power song. Adopt it as your personal anthem. Connect with the lyrics, melody, and energy … If you feel so inspired, you can write your own power song by using a melody you already know but set to your own lyrics, or you can make up your own tune (p. 74).

Power songs may be the ultimate agent of empowerment. Consistent with Sam Hanser's philosophy, self-empowerment can release the inner healer, while the mastery of self-proclamation can lift one to a state of flow or awe. Mind, body, and spirit are strengthened with such awakening songs.

Awakening the Self

Paul Pearsall (2007) speaks of awe as the eleventh emotion:

> Life can feel busy and interesting (and a lot easier) when we automatically and quickly react to our world, but it becomes an awe-inspiring, tremendous mystery when we take responsibility for the fact that how we see, think about, and experience our world is largely a matter of our own conscious choice to embrace and think longer and more deeply about its mystifying grandeur. We can go through the ten basic human emotions (love, fear, sadness or loneliness, embarrassment, curiosity, pride, enjoyment or joy, despair, guilt, and anger) or be open to the unique eleventh by becoming more deeply aware of nature … Being aware is much more than reacting. It's experiencing that we are experiencing and applying our full and deepest consciousness to where, with whom, and why we are, and that's what can inspire profound awe (p. 12).
>
> A good life is about meeting the challenge of carrying pain without amplifying it into suffering and savoring pleasure without becoming a slave to pursuing more of it. It's our eleventh emotion, and it is its capacity to expand our imaginations and open our minds to all that is available to us in the present moment—be it good or bad—that offers creative ways to meet that challenge. The capacity to meet challenges in creative ways refers to a creative consciousness that facilitates a fuller engagement to try to understand, rather than the easier awe of ignorant acceptance and a sense of confirmation (p. 73).

In Chap. 8, you saw how Helen and her music therapist uncovered her creativity and talent when she began to learn to play the piano during her hospitalization. She began to realize the dream of learning piano when she least expected it. To see Helen's giant grin as she performed a folk song from her native Puerto Rico was to witness a state of awe.

Montello (2005) enlightens us:

> The key to successfully walking this musical path is to accept yourself and all your permutations right now, not when you have fixed what ails you. To walk this path to the spirit of self-acceptance, patience, curiosity, and positive expectations is to walk with joy (p. 77).

Songs to Awaken

For some, the songs in Fig. 11.1 engender hope or awaken the spirit. This list includes some of the dreamiest songs, like "Somewhere Over the Rainbow" and "Songs of the Heart." It exudes optimism with "Let It Go" and realism with "Heal the World." My favorite is "Here Comes the Sun" by the Beatles. It reminds me of the Sun-self that Sam Hanser refers to when he speaks of us as rays of sunshine. So sing, keep singing, and take Sam's advice: "Own your light. And keep beaming!" In the next chapter, we will explore ways to ignite the musical self and uncover the inner source of creativity.

12

The Way to the Musical Self

Laws of Creativity
(some observations)
spirit creates form
every thought is ultimately an event
as you think so you become
like attracts like
each soul must walk its own path
it is a free will universe
all being is becoming
nothing that is created is ever extinguished
you experience what you concentrate upon
A note: If you're looking for meaning, then it is yours to create. You set the
destination for your life and if you persevere, you will get there. Be careful
though. Even purpose can be an addiction. It's how you get there that mat-
ters. That means staying present with your experience whatever it may be
(Samuel Hanser, 2010, p. 17).

Sam's creative meanderings leave us with a paradox between staying
present for creativity and following the laws, destinations, and purpose

© The Editor(s) (if applicable) and The Author(s) 2016
S.B. Hanser, *Integrative Health through Music Therapy*,
DOI 10.1057/978-1-137-38477-5_12

that guide the process. He states that we can create meaning when we are present and allow spirit to create form.

As we have been exploring, there is a healthy spirit that dwells below the surface of pain and suffering. It longs to express the meaning of the journey to wellness from a source of wholeness that accepts and knows the path to true healing. Part of this path is giving voice to the unique story of each of our companions as they traverse the terrain of illness.

Everyone has a story, a story that must be told. You have an important story that identifies who you are, one that can only be told by you. Sadly, many of our stories are first revealed in eulogy. But we music therapists can open up these authentic narratives so that the storyteller can speak them (actually sing them!) out loud. At times, the stories bring insights and existential highlights. Once vocalized, they can be heard, shared, and recorded as keepsakes for anyone to read or hear.

Our music stirs up the deepest inner recesses and provides a frame and vocabulary of expressive language. It is a safe language to use, since it can be metaphorical and indirect. But, if desired, and with the addition of lyrics, it can be rather concrete and insightful. The human spirit can conjure beauty never before realized—something so original that no one has ever thought of it. Such is the case for Brad and Darcie.

The Musical Journey

Brad's Journey

An accountant in international development, Brad Else spent his career making meaning of numbers for his clients. Then, when he got sick, numbers controlled him—told him whether he was going to live or die. But Brad found a remarkable way to make his numbers count, and he produced a movie called *Behind the Numbers* to describe this process. The numbers he refers to are the platelet counts that determine whether cancer is inhabiting his body. Here is Brad's medical history, according to his own account:

- Diagnosed with leukemia in early 2012 ... and promptly lost my career.
- Spent 62 days in the hospital and received chemotherapy and an allogeneic bone marrow transplant.
- Discharged in June of 2012. In early 2014 fell out of remission and recently underwent a donor lymphocyte infusion.
- The leukemia appears gone but now I've been diagnosed with another challenge ... MDS (from the film, *Behind the Numbers*).

MDS is myelodysplastic syndrome, wherein abnormal bone marrow cells are not producing healthy new blood cells. This condition can lead to acute myeloid leukemia, so Brad's cancer story continues. Brad sustained 23 treatments over 4 years, including a lengthy hospital stay for a bone marrow transplant. Since his initial screening, he has had regular blood tests and oncology visits, but found that rarely was he asked, "How do you feel?" The question was always, "How are your numbers?" The medical team was referring to his platelet counts that would reveal whether the unwelcome guest, cancer, was present in his bloodstream. Brad described the routine:

Who you are—are the numbers; numbers are a proxy for you. When my numbers dipped, I felt that the leukemia was returning, and my pessimism came true. I was tracking them all along. It was natural for me to write up Excel graphs, given my background. So I said, "Let's look at these numbers in a completely different way." There was a different way: Sonification.

This is a transcript of *Behind the Numbers*:

No matter what your blood count numbers indicate,
Within your numbers lie unique melodies.
Melodies that transcend disease.
Melodies that flow no matter what the medical intervention.
Melodies that continue, even when insurance denies coverage.
Sustaining rhythms that will last longer than all of us.
Melodies that are unique to you and ONLY you.
In fact, the piano notes you are hearing are my white blood cells ...
Indeed, blood counts can reveal YOUR music.

Let me explain how this is possible.
So that those that follow might hear this music.
So you can hear it.
And so those that provide care can also enjoy it.
The process begins with laboratory results.
Save your lab reports!
Assemble a history of a given test such as WBCs (white blood cell counts).
Consistently map the numerical count to musical notes.
Select a primary instrument to represent your sound.
Add any background instrumentation as you want.
Be prepared to watch others smile at your music.
What about platelet and red blood cells?
At first, platelets sounded like this ... (*low drone*).
A series of digitized notes.
The digitized notes of platelets were then replaced with piano keys.
Other background instrumentation was then added to accompany the piano. You are now hearing the melody of my platelets ...
My platelet counts are represented by the piano. The platelet-music began with low tones during chemotherapy and the transplant in 2012, then rose somewhat in 2013, and then declined when I fell out of remission. Even with large swings in the counts, the "music of platelets" continues with the certainty of their underlying rhythm. As do I.
Notice how music changes the tenor of a lab report ...
Red blood cells were approached the same way.
At first, just a series of digitized notes.
But I wanted a higher energy sound, so an electric guitar replaced the digitized sounds accompanied by some acoustic rock.
Again, the entire outlook on red blood cells changes with music ...
Yep. You're listening to my red blood cells.
Cool, huh?

I interviewed Brad in person, and he described the process for me in greater detail:

I have a 2-year data set. I needed to write an algorithm to map them, and found one produced at Washington State University (Sommerfeld, n.d.). But the platelets data sounded dry. Yet you hear the affirmation of feeling well in the music.

Then music therapist Michael Plunkett translated the algorithms into GarageBand music recording software. "When I assigned the piano to the tones, it was a quantum leap—at last my numbers were music!" Brad said. When I asked him how this made him feel, he commented,

> You have music coming out of bad numbers—It's mind blowing. Taking these data and making them approachable and using them in a new way fits together in interactive medicine. An orchestration that had coherence could separate out the complexity. This music was me—I can trace that … The creative process absorbs you in something other than the battle.
>
> In the end, I think the effort enabled me to do many things, including better separating a disease process from *who I am*. When you get a disease like this, there is a tendency for internal and external conversations to overwhelm *who you are* with the disease … Indeed, underneath all of the cancer-hoopla remains a unique, sustaining and interesting melody. We all have that—it just took a cancer as well as some music to remind me of that.

Brad's Heroic Journey. Brad resisted being a set of numbers. Instead, he traveled the Hero's Journey, and found a guide in his sister, Barbara Else, who is a board-certified music therapist. As they discussed ways to bring music into his life, they conceived this ingenious plan. As Brad trespassed many zones of treatment, his inanimate identity as "the one with plunging numbers" morphed into composer of music. It was not simply original music, but an invention emanating from his blood. Later, music therapist Michael Plunkett appeared as a new guide for Brad's journey, and they were on their way to recording this music. While under serious threat of death, Brad prevailed and produced a film to depict his expedition behind the numbers and give others a roadmap to inspire their creativity and redefine themselves. The film concludes with this:

> The music (the score of the movie) covers the 2-year period up until the lymphocyte infusion. The "numbers" have varied greatly over this time-span, but the music seems to have remained steady. I encourage you not to be defined by your "numbers" … there is much more behind those numbers. All we have to do is listen.

Darcie's Journey

Darcie Nicole is also changing the way she looks at her disease. Her EEG graphs are creating original music scores. Here is her story:

> I am a neurology patient with idiopathic, myoclonic, generalized, petit mal seizure disorder with pediatric onset, and I really feel that epilepsy is misunderstood. People associate it with grand mal episodes. They don't understand that there are cohabiting personalities that can emerge from being an epileptic person. We can get really self-conscious and explain ourselves too much. In my case, I have a form of epilepsy where calcium and sodium are crossing pathways, and they are creating combustion. I am overprocessing and neuroprocessing constantly. When that happens, any thought in my brain has to be rerouted. People don't realize how hard my brain is working. My brain is constantly shifting and resorting, so I tend to do things in a different way.
>
> I am a vocalist and songwriter, and my mother was also a musician. One day, while still a music student, I was doing really badly in a music composition class, and I called my mother. She said, "I bet you would get A's if you did this differently." She encouraged me to take some power back regarding my epilepsy and get printouts of my electroencephalograph (EEG) readings, enlarge them, superimpose staff lines, and compose—by hand—free notation on top of the spikes and waves. Then each little composition could also be named for something related to neurology.
>
> I reached out to my doctor, Dr. Dan Hoch at Massachusetts General Hospital, who loved the idea. He printed out some very active, lively and interesting sections of my most recent EEG, and I did the rest. I am using my own EEG patterns as a guide for the notation, and then making the adjustments.
>
> You know, I can manage this condition of mine, but I can't control it. This musical exercise, turned inspiration, is also an opportunity to use my lack of control as a tool for creativity. I think it's empowering. Oh, and by the way, I passed the class!

Take a look at Darcie's creation in Fig. 12.1.

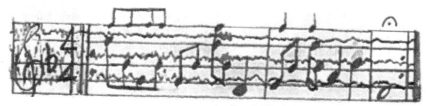

Darcie Nicole EEG sample composed over a
sourced anonymous EEG scan segment

Fig. 12.1   Darcie's music

A Journey through Grief

Music therapist Brian Schreck is creating musical tributes of a very different kind. An ABC News reporter interviewed Brian and the Bennett family:

Margaret and Jeremy Bennett's son died in February, but they still listen to his heartbeat every day. As 14-year-old Dylan Bennett lay dying in the intensive care unit of Cincinnati Children's Hospital, Brian Schreck recorded his heartbeat. He then paired rhythmic thumping with some of Dylan's favorite music to create a song for the Bennetts to keep.

"Our son was dying in front of us, and it was very tough," Jeremy Bennett said in a short film about the songs. "So just to hear that music, it really, really got my spirits up and I needed that."

Over the last six months, Schreck has made a dozen songs for the families of dying patients at Cincinnati Children's Hospital to help them cope with loss, he told ABC News. He said families worry that they'll forget the feel of their loved ones after they die, and he wants to preserve their "humanity" through music. He said the songs vary just as much as the patients, and has included music by artists from John Legend to Metallica. He plays the music himself but leaves the vocals out.

Schreck has been a music therapist for 10 years, but he only recently started making music for patients in the intensive care unit, which he said can be tense.

"People are very on edge all around," he said. "A lot of times, it's quiet when I go into the room, people don't really know exactly what to do or say. To let me know that it's in some way helping with their ability to cope with the very early onset of grief is a very rewarding thing," he said (Couch, 2014).

There is something about keeping the heartbeat alive that is enlivening. I actually have a recording of Sam's heartbeat, but his was recorded in utero. I set his fetal heartbeat to Vivaldi's *Winter* from *The Four Seasons*, and used it as the score for a film to promote my research project on music therapy in labor and delivery. It is surprisingly and curiously comforting to listen to it.

Writing Our Stories

Our stories must be told. They speak our Truth and reveal our Self. They contain the treasure map that will guide us along the road to wellness. When set to music, they bring out our unique, creative selves. Through this process, a talented music therapist can unearth the joy, hope, or resources that reside in all of us.

Songwriting

What does it take to write a song? Music therapists use a wide variety of methods, as presented in the comprehensive text, *Songwriting*, edited by Felicity Baker and Tony Wigram (2005). In the final chapter of that book, Wigram provides guidelines for a *Flexible Approach to Songwriting in Therapy* (*FAST*) model that incorporates common features of protocols published by music therapists. For our companions, the stages might include these options:

1. Introduce the songwriting experience by:
   a. improvising a story line
   b. therapist-initiated discussion
   c. companion-initiated idea after singing songs

2. Write lyrics through:
   a. brainstorming.
   b. words suggested by therapist or companion
   c. words about the companion's issue(s)
   d. companion's sources (favorite poem, original poetry etc.)

3. Compose music through:
   a. improvisation
   b. providing harmonic structure
   c. companion's ideas for melody and/or harmony
   d. therapist's ideas for vetting by companion
   e. offering music created by therapist (or pre-composed)

4. Transcribe the song
   a. lyrics
   b. lyrics and melody
   c. lyrics, melody, and chord chart
   d. lyrics, melody, chord chart, and accompaniment

5. Perform
   a. by therapist and companion
   b. for hospital personnel or other companions
   c. for friends and family

6. Record
   a. the original rendition
   b. the song sung by others
   c. with professional musicians (with or without orchestration)

The *Guiding Original Lyrics and Music* (*GOLM*) songwriting method was designed by Clare O'Callaghan (1996) and expanded for people with cancer by Emma O'Brian (2005). This approach incorporates the same stages of development, but GOLM emphasizes the need for companions to be presented with choices, allowing them to take ownership of their creations. The ideas generated by companions and the words of their stories are preserved by the therapist and grouped into a song structure. The companion decides upon the style of music and provides melodic ideas, enabling the song to evolve organically. Re-evaluation of the lyrics after the melody has been established offers the companion more choices, and the accompanying harmonies and instrumentation can be managed and morphed into the final creation.

Songwriting is a platform for exploring new metaphors for living, meaning, coping, and acceptance. The product is a visceral and fundamental manifestation of identity, life story, spontaneous expression, or meticulously designed creation. Each person has an inimitable style of engaging with and in music. Here are three songs composed by some of music therapist Dr. Maria Hernandez's companions.

Helen's Song. Back in the hospital for pain management of her sickle cell disease, Helen was more interested in playing the piano than in composing a song. But her music therapist knew that there was much that Helen had to say. When Hernandez guided her in the *five-finger exercise* for relaxation and focus, they had talked about what brought joy into her life when she was feeling so ill, and what allowed her to "get up" every day. Hernandez set Helen's words to music and sang the song to her at a subsequent session. Helen requested hearing her special song again at her last session before discharge, and Hernandez recorded it for her so that she could listen whenever she chose. Here are the lyrics:

I WILL GET UP
I live my life as if I only had today
I keep strong when life throws
Hardships my way
Chorus:
NO FEAR, NO PAIN CAN KEEP ME DOWN
I WILL GET UP WHEN LIFE WANTS TO PUSH ME DOWN
I live my life with God and love on my side
Laughter of children bringing
Joy to my heart
(Chorus)
I live my life with all the courage that I need
A castle in the clouds gives me
Some peace
(Chorus)

As is evident in these words, Helen's healing has required the determination, strength, full engagement, and fortitude that she articulates in her song. She was discharged from the hospital with more than new medications for her symptoms. Helen's heroic journey continues with the benefit of a power song to remind her that neither fear nor pain can keep her down, supplementing the piano as an additional outlet for her self-expression.

Michael's Song. Michael is a 40-year-old man with a history of morbid obesity and generalized anxiety disorder. He was admitted to Boston Medical Center with severe cellulitis, a subcutaneous infection that is capable of invading the lymphatic system. Michael was physically immobile in the hospital and psychologically depressed, and when his physicians could not easily diagnose the cause of his symptoms, his anxiety intensified. Michael wrote the lyrics for "The Music Within the Noise" while Dr. Hernandez strummed a progression of guitar chords. Here are his lyrics:

THE MUSIC WITHIN THE NOISE
My life right now
Is pretty much on hold
My time is spent
Waiting to heal
I feel stuck on an island
Watching others sail by
Their lives moving forward
While mine is still standing by
Chorus:
TRYING TO FIND THE MUSIC
WITHIN THE NOISE
THE EYE WITHIN THE STORM
A CALM INSIDE THE TENSION
THE PEACE INSIDE THE WAR
What used to be easy
Is a struggle now
Everyday tasks a real challenge
Finding the focus is often elusive
Every day getting harder to manage

208   Integrative Health through Music Therapy

(Chorus)

These lyrics portray Michael's struggles with intensity and clarity. Deconstructing "the music within the noise" exposed a powerful existential, psychotherapeutic channel leading toward insight and acceptance.

José's Song. When Dr. Hernandez suggested that José compose a song, he was ready. Hospitalized with a bout of chronic pancreatitis, he seemed anxious to share his history with his music therapist. In his first music therapy session, he explained the challenge of losing two brothers within a very short period of time. So, during his second session, Dr. Hernandez asked if he would like to write a song for his brothers. Wearing a downcast expression, he immediately spewed the words to his song. With Hernandez providing an accompaniment on guitar, José played the conga drums while they recorded this special memorial to his beloved brothers. When his sisters visited him in the hospital, José played the recording, and they all cried and embraced. José's song is in Spanish, and the English translation is shown alongside:

MIS QUERIDOS HERMANOS LEGENDARIOS (MY DEAR LEGENDARY BROTHERS)

Me levanto en la mañana	I wake up in the morning
Extrañando a mis hermanos	Missing my brothers
Los extraño porque se	I miss them because I know
Que no estarán a mi lado	They won't be at my side any longer
Ellos están en la Gloria	They are in the Glory (Heaven)
Y ya no están sufriendo	They are no longer suffering
Los que sufrimos somos	We are the ones who suffer
Los que nos quedamos	We who stay behind
Aquí en la tierra	Here on Earth
Lo que mas me duele	What hurts the most
Es cuando veo a la vieja mía	Is when I see my mother
Y cuando me pregunta por ellos	When she asks for them
Le digo que hace tiempo	I tell her I have not seen them
Que no los veos	For a while
Me siento mentiroso	I feel like a liar
Y solo le veo la tristeza	And only see her sadness
Y el corazón se me rompe	And my heart breaks
Éramos nueve y quedamos siete	We were nine and now we are seven
Vamos pa'lante toda mi gente	Let's move forward, my people
Porque nos queremos mucho	Because we love each other
Y el amor es incondicional	Love is unconditional

Me levanto en la mañana	I wake up in the morning
Y siempre estamos a nuestros lados	And we will always have each other
El cielo esta lleno	The heavens/sky is full
Y vamos a quedarnos	We will stay here
R ... y E ... como los extrañamos	R ... and E ... you are so missed
Pero un día nos veremos	But one day we will see each other
Pero no tan temprano	But not yet or too soon
Porque todavía me queda mucho	Because I still have much left
Para estar a sus lados	Before we meet again
Pero siempre recordando	Always remembering
sus presencias	Your presence
Mis queridos hermanos legendarios	My dear legendary brothers

Was it his vulnerability in the hospital, the relationship with Dr. Hernandez, his grief ready to emerge, or something else that incited José's desire to write this song? We may never know, but we can see the bereavement process materialize in this poignant example.

Lyric Substitution

Helen, Michael, and José entered into songwriting at their own gateways, with different levels of engagement and therapist intervention, to sculpt a musical way to express what they wanted to say. In these cases, their words revealed an important message, and the music heightened the underlying emotions.

When your companion is cognitively unable, too ill, or too tired to exert the effort, it may not be feasible or desirable to write a song. In these cases, lyric substitution provides an alternative for self-expression. By sprinkling some original lyrics into those grand old songs, the punchy contemporary ones, or the ones that are simply cute, the songs become their own. The process can be as easy as identifying a singable song that they know and like, and replacing a few key words with personal ones.

For a seamless process, you can find a folksong or other well-known ditty that has repetitive phrases within the text. A few favorites are: "Peace Like a River," "He's Got the Whole World in His Hands," "Down By the Riverside," and "We Will Rock You." Ask your companions to fill in the blanks, or answer your questions about their perspective on the subject, and they will have a personalized song that may offer a few surprising insights about their journeys. Of course, you may also want to begin with songs on your companion's own playlist.

Just Say It

W.A. Mathieu makes composing music fun with a variety of simple techniques, in *The Listening Book: Discovering Your Own Music* (1991). He has a recommendation for those who may be reticent to write a new song of their own:

> The secret to setting words to music is to say the words and to hear the words you are saying as if they were music ... If you write poems, or lyrics or lyrical prose ... first say the lines you write and then sing them as an extension of your patterns of speech ... Proceed line by line, taking the time to refine each phrase (p. 104).

Intonation is what communicates the emotion underneath the content of our language. Enhancing this intonation, as Mathieu suggests, not only produces our incomparable song, but also provides us with immediate feedback on what we really mean to say.

Musical Autobiography

In Chap. 7, you assessed the music that was and is important to your companion by fashioning playlists for many moods. A *Musical Autobiography* playlist is one that you can assemble with your companions to help them tell their life stories. What music do they associate with their earliest memories? What music did they enjoy as a young child? Was there music that they loved to hear, play, or sing during early schooling? During adolescence? During significant stages of their adult lives? Draw from the playlists already recorded, and add other music that is key to these developmental milestones. Listen, and with permission, record the stories (spoken or sung) that are associated with turning points in their lives. To pursue this further, ask them to create musical life maps on construction paper, with key songs noted at important junctures of their lives. There are quintessential lyrics within.

Inventing Music

A Child's Music

The University of the Pacific in Stockton, California used to hold "kiddie college" during the summers. During my tenure there as chair of the Music Therapy Department, I decided to offer a couple of music classes, one for children of preschool age and the other for those who had just completed kindergarten. I remember beginning the preschool class with a tambourine. I chanted, "This is a tambourine, a tambourine, a tambourine. This is a tambourine, but what else could it be?" I put it on my head, then flipped it and pretended to drink soup, next attempting to eat it. The children laughed and yelled, "A hat, a bowl, a cookie," and then, someone shouted out, "A pizza!" then, "The sun!" and "A circle!" We passed around the tambourine, and the children made new sounds with its cymbals and surfaces.

The kindergarten class came immediately following. Once again, I started with "This is a tambourine, a tambourine, a tambourine. This is a tambourine, but what else could it be?" Hands went up in response to my question.

"No," I said, "You don't need to raise your hands. We'll pass it around."

The first child said, "It's a tambourine," and I followed with, "But what else could it be?" I fumbled with it on my head, and the child said, "A hat."

As we passed it around the circle, the next child said, "A hat," but the enthusiasm had subsided. I had succeeded in reinforcing the "right answer," rather than stimulating curiosity and creativity.

That experience taught me how early on the rules of engagement (raising hands) can become the norm, how developmental stages of growth contribute to concrete thinking (having the right answers), and how cultural attunement to the social collective predicts group behavior (repeat what I heard, rather than risk an individualistic response). Once becoming socialized in kindergarten, these young children seemed to have lost some of the imaginative ways they approached the world.

As adults, of course, there are even more incentives to conform, comply, and cooperate. There are routines and rules to be followed in order to preserve order. But, does growing up have to mean sacrificing our imaginative sides? Those of us fortunate enough to pursue the arts, or to have the freedom to write and express ourselves individualistically in our work and home environments, know the benefits of engaging the intuitive and artistic side of the brain.

As music therapists, we have the opportunity to bring the freedom and playfulness of the young child back into the psyche. For this, improvisation is a fine tool.

Improvisation

Improvisation is an expressive art form that requires or creates flow. After years of classical musical training, it was particularly difficult for me to loosen up and allow myself to make the "musical mistakes" that improvisation requires. Musicmaking was always embedded with technique, repeated practice, and perfectionism. I could not see how the production of music could ever be free-floating or intuitive. Then I learned clinical improvisation.

Dr. Kenneth Bruscia's comprehensive text, *Improvisational Models of Music Therapy* (1987), includes an astounding number of improvisation techniques—I counted 64. Just as becoming a music therapist is a lifelong endeavor in honing one's skills, there is always more to explore and understand about clinical methods of improvisation. But one of the most important lessons was: "Be you, just be you, and you, too, can succeed at improvising."

Then I co-led a summer retreat in northern Sweden with Dr. Louise Montello that we called, "The Vision Quest." Although we trekked through the forests and rivers of Sweden, the journey was internal. Every time we experienced a new view of nature, Montello asked us to "play it." Every time we encountered a new insight, we "played it," and we really played with it. We used only our voices, bodies, and implements available in the natural environment to make music out of our feelings. Whenever we became aware that something inside us was changing, even if it was hunger or fatigue, we "played it." Whenever we imagined our future, we "played it." At the end of 10 days, we arrived home with more than visions of our future. We had created symphonies of ourselves for the present and for our forthcoming lives.

In *Outside Music/Inside Voices: Dialogues on Improvisation and the Spirit of Creative Music*, Garrison Fewell (2014) says:

> Improvisation is a process of discovery, a conversation or dialogue through spontaneous generation of sound that involves our entire being in an act that reveals the inherent connectivity between the inner microcosm and the outer macrocosm and creates unity between the inner self and the cosmic universe ...
>
> Improvisation is a way of life that involves all the senses and requires a total surrender to the moment ... I often use the French expression "l'instant du moment" to describe being in the moment—literally an instant within a moment.
>
> Developing a comfortable attitude toward "not knowing" is a theme ... I would add that many "abstract" descriptions of improvisation intersect with the metaphysical, in that an activity so deep and complex requires indirect approaches such as those implied by words and phrases like "mystery," "letting go," and "a leap into the unknown." Improvisation requires a thorough study of the fundamentals of music—harmony, melody, and rhythm—but for it to "happen" successfully, the improviser has to stop controlling the process and "get out of the way."
>
> Many believe that creative consciousness exists within each of us. Improvising musicians often talk about being a "channel" through which creative energy flows, becoming manifested in sound, and that it works best when we step back ... (pp. 16–19).

Fewell's words remind us how freeing it can be to "stay out of your own way," and not just musically.

When Dr. Colin Lee joined the Berklee music therapy faculty, he offered a new perspective on clinical music therapy improvisation through what he called *Aesthetic Music Therapy* (*AeMT*). Because we were both classically trained pianists, I had performed many of the musical resources that he used as building blocks for his approach and later introduced in his book, *Architecture of Aesthetic Music Therapy* (2003). Lee's model relies on musical idioms, melodies, harmonies, and rhythms from the classical repertoire in order to support improvisations by our companions. His approach is to galvanize our trust in our musical instincts and build on the music that we know best. Then, musical interactions with our companions can bring out our best, and theirs, too.

Music therapist Kimberly Khare is trained in *Creative Music Therapy*, an approach founded by Paul Nordoff and Clive Robbins (1977). Its hallmark is clinical music improvisation that brings out the music child within everyone. Khare applies guitar progressions that ask a question with a certain progression, provide a reassuring foundation with another set of chords, and reflect her companion's nonverbal intentions with other harmonic accompaniments. Khare creates an alliance through an intimate musical conversation. She says that the most important ingredient is learning to take musical risks, and experiment with new melodies, harmonies, and rhythms.

In *Improvisation: Methods and Techniques for Music Therapy Clinicians, Educators and Students*, Dr. Tony Wigram (2004) distinguishes between musical improvisation and clinical improvisation, the latter being: "the use of improvisation in an environment of trust and support established to meet the needs of clients" (p. 37). He emphasizes mirroring and matching, grounding and holding, modeling and cueing, and reflecting and empathizing.

Take a tip from these experts: "Be you," "Just play," "Stay out of your way," "Do what you know best," and "Take a risk." My advice is: "Practice, practice, practice." Yes, improvisation is a practice, and one that is sublimely in-the-moment. Improvising is a master class in letting things go, without judgment. Try it, and like Garrison Fewell, you might experience the awe of "leaping into the unknown."

Musical Selves

In this musical journey, I have been encouraging you to pursue your own musical quest while you foster your companions' musical abilities and creativity. Displaying your own vulnerability as you introduce activities that are new to you as well as to your companions may have the effect of enhancing empathy between you. Experimenting together and inspiring each other may extend the creative limits of both of you. Meanwhile, you are turning off your companion's ill persona and turning on the musician. With you as guide, your companions can reframe the experience of illness to one of musical discovery, whether or not they are aware of any latent talents. By making music integral to the journey toward wellness, your companions will be uncovering their creative, musical selves, and you might be surprised to find a more musical self in yourself as well.

13

The Way to Cope

Know that the reality within which you operate is created by your beliefs. Know that this realm of the relative is an opportunity to express your being to its fullest, its brightest, and your inner source, the realm of the absolute is unaffected by the "trials and tribulations" of your current personality.

My desire for you is to realize that now, as ever, your being rests within the ubiquity of love and *nothing* can threaten it. Doubt you this truth and you will have bowed to the voice of fear. You may recognize fear by its promise of "some day," "elsewhere," and "without." Love, however, is the fabric of your being, the yarn by which you knit your reality. It is inescapable, unconditional, and inextricably part of *you*. Even as you deny love its validity, know that you are embraced by love always. It waits patiently for you to lift the veils of illusion so that you may claim it as yourself. All masters know this.

And when you have realized the unity of love, then you shall create with it and all your dreams may be manifest (Samuel Hanser, 2010, p. 23).

This chapter is about applying the head and the heart to foster resilience to physical and emotional suffering. It is about challenging the beliefs that too easily blot out love. It is also about accessing inner resources that counteract fear. It is about retrieving love's core and more, to cope with stress, fear, and pain.

© The Editor(s) (if applicable) and The Author(s) 2016
S.B. Hanser, *Integrative Health through Music Therapy*,
DOI 10.1057/978-1-137-38477-5_13

Coping Through Head and Heart

Yet this struggle may be far more distressing when the subject matter is grief. The bereaved heart is desperate for reason, logic, more rationale thoughts and clear thinking, or to hear a different truth from the mind's meandering. In the poem, *Head, Heart*, Lydia Davis (2007) writes: "I want them back, says heart. Head is all heart has. Help, head. Help heart (p. 191).":

> Heart weeps.
> Head tries to help heart.
> Head tells heart how it is, again:
> You will lose the ones you love. They will all go. But even the earth will go, someday.
> Heart feels better, then.
> But the words of head do not remain long in the ears of heart.
> Heart is so new to this.
> I want them back, says heart.
> Head is all heart has.
> Help, head. Help heart (p. 191).

When there is illness to contend with, the head can lead the heart further astray. Following inconclusive diagnoses, bad news, or poor prognoses, the thoughts and worries that pervade the mind pluck the heartstrings. Ironically (or perhaps not so ironically), the Indie band "The Head and the Heart" proffers a solution in their song, "Let's Be Still":

Let's Be Still
> You can get lost in the music for hours, honey,
> You can get lost in a room.
> We can play music for hours and hours
> But the sun'll still be coming up soon
> **Chorus:**
> THE WORLD'S JUST SPINNING
> A LITTLE TOO FAST
> IF THINGS DON'T SLOW DOWN SOON WE MIGHT NOT LAST.

So just for the moment, let's be still.
You can get lost in the music for hours, honey,
You can get lost in a room.
We can play music for hours and hours
But the sun'll still be coming up soon.
The world's not forgiving
Of everyone's fears.
The days turn into months, the months turn into years.
So just for the moment, let's be still
They're tearing down
So we can rebuild
And all this time
Is just circles in my mind
So just for a moment,
Just one moment,
Just for a moment let's be still. (*4 times*)
(Chorus)
Just for a moment let's be still. (*6 times*)

Let's be still—good advice, but how is it possible to be static when the mind's thoughts are circling like a tornado? The music may be a haven, but is it just an escape when you are not really listening? Then the sun comes up again, the world spins, and the cycle of life rolls on before we even know what is happening. How can we be still and also mindful?

Analyzing these lyrics with your companions can open a dialogue about everything from how they use music in their lives, to the passage of time, to how challenging it can be to be still. Then you can spend some time in silence, as the overactive mind slows down to make the morning last.

Syncing the Head and Heart

Chapter 4 introduced the HeartMath Institute (HMI) and its study of the dynamic interactions between head and heart, thinking and feeling. In *Transforming Anxiety: The HeartMath Solution for Overcoming Fear and Worry and Creating Serenity*, HMI founder Doc Childre and Deborah

Rozman (2006) describe techniques designed to enhance synchronicity between mind and heart, and serve as coping techniques for stress and fear, consistent with many music therapy methods. Here is an adapted HeartMath protocol for you to try first. Then decide whether an individualized music therapy application will suit your companion's needs.

- **Notice and Ease.** Take note of feelings and attempt to name them. Focus on the heart, breathe, and relax.
  Music Therapy Application. As you improvise some music, ask your companions to listen to the music and listen to what is happening inside. Ask about the feelings that are generated. Modulate to a different mode, vary tempo and dynamics to create a new mood, or ask about changes in feeling states. Maintain music that evokes positive feelings, and invite your companions to close their eyes and imagine the music flowing into the space around the heart.
- **Neutralize Feelings.** Breathe deeply. Imagine the breath entering and exiting the area around your heart and chest. To neutralize worries or stresses, focus on the breath, and let go of these negative thoughts and feelings. When you notice a worry or negative thought, be kind to yourself, and let it go.
  Music Therapy Application. Ask your companions whether you should continue with your improvisations or play some favorite, relaxing music. Suggest that they breathe along with the music, and pay attention to these deep, rhythmic breaths. If worries or negative thinking surfaces, have your companions focus on the breath and music again, gently letting go of the thoughts. Remind them to notice if the worries return and then, to bring an attitude of acceptance to them, before letting them go.
- **Replace Undesirable Attitudes.** Identify a feeling or attitude that you wish to modify, such as fear, worry, anger, frustration, or hopelessness. Select a more positive alternative, such as confidence, calm, excitement, strength, or contentment. After you select one of these, breathe the feeling of that attitude through the area surrounding the heart. Savor these positive feelings.

Music Therapy Application. Ask your companions if they would like to identify a negative attitude or feeling and its more desirable replacement, as above. Improvise some sounds to reflect the negativity, and move quickly to represent the sounds of a positive attitude. Ask companions to breathe that replacement attitude gradually around and through the heart. Have them dwell there, as you continue to play soothing music. Remind them that they can cope with stressful feelings by breathing a new attitude into the heart.

- **Cut through Emotions.** Explore feelings about the current illness or episode. Breathe deeply, and allow a sense of love and appreciation to flow through the heart for at least 30 seconds. Return to the original feelings, and give them objectivity, as though they were somebody else's response to illness. Rest in the space around the heart. Soak any undesired feelings or confusion in the compassion of the heart. Relax those feelings as you bring them into the heart. Ask for guidance from your heart to cope with these feelings. If nothing comes from this, focus on something that you appreciate.

Music Therapy Application. Ask your companions about the feelings they have about their illness or hospitalization. Then initiate a conversation about love and appreciation. Ask, "What does love sound like to you?" Have them select some instruments, vocal sounds, or songs that represent love. Improvise or play/sing the music of love. Create a (self) love song. Ask them to rest in the silent aftermath of this music. Repeat the instructions above that might resonate with your companion.

- **Lock-in the Heart.** Focus on the heart and breathe deeply. Consider someone or something that you truly appreciate. Bring awareness to these feelings of appreciation. Next direct these feelings toward yourself and others in your life.

Music Therapy Application. Continue with the music of love and appreciation or some favorite relaxing music. Ask your companions to imagine someone who they appreciate or something that they love. Have them free-associate their thoughts about this person, activity, or object, the reasons that your companions appreciate them, and stories or details. Notate these ideas and help your companions compose a song for or about this person or about the beloved object/activity. The lyrics can be set to the music of love/appreciation, a love song, a favorite melody, or something completely new that supports the intentions of this exercise.

Opening the Heart

The adages to "listen to your heart" and "open your heart" may be trite and true. But some of our companions (and some of us) have great difficulty being compassionate with themselves (ourselves). When ill and vulnerable, it is particularly challenging to be kind to one's self. But all of us protect our hearts with thick fortification, at times. When this happens, I think about the text in the Nitzavim, a portion from the Book of Deuteronomy (29:9–30:82) in the Hebrew bible. It states:

> God ... will circumcise your heart and your descendants' hearts so you can love God with all your heart and with all your soul, so that you will live (Deuteronomy 30:6).

Rabbi Shefa Gold recommends a practice for the week in which Nitzavim is chanted:

> Take special care to notice when your heart closes. Really notice. Does your heart close when you feel judged? When you are in the presence of suffering? When you are stuck in traffic? When you disagree? When you get too busy? When you're in pain? When you read the newspaper? In the moment when you notice that your heart is closing, take a slow gentle breath into the heart (http://www.rabbishefagold.com/nitzavim).

Later in the text, there is the advice to "Choose life!" Rabbi Gold chants the Hebrew:

Uvacharta Bachayyim

from the portion: "I have set before you Life and Death, blessing and curse. Choose Life!" (Deuteronomy 30:19). She goes on to suggest:

Not just every year, week or day, but every single moment we can choose Life. This means choosing to let go of a negative thought or judgment; it means choosing to live with uncertainty; choosing the kind word or generous attitude; choosing to let go of tension and relax. In every moment we can choose to "be chosen" by God for the best possible Life, for the life we were meant to live fully. In each moment, we can choose to accept the gifts, challenges, opportunities and responsibilities that we are being given. (http://www.rabbishefagold.com/nitzavim).

Beginning to Cope

Removing Obstacles on the Path to Coping

There are many obstacles beyond a metaphorical thickening of the heart that erect barricades to effective coping. For one companion, it may be the constant worry about how illness will affect the future; for another, it may be fear of pain; for some, it can be relentless hopelessness that permeates the mind. Vidyamala Burch and Danny Penman (2013) say, "You are not your pain" in their book by that name, subtitled: *Using Mindfulness to Relieve Pain, Reduce Stress, and Restore Well-being*. They also say, "You are not your thoughts." While it may not be possible to remove a stressful or painful stimulus, it is entirely possible to remove the negative and dysfunctional thoughts that can circulate into whirlpools of anxiety, depression, and panic. The authors differentiate between the "doing" and "being" modes of thinking, and point out the advantages of the latter:

- **The doing mode** maintains automatic pilot by repeating habits without giving them much thought. Without being aware of what is happening, a tendency to predict the future, or black and white thinking may invite suffering.

The being mode makes choices to change by staying present. Paying attention to the breath and to relaxing music represents a choice to cope.

- **The doing mode** analyzes what is happening. Thinking too much keeps negative thoughts spiraling down into depression or up into anxiety.
  The being mode experiences the moment, and witnesses without judgment. Savoring musical moments can break a cycle of negativity.

- **The doing mode** holds on for dear life. In an attempt to evade suffering, avoidance keeps the mind focused on those very things it wishes to avoid. Don't think of a pink elephant!
  The being mode approaches experience with openness and curiosity. Engaging in new musical activities expands this positive outlook.

- **The doing mode** strives. It works overtime to compare what is with what should be.
  The being mode accepts reality. Improvising, writing songs, singing, interpreting music, and discussing music, explore the current reality in a safe and creative manner.

- **The doing mode** views thoughts as solid and true, as it develops theories about the world that can easily prompt worry and fear.
  The being mode views thoughts as "passing mental events" that may or may not echo the way things are. While meditating or breathing with music, it is possible to notice and allow negative thoughts to enter the mind, and then let them go with a compassionate heart.

- **The doing mode** compounds suffering.
  The being mode is the mindful way to cope with illness and change the experience of suffering.

Committing to Coping

Shapiro and Vivino's *Freedom from Anxiety* (2014) tells us:

... well-being does not just happen. We are not passive participants. We are active creators of our experience ... Anyone or anything else along the way ... is just a vehicle for you to get in touch with you (p. 29).

This sensibility can be empowering to our companions who are having difficulty coping with their conditions. When cognitive and emotional barriers block the path toward wellness, it may be easier to give in to the obstacle by feeding it attention, or to give up hope by granting it importance. So for example, when a biopsy causes scarring but reveals a benign tumor, the tendency might be to bemoan the scar instead of feel gratitude for the benign finding. Considering the temporary nature of the scar and turning the attention to the favorable diagnosis opens a wide angle, holistic lens. Likewise, pain can naturally signal panic and distress. Yet looking at the pain as impermanent and as a necessary step in the longer process of recovery offers a perspective that changes the thinking patterns and emotions associated with pain. Taking responsibility for looking at challenges and barriers to health through a different viewpoint can be an important coping strategy itself. This philosophy is also a great start to generating some profound lyrics. In the course of discussing these issues, consider writing a song about your companion's insights.

It is also possible to decide to take charge of the journey to wellness and move forward with positive coping strategies and healthy habits. Jim Nicolai (2013), in *Integrative Wellness Rules: A Simple Guide to Healthy Living*, says:

The word *decide* comes from the Latin decider, which means "to cut off from." It means to take all of your options, select the one you want, and throw the others out the door. When people truly decide to do something, it gets done regardless of the obstacles because they have "cut away" any other option from happening (p. 3).

Deciding to move away from the ill persona and toward wellness can itself be a positive strategy that modifies the way to approach health. Making a commitment to learn techniques that facilitate the process of coping is another constructive step toward change.

Giving Back

Giving back is an alternative to giving in or giving up. Your companion may wish to record a song for a loved one, prepare a playlist of favorites for an important someone, or write an original piece of music in his or her honor. The act of shifting the focus away from the self to the other opens the door for the ego to depart, expands the heart, and reminds companions of a broader sense of purpose. Altruism is a healing art in itself. You can help your companion cultivate generosity and selflessness in the wide world beyond the hospital. A simple creative act opens the door.

Ben's gift. Angela Wibben is a music therapist at Cardon Children's Medical Center in Mesa, Arizona. Her work with Ben exemplifies the healing heart of song:

> When I met 17-year-old Ben, he had recently been admitted to the children's hospital. He was brought in by our state's Child Protective Services, due to malnutrition, possible medical neglect, and psycho-social concerns within his home environment.
>
> During the first music therapy session with Ben, I introduced drum improvisation, utilizing imitation and reflection techniques, so that he could verbally and musically express his emotions. He demonstrated anger and resentment towards the hospital staff because his parents were prohibited visitation and his siblings were under the care and protection of the state.
>
> He stated: "No one gets me. I don't even think they [nurses] know why they are keeping me here … I just want to get better, go home, take care of my brothers and sister again, and make sure that my mom and dad are okay."
>
> Throughout our initial musical dialogue, not only was therapeutic rapport being built, but music experiences also gave him the opportunity to express himself in an improvised way, through his stream-of-consciousness, as a means to share and play out his story.
>
> At our second session, Ben's family had been granted brief, supervised visitation and phone calls. It was at that point that I mentioned the idea of taking the words that he shared with me, and turning them into a song as a means of reaching out to his family. The end result was a song that

addressed each of his family members individually, and ultimately his own emotional state. Here are the lyrics:

Loving You Always
(To my mom)
I can look at you and see how you are
You're trying to get me home 'cause I've been so far
I wish that being apart would end soon
'Cause there are times we get stuck, but we help each other make it through
Chorus:
I WISH THAT I COULD TELL YOU WHAT IS GOING ON
BECAUSE I'M LOVING YOU ALWAYS EVEN WHEN I'M GONE
'CAUSE YOU'RE MY FAMILY, AND NO MATTER WHAT YOU DO
I WILL STILL LOVE YOU AND WOULDN'T CHANGE A THING ABOUT YOU
We try to make each other better, and we'll always be there
Through thick and thin I love you, wantchu to know that I care
And I want to be with you all the time
So we know what's happening in each other's lives
Ooooooh, oooooh, oooooooh
Loving you always
(To my brothers and sister)
We take care of each other, we try to help out
I know we all need someone to trust and you can trust me now
You think it's funny to joke with me every single day
But you can't trick me so you try again in a different way
(Chorus)
(To my dad)
You can be as extraordinary as you want to be
You're waiting for the right thing, but you'll know it when you see
We all make mistakes we just gotta let go of
And happiness is just to be with the ones that you love
(Chorus)
(For me)
I want me to be better, to grow up, to get stronger
I want me to feel better, be a good husband, a good father

Cause I'm feeling good and I wish to come home
I'm waiting for my purpose and to know the way that I'll go
(Chorus)
Ooooooh, oooooh, ooooooooh
Loving you always

Just Singing

S.O.S. is the international distress call that was conveyed through Morse Code in the early twentieth century. Colloquially, it has been known in some circles as the abbreviation for "Save our ship" or "Save our souls," but a twenty-first century behavioral coping technique might also be identified by the S.O.S. initials. When all else fails, try this S.O.S. as one of the simplest replacements for distress—**S**miling **O**r **S**inging. While this may sound ever so simplistic, it is amazing how a smile or a familiar song can deactivate a surge of advancing negativity. One motto of the behavioral approach is to act your way into a new way of thinking (Madsen & Madsen, 1981), and there is little doubt that a bit of humor can be a benign way to place a full stop sign in front of a distress call. When your companions learn that choosing to turn their focus to something positive really can affect their moods, they will have mastered an important skill. Obviously, this approach is not meant to dismiss any underlying distress, but rather is an immediate intervention to unravel a spiraling downturn.

Coping with the Stresses of Illness

Reframing

Recently, I had the pleasure of training a group of women in Beijing, China about managing their stress and pain through music. When I began to assess the stresses that each of them was under, one woman wailed that the air she and her family were breathing was seriously polluted, causing waves of respiratory illnesses for all of them. She said that she thought about the poison every time she inhaled and asked me what she could do about this dangerous situation. I had come to China to teach positive and creative coping techniques, but I certainly couldn't tell her how to fight the air contamination in her city. Then I thought about Louise Hay's words, from *You Can Heal Your Life* (1999):

> Thoughts have no power over us unless we give in to them. Thoughts are only words strung together. They have NO MEANING WHATSOEVER. Only we give meaning to them. Let us choose to think thoughts that nourish and support us (p. 101).

I told the woman that neither of us could change the level of pollution in the air, but her worries were polluting her emotions. What she could change were the negative thoughts that took over her consciousness. In place of her obsessive thought, "This pollution is making me sick," I asked her to reframe the problem and substitute an alternate phrase. She stated, "Worry is making me sicker." She decided to wear a mask more often and use thought-stopping power as soon as a worry about pollution surfaced. She even set those alternative words to a personal jingle and found herself smiling while she sang to herself in place of the anger, frustration, and hopelessness she had been feeling.

For our companions, we can help them reframe their negative thoughts about illness and hospitalization. Here are a few examples:

- **Replace:** I am really nervous about this procedure.
  With: I am as prepared for this procedure as I can be, and can use my coping techniques.
- **Replace:** I am fearful of the pain.
  With: I am fearful of the pain, but I can breathe through it.
- **Replace:** I am afraid of what will happen during this surgery.
  With: I trust my surgeon.
- **Replace:** I am worried that I won't recover quickly.
  With: I am in good health, and can get through this surgery with a full recovery.
- **Replace:** This surgery could lay me up for a long time.
  With: This surgery will cure my disease.

- **Replace:** This treatment is making me tired and sick.
  With: I am confident that this treatment can treat or cure my cancer.
- **Replace:** The pain is terrible.
  With: I can turn my attention to my music, and I won't feel as much pain.
- **Replace:** Will these aches ever stop?
  With: The aches come and go, and I have my breath and my music to help.

Follow up with a large dose of energy-boosting or relaxing music.

Emotional-Approach Coping

While using a mask to deal with air pollution is a problem-focused coping technique, it is not always possible to cover up a problem as simply. Emotional-approach coping (EAC) is a way to get up close and personal with emotions associated with a stressor, as a means of coping. For our companions, it often entails identifying, acknowledging, communicating, and expressing emotions in order to understand their responses to illness and its many concomitant conditions. While many stressors, like a chronic illness or painful symptoms, are impossible to control willfully, getting in touch with and processing the resultant emotions can foster healthy attitudes and contribute to a sense of wellness. EAC allows for an appraisal and reappraisal of conditions, while realigning the feelings and thoughts that tend to arise from them. In their landmark text, *Stress, Appraisal, and Coping,* Richard Lazarus and Susan Folkman (1984) elucidate how the amount of stress perceived by people is due to the appraisal of their circumstances, as opposed to actual conditions. Therefore, reappraisal is part of an effective coping mechanism:

> There is a dynamic, continuous evaluation of both the situation and one's readiness to respond to it. People don't always respond to stress reflexively. They often appraise their chances of being able to deal with the stressor effectively. They weigh various options and consider the consequences of those options before acting. Decisions about how to cope depend in part

on implicit confidence or doubt about the usefulness of a particular response (p. 165).

Dr. Claire Ghetti (2011b) describes a music therapy protocol based on EAC in her doctoral dissertation, *Effect of Music Therapy with Emotional-Approach Coping on Pre-procedural Anxiety in Cardiac Catheterization*. Dr. Ghetti also published experimental research with individuals undergoing kidney and liver transplants (2011a) and cardiac catheterization (2013), supporting its efficacy. The method she called *Music Therapy with Emotional-Approach Coping* (*MT/EAC*) involves a session of approximately 30 minutes. Its main components are:

- active engagement verbally and musically by companions
- invitation to family caregivers to participate
- prompting and validation by music therapist of attitudes, nature of stress, coping, and coping resources prior to cardiac catheterization
- assessment of mood and attitudes regarding procedure in order to determine needs
- assessment of music preferences
- demonstration and invitation to play any of a wide variety of rhythm instruments
- introduction of a songbook with seven genres of music spanning several eras, with discussion themes, including support, companionship, determination, gratitude, praise, faith, suffering, transition, perseverance, optimism, relationships, memories, love, coping with challenges, loss, home, pride, and the like.
- singing selected songs with rhythmic accompaniment by companions and caregivers
- soliciting companion's choice of two or three songs, and identifying themes common to issues presented during initial discussion and assessment
- for companions who participated actively, verbal processing of song themes and emotions; for those who did not, encouragement, additional options, and new song selection

- continuation of discussions regarding lyrics and themes, based on thoughts and emotions triggered by the music, feelings about the procedure, and ways of coping
- selection of a final song, based on these themes and designed for closure
- farewell and wishing well.

Songs included a rich collection of material for analysis, a sample of which appears in Fig. 13.1. These classics tell life's stories, struggles, and universal themes in singable melodies with memorable lyrics, facilitating effective coping for those who are ill.

Coping with Pain

Pain is a perception. It may result through injury to the physical tissue, but before feeling pain, we interpret the sensations caused by the damage. In this process, thoughts and emotions affect the quality and quantity of pain that is perceived. Primary suffering refers to the unpleasant feelings aroused by pain stimuli, but secondary suffering results from anxiety, depression, fear, hopelessness, and other distress that may coexist. While it may not be possible to affect the pain-producing stimulus, it is possible to change the thoughts and emotions, thus reducing the perception of pain.

Dissecting Pain's Neurosignature

In the neuromatrix theory of pain, Melzack (2001) asserts that pain is a multidimensional, body-self construct that is modifiable, due to its widely distributed neurosignature. The pain stimulus travels to the brain and is then mediated by three psychological domains, the sensory-discriminative, motivational-affective, and cognitive-evaluative. These determinants affect the subsequent signal descending from the brain, which ultimately defines the perception of pain. The sensory-discriminate

Songs for Emotional-Approach Coping

59ᵗʰ Street Bridge Song (Feelin' Groovy)	Simon and Garfunkel
A Change is Gonna Come	Sam Cooke
A Hard Day's Night	The Beatles
All Shook Up	Elvis Presley
Beautiful Dreamer	Bing Crosby
The Boxer	Simon and Garfunkel
Breathe	Faith Hill
Close To You	The Carpenters
Don't Stop Believing	Journey
Don't Stop Thinking About Tomorrow	Fleetwood Mac
Down By the Riverside	Pete Seeger
God Bless America	Kate Smith
Good Day Sunshine	The Beatles
Great Balls of Fire	Elvis Presley
I Feel Good	James Brown
I'm a Survivor	Reba McEntire
Keep Breathing	Ingrid Michaelson
Love Me Tender	Elvis Presley
On the Sunny Side of the Street	Louis Armstrong
River of Dreams	Billy Joel
Scarborough Fair	Simon and Garfunkel
(Sittin' On) The Dock of the Bay	Otis Redding
Sixteen Tons	Merle Travis
This Train Is Bound For Glory	Sister Rosetta Sharpe
This Land is Your Land	Woody Guthrie
Try to Remember	from The Fantasticks
Unchained Melody	Righteous Brothers
Unforgettable	Nat King Cole
Wade in the Water	Eva Cassidy
Walk Away	Kelly Clarkson
What a Wonderful World	Louis Armstrong
Wind Beneath My Wings	Bette Midler
With a Little Help From My Friends	The Beatles
You Are Not Alone	Michael Jackson
You Needed Me	Anne Murray
You'll Never Walk Alone	from Carousel

Fig. 13.1   Songs for emotional-approach coping

domain allows pain to be viewed as a changing phenomenon. When music-facilitated relaxation techniques, such as guided meditation, suggest that the pain becomes more diffuse and spreads out with each musical phrase, this can challenge the conception that pain is solid and unmovable. The motivational-affective domain refers to the reasons and feelings associated with pain. When music-facilitated imagery evokes a beautiful or peaceful setting, it can, likewise, affect pain perception. In the cognitive-evaluative domain, the way one conceptualizes pain affects how it is experienced. Music-facilitated breathing techniques can reframe pain sensations with the rising and falling of the breath. Thus, the neuro-matrix explains some of the mechanisms underlying the effectiveness of music therapy strategies.

Accepting Pain Compassionately

Burch and Penman (2013) recommend a mindfulness exercise that they call "compassionate acceptance" of pain. Notice how they guide the listener to observe the correlates of pain and move them about with kindly acceptance. Consider integrating music-facilitated techniques into this script:

> Now, with great tenderness, gently open your awareness to include your pain, discomfort, fatigue, or difficulty of whatever kind you're experiencing. Include it in your awareness with the kind of attitude that you would naturally have toward a loved one who was hurting or injured. Softly breathe with this experience for a few moments. If this feels frightening, then breathe with the fear with gentleness, coming back to rest your awareness on the breath in the body, over and over …
>
> Now, allowing your awareness to become a little more precise, investigate the exact sensations of pain or discomfort. What do you feel? Do you notice the way the sensations are always changing and how no two moments are precisely the same? As you come closer to your actual experience, you may realize, for example, that it's just your lower back that's hurting rather than your whole back, as you'd previously thought.
>
> … Are you having any thoughts or emotions about your pain or difficulty? Can you let them come and go moment by moment, neither suppressing them nor overidentifying with them? Can you let them go a little bit as you rest with the basic sensations in the body, moment by moment, held by the kindly breath?

Now saturate the breath with self-compassion. As you breathe in, imagine a sense of kindliness flowing into your whole body, and as you breathe out, imagine the kindness seeping ever deeper, saturating the body with warmth and compassion (p. 119).

Surrendering to pain without fighting or struggling with it can be freeing. Quietly witnessing the experience with compassion is the Buddhist way to approach a challenge like physical pain.

Entraining Pain and Music

There are other ways to actively cope with pain, and entrainment has been employed successfully. To entrain is to draw along or fall into step with a particular element. In music therapy, it refers to the way that the body's behavior and physiological responses synchronize to the period and phase of a sound wave form. There is impressive evidence from the fields of chronobiology, biomusicology, and music therapy, that as the tempo of a piece of music changes, the listener's behavior comes into correspondence with that pace and moves in the same direction.

Music therapist Joke Bradt (2010) tested a pain management/entrainment strategy for children who were hospitalized for orthopedic surgery, but the basic methodology is the same for adults. The children first experimented with a variety of simple instruments and were asked to describe their pain. Based on an entrainment technique that she and Dr. Cheryl Dileo describe in "Entrainment, resonance, and pain-related suffering" (Dileo & Bradt, 1999), Dr. Bradt asked each child to select from a variety of musical instruments and mimic what pain might sound like. She asked them, "Which of these instruments sound most like the pain you're having right now? Does your pain have a beat? How strong/intense is your pain right now?" (p. 152). Bradt improvised around those sounds and asked the child to suggest modifications to create sounds that were more resonant with the sensation of pain. Once the child agreed that the sound match was accurate, Bradt attempted to improvise sounds that soothed, or represented "pain-healing sounds." She played with these new sounds and instruments until the child agreed that the effect was soothing. The child was asked to find a comfortable position, close the eyes, and listen, as Bradt played the sounds of pain, gradually morphing the musical elements until she was replicating the suggested soothing sounds. In a subsequent session, child and music therapist reviewed the improvisations, made any necessary adaptations to reflect the current experience of pain, and repeated the process in a 5- to 15-minute improvisation, the exact duration of which was determined by the child. The results of Bradt's randomized trial revealed significantly greater effects on pain for those who were treated with the music entrainment intervention, as compared with a control group.

Supporting Medical Procedures

Claire Ghetti (2012) developed a conceptual model to identify the types of procedural support described in the music therapy literature. This includes multiple methods through which music therapists assist their companions to cope and tolerate pain during medical procedures:

- **Music alternate engagement (MAE)**, also known as music engagement, invites active participation from the companion with the purpose of drawing the companion's full attention to the musical task or activity.
- **Integration** is a method first described by Dr. Joanne Loewy (Loewy, MacGregor, Richards, & Rodriguez, 1997) as an approach that asks the companion to focus on what is happening in the body, including breath, emotion, intention, and subsequent resonance with the music. One technique is transformational toning, the use of dissonant and consonant music to reflect the sound of pain, similar to Dileo and Bradt's technique (1999).
- **Music-assisted relaxation (MAR)** refers to the many strategies that generally employ more passive music listening to induce a relaxation response. Entrainment, music and imagery interventions, audio-analgesia (music/sound to minimize perception of pain), and anxiolytic music (music/sound to minimize anxiety) are all considered MAR techniques.

Dr. Ghetti explains the main elements of the model in Fig. 13.2:

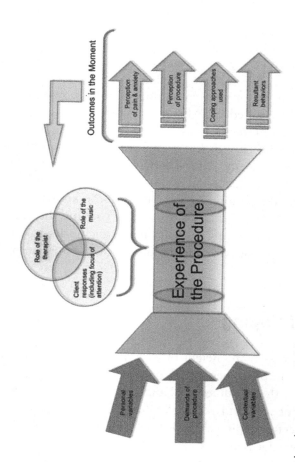

Fig. 13.2 Procedural support model (reprinted with permission from Figure 1, Ghetti, C.M. (2012). Music therapy as procedural support for invasive medical procedures: toward the development of music therapy theory, *Nordic Journal of Music Therapy, 21*(1), Taylor & Francis)

Multifaceted moderators including personal variables, demands of the procedure, and contextual variables enter into the individual's experience of a procedure. Factors relating to the therapist, role of the music, and patient responses combine to serve as a lens that filters the individual's experience of the procedure. This filtering process results in the individual's perceptions of the procedure, perceptions of pain/anxiety, coping approaches, and resultant behaviors. The music therapist uses these outcomes in the moment within a reflexive process of re-assessing and re-focusing the intervention "lens" in an on-going manner to positively alter outcomes (p. 28).

In their systematic review of research on music-based approaches to procedural support, Olivia Swedberg Yinger and Lori Gooding (2015) note that there is a wealth of interventions in music therapy and music medicine, but sadly, this diversity makes it challenging to determine which techniques to choose. Clearly, clinical judgment plays a significant role in the selection of best practices and the most potentially effective strategies for a particular companion. What is important to know is that there are ways to cope with pain through music, when you find the music that bathes the mind in rhythms, resonance, images, memories and associations, and apply that music with a method that meets your companion's needs.

The Heart of Coping

At the worst of times, at the height of pain and suffering, it is hard to grasp that pain is impermanent. It is particularly challenging to keep faith that you have the resources to change your perception of physical or mental pain. But you (and your Self) do have the ability to focus on healing and to practice coping skills to overcome suffering. The heart of coping is the knowledge that music can embrace you with beauty and the ineffable when your heart is open. "You are embraced by love always ... In the name of love," said Sam Hanser (2010), "that is why you are here" (p. 23).

14

Conclusion: The Way to Peace

Your inner state of being is not dependent upon your outer state of being.

Your inner state, your own divine essence, is happiness—I would bet my life on this truth. It may seem at times that there is much in the world that would take you away from your own essence—this happiness. That's when it becomes a choice.

Happiness is a gift you give yourself, not by doing anything, but by being.

Now, I'm not saying don't do things that make you happy. Please do. Just know that your happiness is not dependent upon those things. Happiness can only be realized within. When you look without, e.g. in relationships, places, things, you actually remove yourself from happiness.

The one thing life guarantees is that all things die. Happiness won't. And it won't because it's not a thing—it's who you are (Samuel Hanser, 2010, p. 5).

© The Editor(s) (if applicable) and The Author(s) 2016
S.B. Hanser, *Integrative Health through Music Therapy*,
DOI 10.1057/978-1-137-38477-5_14

Finding Your Way Home

This is no one path to happiness. Through this journey called life, you will find your own way home, to the place of true happiness, where all treasures reside. At the heart of a folktale shared by countless cultures is the notion that one can journey far and wide, only to find the real treasure at home. We must live out our personal legends and tell our stories to earn the real treasure—the lessons of the journey and the meaning of life.

Finding the Way to Acceptance

When taking this precious inward journey, we are bound to see the faults and flaws among the treasures that reside in our core. In *Mourning and Mitzvah*, Anne Brener (1993) tells a fable from the Dubner Magid, advisor to Elijah ben Shlomo Zalman, an eighteenth century leader of Ashkenazi Jews in Vilnius, Lithuania:

> Once there was a king who had a beautiful diamond. But this beautiful diamond had a flaw—a scratch in the middle. The king sent word throughout his kingdom that great riches would come to anyone who could rid the diamond of its flaw. Gem cutters, jewelry makers, and artisans from around the kingdom came to the castle, but no one could erase the diamond's scratch. Finally, a young man came and announced that he could make the diamond more beautiful than ever before. Everyone scoffed as he disappeared into the king's treasury, but they gasped with awe when he came out—and presented the king with the stone. The scratch was still in the diamond but it was—indeed—more beautiful than ever before. For in the center of the diamond the young man had carved a beautiful rose, using the scratch for the stem (p. 231).

Brener advises us how to live with the imperfections that can take the life out of our lives. She writes,

> Acceptance is more an ability to make peace with a situation. It means being able to look forward to the future after integrating some of the reality

and the repercussions of the loss. It means approaching a sense of completeness with issues that were unresolved … Acceptance means finding a way to feel some harmony … with the universe. By eventually embracing themselves, they come to know their own stories with compassion.

In Hebrew, the word for wound, *petzah*, is closely related to another word which is used to describe the break of day, *miftziah hashachar*, the moment when the sun breaks from behind the clouds. This transformation which comes through the opening initially caused by a wound, can be the foundation of a bright future (p. 233).

It is notable that Brener uses the word *harmony* to define acceptance. Those fortunate companions who are tended by music therapists literally create musical harmony in their quest to achieve this more esoteric sense of harmony, or wellness. Their music is a testament to their insights and may hold the key that unlocks their power to transform.

Finding Your Way at the End of Life

In *Being Mortal*, surgeon Atul Gawande (2014) notes how perspectives and priorities change when illness draws our companions near death:

As our time winds down, we all seek comfort in simple pleasures—companionship, everyday routines, and the taste of good food, the warmth of sunlight on our faces. We become less interested in the rewards of achieving and accumulating, and more interested in the rewards of simply being. Yet while we may feel less ambitious, we also become concerned for our legacy. And we have a deep need to identify purposes outside ourselves that make living feel meaningful and worthwhile (p. 228).

Hospice music therapists are the midwives who witness and guide their companions through their final transitions. They can coach their companions through their concerns by various means, including teaching coping techniques, facilitating creative activities for loved ones of all ages, helping focus their attention, empowering them to express their needs, and creating legacy projects that articulate the messages they wish to leave behind.

Some years ago, I was blessed to give a lecture at St. Christopher's, a hospice in London that was the model for the worldwide movement to care for the dying in a holistic fashion. St. Christopher's has long recognized the immense contributions of music therapists in providing palliative care through spiritual guidance, in addition to psychological and physical treatment, so it was an honor to be invited to this historic place. Moved by the peacefulness of the setting, I found that my sentences flowed more easily, yet deliberately, as I stood in the presence of professionals who have devoted their lives to the end of life. When I returned home, I found a beautiful book, *Graceful Passages: A Companion for Living and Dying* (Stillwater & Malkin, 2003), that captured the awe of my experience. I opened the text to a poem by modern Confucian scholar and Harvard Professor, Tu Weiming. His words were addressed to the dying, but they spoke the message that I brought back with me: "You have heard the Way; Return Home in Peace (p. 30).":

> Your vital energy is returning to the Source,
> Like the flowing stream returning to ocean.
>
> Heaven is our Father,
> Earth is our Mother,
> All people are our brothers and sisters,
> And all things are our companions.
>
> In this gentle, peaceful journey,
> You are forming one body with heaven and earth.
> Entrust yourself in the transforming and
>   nourishing care of the Cosmos.
> Listen to the voice of love I silence.
> You have heard the Way;
> Return Home in Peace (p. 30).

Finding Your Way through Anxiety

Ali Rapetti is a hospice music therapist in Boston. In an interview about the way her companions find their way through anxiety, Rapetti spoke of the dyspnea, the labored breathing, that can trigger anxiety and suffering at the end of life.

Once the dyspnea happens, you get more anxious. Then you get more dyspnea. Then you get more anxious, and it just keeps going in a cycle. And this can be very dangerous for patients that have COPD, chronic asthma, or poor lung capacity.

One of the techniques I utilize is playing music along with the patient's breath. You could have the music sound agitated so that you both meet each other. And then, once you reach that level of meeting, you can slowly start tapering it, taking it from a place of chaos to calm, slowly. Breathwork is telling a patient, "I'm hearing you. I'm seeing you. I'm with you. I'm validating you." And then, as things like emotions and anxiety are accepted in that sense, they can be recognized and fully accepted. It's only then that the shift can actually happen.

Sometimes just the nature of the therapeutic process is what helps with that anxiety. You can just start addressing the fact that the person is dying. Some people are very direct; some can't face it at all; some can only face it as a metaphor. And so, many times, that metaphor is going on a trip, going on an airplane. You might want to sing a song about leaving on a jet plane, and it turns out, that's the language that the patient needed to feel less anxious.

Anxiety also comes from people feeling like they don't have the permission to go. So if you're able to facilitate the family giving that permission, anxiety washes away. It doesn't always happen that way, but sometimes you find its source, and that gets rid of it.

There was a patient for whom everybody said, "She's so anxious. Go talk to her." I walked into the room and there were five family members with the matriarch of the family in the bed. They clearly adored her, and wanted to do everything right. They probably read every hospice book on the shelf. In fact, what they were doing was bringing all of this expectation. So I said, "I wonder if everybody would just leave and let us talk," and I just sat with her for a long time. I didn't say anything. She just stared at me, and finally said, "They all want me to say something meaningful, and I don't have anything to say." That's what was driving her anxiety, this feeling that "I have to produce." (Rapetti, personal communication, 2014).

Finding Your Way in Silence

As music therapists, we engage in a great deal of sound-making. Are we devoting as much attention to silence? The oft-quoted phrase, "Music is the silence between the notes" is attributed to Debussy, but also to masters of Zen. In a world full of busy-ness and noise, silence is proverbially "golden."

Being in silence can bring a sense of peace to some, but not to others whose inner critics and pessimism are active, particularly when there is no external focus for attention. When guiding our companions into silence, it is important to ensure that they feel safe and protected. There are various ways for preparing to enter silence. Here are some examples:

- Set an intention through song. Sing a meaningful song that sets a positive intention or mood. Instruct your companion to meditate on the words.
- Set a soothing mood through instrumental music. Ask your companion to identify music that usually evokes a calm, peaceful memory or image. Play the music; when it ends, continue to listen.
- Chant a mantra that represents a desired state of mind. Slow the tempo and decrease the volume of the chant until there is silence.
- Listen to the silence. Because there is no such thing as true silence, listen to the sounds outside and inside.

Along the journey, when I come upon my favorite flowers, roses, I make a point to inhale their essence, view their flamboyant colors, uncover their hidden pistils, make tea from their fruity hips, and enjoy the silence.

Finding Your Way through Ritual

One of my favorite Jewish religious practices is "Tashlich," a ritual performed on the first day of the Jewish new year, Rosh Hashanah. Our community assembles after religious services at a nearby body of water, and we clean out our pockets or toss bits of bread into the water. The metaphoric act of discarding something in preparation for a new chapter in the book of life is a liberating experience for me, an opportunity for forgiveness, and a signal to move on.

In the spirit of Tashlich, Sam would often ask his dinner guests on Friday night, the eve of the Jewish Sabbath, to let go of something they wanted to leave in the past and to bring in something they needed in the following week. As is customary on Friday nights, each guest would ignite a candle to light the way for the transition to a peaceful Shabbat, or day of rest, and symbolize the start of a new week. This ritual often took the form of a blessing, for example, "Let me let go of the resentment I have" and "May I find peaceful moments when I least expect them." I am reminded of this sweet tradition, when I guide my companions in similar rituals to help alleviate suffering.

- **Offer an intention.** Identify music that has personal meaning, or review the Songs of Hope in Chap. 11 and Songs for Emotional-Approach Coping in Chap. 13 to find a song that carries a positive intention. Ask your companion to choose the arrangement, perhaps one of you singing it solo or together, accompanying with favorite instruments, or a cappella. Use electronic aides like GarageBand software to provide background, or ask family members, friends, or staff to perform along. Of course, just listening is fine, as well.
- **Create a theme song.** Select a favorite song to be sung or played regularly, if desired by your companion. Notice how your companion responds to it, in order to gauge current status.
- **Send blessings.** What does your companion need today? Articulate a desire in a chant or jingle, and sing it to your companion and/or have your companion sing it alone. One example is, "May you (I) feel better every day," "May your (my) procedure go easily," or "May you (I) feel more comfortable today."
- **Collect special objects.** Find some that symbolize love, peace, or comfort, such as greeting cards from loved ones, photographs, mementos, magazine pictures, books, etc. Write a song that depicts their meaning.

- **Take a small object, such as a pebble or a flower, and imbue it with symbolism.** Write a simple song about leaving something behind and taking in something new. Examples are: "I breathe out my frustration, and I take in a deep breath" or "I want to let go of fear, and bring in optimism." Leave your companion with the object as a reminder.
- **Give a musical gift.** Play a special song for your companion, without asking your companion to do anything besides listen.
- **End with silence.**

Finding Your Way Through Gratitude

Oliver Sacks was a neurologist, music therapy advocate, and best-selling author who passed away during the editing of this book. Being an admirer of Sacks' work over the course of my career, I was saddened to read his article in the *New York Times* (February 19, 2015):

> A MONTH ago, I felt that I was in good health, even robust health. At 81, I still swim a mile a day. But my luck has run out—a few weeks ago I learned that I have multiple metastases in the liver. Nine years ago it was discovered that I had a rare tumor of the eye, an ocular melanoma ... I feel grateful that I have been granted nine years of good health and productivity since the original diagnosis, but now I am face to face with dying.
>
> I have been increasingly conscious, for the last 10 years or so, of deaths among my contemporaries ... They leave holes that cannot be filled, for it is the fate—the genetic and neural fate—of every human being to be a unique individual, to find his own path, to live his own life, to die his own death.
>
> I cannot pretend I am without fear. But my predominant feeling is one of gratitude. I have loved and been loved; I have been given much and I have given something in return; I have read and traveled and thought and written. I have had an intercourse with the world, the special intercourse of writers and readers.

Above all, I have been a sentient being, a thinking animal, on this beautiful planet, and that in itself has been an enormous privilege and adventure (Sacks, 2015, p. A25).

Oliver Sacks was an inspiring and courageous example of expressing gratitude, even at the depths of one's life. When in pain, experiencing fear, or suffering, it may be difficult to find things for which you are grateful. Yet focusing on those things that are right with life and on the parts of the body and mind that are in good shape is an important way to challenge excess stress. Rather than inundate the mind with worries, it is possible to take a deep breath and change the way you think. At this stage of life—near the end of life—existential insights are common, as thoughts are paired down to the most immediate and important aspects of living.

This is the time to sing a song of gratitude. Figure 14.1 lists some popular music with such a theme. You can sing these with or to your companion, or compose one on the spot. To begin, consider those small things for which your companion is grateful, like beauty, loved ones, spiritual beliefs, and the like.

In *Gratitude Works!* Robert Emmons (2013) says that while we cannot always feel grateful, we can just be grateful. He asserts that we can choose gratitude. I ask my students to write about what they are grateful for in a daily journal. You can ask your companions to come up with lyrics for an original song that expresses gratitude for something or to someone. An assignment like that can take up space otherwise used for worry or sadness, and change outlook and mood. Then you both can write a song to someone expressing what has gone unsaid or just to say, "Thanks!"

Finding the Spiritual Path

In *Health as a Path: A Guidebook for Spiritual Healing and Health-care in Everyday Life*, Carolin and Alexander Toskar (2011) present the positive side of illness. They state:

SONGS OF GRATITUDE

All My Days	Alexi Murdoch
All You Need Is Love	The Beatles
Blue Skies	Dinah Washington
Flowers in the Rain	The Move
For Good	from *Wicked*
Happy	Pharrell
Happy Days Are Here Again	Johnny Marvin
Happy Feet	Cab Calloway
Hi Ho Silver Lining	Jeff Beck
I Feel Good	James Brown
I'm Alive	Celine Dion
In My Life	The Beatles
Isn't This a Lovely Day	Ella Fitzgerald
It's a Beautiful Day	U2
Let There Be Love	Nat King Cole
Love Is All Around	Wet Wet Wet
Love Will Keep Us Alive	The Eagles
Music of My Heart	Gloria Estefan
Kind and Generous	Natalie Merchant
Pennies from Heaven	Louis Prima
Place to Be	Nick Drake
Thank God I'm a Country Boy	John Denver
Time After Time	Cyndi Lauper
For the Good Times	Al Green
Shelter from the Storm	Bob Dylan
Shower the People	James Taylor
Somebody's Hero	Jamie O'Neal
Take Me Home, Country Roads	John Denver
Thank You for the Music	Abba
That's What Friends Are For	Dionne Warwick
Turn, Turn, Turn	The Weavers
To Build a Home	The Cinematic Orchestra
Walking on Sunshine	Katrina and the Waves
What a Wonderful World	Louis Armstrong
When You're Smiling	Louis Armstrong
Wind Beneath My Wings	Bette Midler
With a Little Help from My Friends	The Beatles
Wonderful World, Beautiful People	Jimmy Cliff
You Are So Beautiful	Joe Cocker
You Raise Me Up	Josh Groban

Fig. 14.1 Songs of gratitude

Illness is … an invitation for transformation and harmonization of the self; diseases are an opportunity to examine and change our way of thinking, acting, and feeling. Every person has the ability to regain their equilibrium and true wellbeing (p. 22).

Spiritual wellbeing is a significant ingredient in a holistic definition of health and wellness. As music therapists, we are working in the spiritual realm as soon as we observe a change or transformation of a person's mood, outlook, or disposition that we cannot easily measure or explain. The deep connections we instill and the music we produce sometimes evoke insights that cannot be interpreted in words or through customary ways of thinking. When these experiences allow our companions to feel a sense of peace or comfort, this contributes to their health and wellbeing. Whether it sparks the healing process is more difficult to document. But there will always be things that are inexplicable, unexplainable, invisible, maybe even impossible. When these experiences move beyond our understanding, we tend to place them in the realm of the spiritual. While established religions are perhaps the most likely to name spirituality in their precepts and practices, there is a much broader perspective to consider. Religious belief systems may provide images, persona, and vocabulary, yet every person who wonders, considers, questions, feels, and seeks is defining spirituality in his or her unique way. While many enter the spiritual realm to find God, the Divine, the infinite, or the life force, others reject the term but still ache to find meaning, faith, and hope. When encountering disease, pain, or physical ailments, some of our companions question the meaning of their symptoms and illness, and examine the greater context of their lives, especially when confronted with the possibility of death.

We music therapists work by their sides and become privy to their thoughts, feelings, and expressions of their experience as whole persons. We are the witnesses to their journeys and share a relationship with them and with music that is filled with awe, beauty, inspiration, creativity, and the numinous. There is more to life than what we experience through our senses, think with our minds, and feel with our bodies. As music therapists, we bring the awesome, sublime, and supernatural into the room, and into the path to wellness.

In his senior thesis on the "Healing Empowerment Center," Sam Hanser (2004) writes about the resources that every individual holds within: "It is not external force but internal source that gives rise to the lasting change we direly seek ... Do our belief systems work? Do they foster peace, do they honor love, do they uphold the utter joy and freedom of our being?" (p. 3). These are the internal resources we are capable of developing, even, or especially, when diagnosed with a chronic or terminal illness, in order to be empowered to heal ourselves.

A Story of Faith

Jeniris Gonzalez is a music therapist who had the privilege of journeying for about 18 months with a woman named Faith. Gonzalez tells their story:

> Faith began her music therapy journey in the spring of 2014. A vibrant woman always full of surprises and jokes, she was referred to music therapy by her hospice team. While Faith resided in a skilled nursing facility, her first music therapy sessions consisted mainly of the music therapist playing her favorite music, while she sang along and occasionally played an instrument. Some sessions consisted of only soothing, continuous music played at her bedside, when she was tired, in pain, or not alert.
>
> As the weeks progressed, Faith became more active musically, rewriting lyrics to her preferred songs and asking for instruments before they were offered. Over a few months, she began to open up emotionally, disclosing much of her past, her family history, and significant life events. One day, while I was playing one of the songs she typically requested, "My Blue Heaven," Faith stopped me and asked, "Could you do me a favor? Could you come play that song when I die?" I invited Faith to explore her beliefs about the afterlife, as well as her feelings about her current state. Faith began to speak about what she regretted, felt proud of, and made her happy. It was during this time that Faith's legacy song project was born.
>
> I explained how songwriting might serve as an emotional outlet and "blank canvas" for Faith to paint a picture of her life. She decided to dedicate a song to her family and loved ones. She came up with the following:

> **Faith's Song**
> **Verse 1:**
> I've traveled many rough roads
> Met people from all over the world

Found things that bring me peace
Like my family, my music, my God.
Since I laid down on this bed
My steps have come to a stop
But in the midst of the loneliness
People have made me smile ...
Chorus:
WHEN I'M GONE, PLEASE REMEMBER
THAT I'M OKAY
I'M ON MY "SENTIMENTAL JOURNEY" ...
WHEN I'M GONE, PLEASE REMEMBER
THAT I'M OKAY
TO THE HEAVENS I WILL FLY AWAY.
Verse 2:
I must admit I'm scared
I don't know what comes after this life
But like a tree, I'm strong
On my way to my loved ones.
My blue heaven is a blank in my mind
Don't know what it's like
But I hope that angels come and carry me up
'Cause I'm ready to fly!
(Chorus)
Bridge:
I am the sound that carries on
In the wind, you will hear my song ...
(Chorus)
Ending:
And if you're feeling lost and scared,
To the heavens you can look...and I'll be there.

Faith chose her favorite photos of family members to be shown as the song was played. Faith also spent time carefully choosing the music she wanted to have played at her wake, compiling a list "so that people could remember me as a joyful person."

After working with Faith for about a year and a half, I arrived one day to find that Faith had fallen into a coma. The family mentioned the joy with which Faith described her time in music, and thanked me for working with her. Later that day, Faith passed away peacefully in her room. There is no doubt that Faith's story is filled with light and hope, and that she lives on through her music.

Finding Life through Death

Learn to die for they who know how to die shall truly know how to live.

Death may be the grandest, happiest moment of your life. It is the awakening from your dream, your return Home. Ironically, birth is a far more traumatic experience than death. It marks your arrival into the relative, into an illusory separation. Be assured that there are many beings who assist you in these transitions. At no point in your experience are you ever alone.

In truth there are no deaths, only transformations of consciousness. Embrace these transitions, befriend them because on their arrival you will have no choice but to face yourself. Do you like what you see?

Fear not my beloved. Each death is but an opportunity to create yourself anew (Samuel Hanser, 2010, p. 36).

In the concluding chapter of her book, *Music and Soulmaking: Toward a New Theory of Music Therapy*, Barbara Crowe (2004) articulates a model for the future of the profession. Dr. Crowe embraces complexity and the profound questions that have accompanied the study of music and music therapy. Her concluding words are:

We have wondered for centuries, "Why have music at all?" It has no survival benefit we can determine, no evolutionary advantage. Yet every human culture has had music. Why? Perhaps it truly is a gift programmed into our brain and central nervous system that set us on the road to knowledge. And if music is about multiple levels of deep relationship, of experience in all aspects of human functioning, of the fundamental way the world works, then, perhaps, we are hearing the mind of God when we listen to an Indian raga or a Brahms symphony. Music is the implicit order of the universe made manifest. It can now be our vehicle to true wisdom. Music is every aspect of human endeavor. It is cognitive perception and deep emotional expression, social conflict resolution and underlying principles of culture, and emergent entity and human internal imagination. It is, indeed, the map to knowledge of our world and ourselves. The tool we need to learn about ourselves and our world has been in our hands all along. We play it every day (p. 360).

This wisdom is beautifully expressed in the story of Kalu, in *Dancing to the Flute* by Manisha Jolie Amin (2013):

Guruji had taught him to breathe. To close his eyes and simply breathe, starting at the belly and filling his body with air before releasing it again. Feeling the breath moving through his body and slowly out through his mouth. That breath, sometimes soft, sometimes strong, was the key to making his flute sing. Kalu would silence his mind, and in this void, just as the sky turned pink over the mountains, he'd start to play. (p. 156)
    The sound of the flute grew louder, surrounding him. Now it mocked him in his sadness, forcing him to think about the impact of his choices. Moved him to anger, buffeting him with sounds from his childhood he had chosen to forget. Laughed at his self-absorption, and then, calming him, helped him to see, through the long, slow notes, that grief was a part of living … He pushed away from the rail, away from the water, and made his way back to the city he called home (p. 290).

The continuing journey is one of continuing discoveries of the power of music and the impact of music therapy.

Endings and Beginnings

During the writing of this chapter, Garrison, who was introduced to you in Chap. 9, died. Unlike Sam's passing, Garrison's death was "expected." Yet I still experienced shock, and I am certainly experiencing grief. His legacy is not only his beautiful music and inimitable improvisational style, but also the lessons he offers to us on illness and wellness. Garrison's physical body has been cremated, but his music, his music lessons, his soul, his soul lessons, and every person and student who met him, carry his spirit.

There is no prescribed bereavement process for a therapist who loses a companion. The love and intimacy that grows with every music therapy session suddenly comes to an end, with the passing of a companion. Because we are neither family nor friends, we cannot share in the rituals for grieving, nor reveal our emotional connections with those who knew the deceased. In a poignant essay on *How Therapists Mourn*, psychiatrist Dr. Robin Weiss (2015) relates the challenges of ending the therapeutic relationship:

> Just as what takes place in therapy occurs behind closed doors, so too does the therapist's grieving after a patient dies … Here is a secret that therapists rarely acknowledge: We often grow to love our patients … Few encounters are this deeply honest, and therefore intimate. The attachment engenders profound feelings, a particular kind of love.

Sam's master's thesis (2009) concludes with this:

> Over the months that I spent with Debra (his companion in somatic therapy), I have been blessed to engage the dance between pain and grace through the container of a loving relationship. I have witnessed how a human being reaches for their potential through the body and that potential reaches back through grace (p. 22).

Ancient Chinese poet and presumed author of the Tao Te Ching, Lao-tsu, has stated: "New beginnings are often disguised as painful endings." Sam's words capture the process in between: "We are not human beings, but human becomings."

Writing this book has entailed a journey of becomings, beginnings, endings, grief, and awe. As I bring it to completion, I begin again. My friend, violinist and composer Daniel Kobialka, wrote some music to accompany quotations from two mystical sources: the great Tao Te Ching and the young Sam Hanser. Dr. Kobialka gave me the honor of speaking these words on his album by the same name as Sam's subtitle, *The Remembrance of One*. Suzy Conway wrote this for the program notes:

Light is an appointment we must all keep
  when we are quiet and can find the way. —Tom Crawford

Sam married the light long before he dissolved back into it. An infinite soul in a diminutive body you could see him coming in the dark, he was so lit up. Not that he knew it all along, he didn't, but he grasped it soon enough. Like most light workers, he found it hard to fit in, no niche appealed or appeared. His search for one prepared him for an emergence that was coming and he simmered in the growing intensity of it. He was 20 when I met him, just awakening. He took me for a long walk on a mild winter afternoon. His personality didn't come through as much as his soul. We wasted no time in turning the conversation to the divine and we found ourselves perched side by side on the same spiritual limb.

Sam opened up a space large enough to include me in it and because my body and spirit were weakened due to a recent illness; his willingness to talk to me about it vanquished its lingering. He was drawn to help me, I believe, because somewhere inside of him he knew he had the map. He didn't urge me to do anything; he rather reminded me of what I already knew, and when he did a field of truths were sown. My perceptions of how things worked did not survive his gentle corrections and my wings grew out of that.

Upon my impending move to Nepal:

"Let your beautiful house go. There are other beautiful houses waiting for you."

A Light exercise:

"Face into the sun and let it fill your body with light. The healing is in the light."

On worry:

"Meditate every day."

Sam intimated that I could heal myself and I took that in, heart and soul. He walked with me into the liminal or as Van Morrison put it "into the mystic," with no more of an agenda than to help me connect with my body, with what was inside. Sam was a direction to take, he swayed me like the wind over the ocean does a sail. He possessed a knowing even then. His sights were set on engaging an invisible energy and he inspired me to engage it too.

When Sam took *Emmanuel's Book* off the shelf at a Brookline bookstore and said, "You must read this," I did. I read it when I swam in the pool, I read it while I ate, I read it in Nepal, Ireland, Thailand, Tibet, and Bali, which gave me the ballast I needed the day his Mother called to tell me that he died. Because I'd experienced one profound afternoon with Sam and built on it, his passing didn't devastate me. I knew he didn't go anywhere.

Sam lives in the stillness between the pulses where we can find safe residence; a healing niche. He invites us to become who we already are, to remarry our true self so long before our inevitable appointment that we will have practiced how to be quiet and find the way making dissolution back into the light a triumph not a tragedy.

Sam sets the table; he smiles and leads us in prayer, he lights the candles, sings the song, and nestles us into him.

If you stay in the center
and embrace death with your whole heart,
you will endure forever.
-Tao Te Ching
Lao-tzu
(Conway, 2015)

References

Achterberg, J., Dossey, B., & Kolkmeier, L. (1994). *Rituals of healing: Using imagery for health and wellness.* New York, NY: Bantam.

Ader, R. (1981). A historical account of conditioned immunobiologic responses. In R. Ader (Ed.), *Psychoneuroimmunology* (pp. 321–352). New York: Academic Press.

Amin, M. J. (2013). *Dancing to the flute: A novel.* New York, NY: Simon and Schuster.

Arias, A. J., Steinberg, K., Banga, A., & Trestman, R. L. (2006). Systematic review of the efficacy of meditation techniques as treatments for medical illness. *Journal of Alternative and Complementary Medicine, 12*(8), 817–832.

Arrien, A. (2010). *The four-fold way: Walking the paths of the warrior, teacher, healer, and visionary.* San Francisco, CA: HarperOne.

Augustin, P., & Hains, A. A. (1996). Effect of music on ambulatory surgery patients' preoperative anxiety. *AORN Journal, 63*(4), 750, 753–758.

Baker, F., & Wigram, T. (2005). *Songwriting: Methods, techniques and clinical applications for music therapy clinicians, educators and students.* London, UK: Jessica Kingsley.

Bailey, L. (1984). The use of songs in music therapy with cancer patients and their families. *Music Therapy, 4*(1), 5–17.

© The Editor(s) (if applicable) and The Author(s) 2016
S.B. Hanser, *Integrative Health through Music Therapy*,
DOI 10.1057/978-1-137-38477-5

Barlow, W. (1991). *The Alexander technique: How to use your body without stress.* Rochester, VT: Inner Traditions.

Barsky, A. J., & Deans, E. C. (2006). *Stop being your symptoms and start being yourself: The 6-week mind-body program to ease your chronic symptoms.* New York, NY: HarperCollins.

Beaulieu, J. (2010). *Human tuning sound healing with tuning forks.* High Falls, NY: BioSonic Enterprises.

Beinfield, H., & Korngold, E. (1998). Eastern medicine for Western people. Interview by Bonnie Horrigan. *Alternative Therapies in Health and Medicine, 4*(3), 80–87.

Benson, H., & Klipper, M. Z. (1975). *The relaxation response.* New York, NY: HarperTorch.

Benson, H., & Proctor, W. (2010). *Relaxation revolution: The science and genetics of mind body healing.* New York, NY: Scribner.

Bernardi, L., Porta, C., Casucci, G., et al. (2009). Dynamic interactions between musical, cardiovascular, and cerebral rhythms in humans. *Circulation, 119*(25), 3171–3180.

Brach, T. (2003). *Radical acceptance.* New York, NY: Bantam.

Bradt, J. (2010). The effects of music entrainment on postoperative pain perception in pediatric patients. *Music and Medicine, 2*(3), 150–157.

Brenner, B. (1988). *Hands of light: A guide to healing through the human energy field.* New York, NY: Bantam.

Brenner, B. (1993). *Light emerging: The journey of personal healing.* New York, NY: Bantam.

Brener, A. (1993). *Mourning and Mitzvah.* Woodstock, VT: Jewish Lights.

Brody, H., & Miller, F. G. (2011). Lessons from recent research about the placebo effect—from art to science. *JAMA, 306*(23), 2612–2613.

Bruscia, K. E. (1987). *Improvisational models of music therapy.* Springfield, IL: Charles C Thomas.

Burch, V., & Penman, D. (2013). *You are not your pain: Using mindfulness to relieve pain, reduce stress, and restore well-being—an eight-week program.* New York, NY: Flatiron Books.

Burns, D. D. (2008). *Feeling good: The new mood therapy.* New York, NY: Harper.

Campbell, J. (2008). *The hero with a thousand faces.* Novato, CA: New World Library.

Campbell, J., & Moyers, B. (1988). *The power of myth.* New York, NY: Doubleday.

Chanda, M. L., & Levitin, D. J. (2013). The neurochemistry of music. *Trends in Cognitive Sciences, 17*(4), 179–193.

Childre, D., & Rozman, D. (2006). *Transforming anxiety: The HeartMath solution for overcoming fear and worry and creating serenity.* Oakland, CA: New Harbinger Publications.

Chödrön, P. (1991). *The wisdom of no escape.* Boston: Shambhala Press.

Chödrön, P. (2013). *When pain is the doorway: Awakening in the most difficult circumstances.* Boulder, CO: Sounds True.

Chuang, C.-Y., Han, W.-R., Li, P.-C., et al. (2011). Effect of long-term music therapy intervention on autonomic function in anthracycline-treated breast cancer patients. *Integrative Cancer Therapies, 10*(4), 312–316.

Clarke, D. D. (2007). *They can't find anything wrong!: 7 keys to understanding, treating, and healing stress illness.* Boulder, CO: Sentient Publications.

Conway, S. (2015). Extended program notes. In D. Kobialka, & S. B. [Suzanne] Hanser (Eds.). *The remembrance of one.* San Antonio, TX: Lisem Entrprises.

Cope, S. (2012). *The great work of your life: A guide for the journey to your true calling.* New York, NY: Bantam.

Couch, R. (2014, July 2). Man creates beautiful songs from dying children's heartbeats to comfort grieving parents. *The Huffington Post* http://www.huffingtonpost.com/2014/07/02/recorded-heartbeats-brian-schreck_n_5552019.html. Date accessed 15 Sept 2014.

Cousins, N. (1976). Anatomy of an illness (as perceived by the patient). *The New England Journal of Medicine, 295*(26), 1458–1463.

Crowe, B. J. (2004). *Music and soulmaking: Toward a new theory of music therapy.* Lanham, MD: Scarecrow Press.

Csikszentmihalyi, M. *Csikszentmihalyi on flow* http://www.ted.com/talks/mihaly_csikszentmihalyi_on_flow?language=en. Date accessed 28 Jan 2015.

Csikszentmihalyi, M. (2008). *Flow: The psychology of optimal experience.* New York, NY: Harper Perennial Modern Classics.

Dabhade, A. M., Pawar, B. H., Ghunage, M. S., & Ghunage, V. M. (2012). Effect of pranayama (breathing exercise) on arrhythmias in the human heart. *Explore, 8*(1), 12–15.

Dalai Lama, XIV. (2000). *The Dalai Lama's book of transformation.* London, UK: Thorsons.

Daniel, E. (2010). *The grammar, history and derivation of the English language, with chapters on parsing, analysis of sentences, and prosody.* Charleston, SC: Nabu Press.

Daniélou, A. (2002). *Sacred music: Its origins, powers, and future.* New Delhi, India: First Impression.

D'Angelo, J. (2000). *The healing power of the human voice: Mantras, chants, and seed sounds for health and harmony.* Rochester, VT: Healing Arts Press.

Das, K. (2011). *The way of music—creating sound connections in music therapy.* Denton, TX: Sarsen Publishing.

Davis, L. (2007). *Varieties of disturbance: Stories.* New York, NY: Farrar, Straus and Giroux.

Davis, M., Eshelman, E. R., & McKay, M. (1995). *The relaxation and stress reduction workbook.* Oakland, CA: New Harbinger Publications.

Davison, G. M., & Reed, B. E. (1998). *Culture and customs of Taiwan.* Westport, CT: Greenwood Publishing Group.

Diallo, Y., & Hall, M. (1989). *The healing drum.* Rochester, VT: Destiny Books.

DiLeo, C., & Bradt, J. (1999). Entrainment, resonance, and pain-related suffering. In C. DiLeo (Ed.), *Music therapy and medicine: Theoretical and clinical approaches* (pp. 181–188). Silver Spring, MD: American Music Therapy Association.

Dowman, K. (1985). *Masters of Mahāmudrā: Songs and histories of the 84 Buddhist Siddhas.* Albany, NY: State University of New York Press.

Ellis, A., & Blau, S. (1998). *The Albert Ellis reader: A guide to well-being using rational emotive behavior therapy.* Secaucus, NJ: Citadel.

Emmons, R. A. (2013). *Gratitude works! A 21-day program for creating emotional prosperity.* New York, NY: John Wiley & Sons.

Fadiman, J., & Frager, R. (1997). *Essential sufism.* San Francisco, CA: HarperSanFrancisco.

Fancourt, D., Ockelford, A., & Belai, A. (2014). The psychoneuroimmunological effects of music: A systematic review and a new model. *Brain, Behavior, and Immunity, 36,* 15–26.

Feldenkrais, M. (1972). *Awareness through movement.* New York, NY: HarperCollins.

Ferrara, L. (1984). Phenomenology as a tool for musical analysis. *The Musical Quarterly, 70*(3), 355–373.

Fewell, G. (2014). *Outside music, inside voices: Dialogues on improvisation and the spirit of creative music.* Somerville, MA: Saturn University Press.

Fischer, R. (1971). A cartography of the ecstatic and meditative states. *Science, 174*(4012), 897–904.

Forinash, M., & Gonzalez, D. (1989). A phenomenological perspective of music therapy. *Music Therapy, 8*(1), 35–46.

Fortney, L., & Taylor, M. (2010). Meditation in medical practice: A review of the evidence and practice. *Primary Care, 37*(1), 81–90.

Friedman, S. (2014). *Zen cancer wisdom: Tips for making each day better.* Boston, MA: Wisdom Publications.

Friedson, S. M. (1996). *Dancing prophets: Musical experience in Tumbuka healing.* Chicago, IL: Univ. Chicago Press.

Galvin, K., & Todres, L. (2013). *Caring and well-being: A lifeworld approach.* New York, NY: Routledge.

Gaser, C., & Schlaug, G. (2003). Brain structures differ between musicians and non-musicians. *The Journal of Neuroscience, 23*(27), 9240–9245.

Gawande, A. (2014). *Being mortal.* New York, NY: Henry Holt & Co.

Geller, S. M., & Greenberg, L. S. (2011). *Therapeutic presence.* Washington, DC: American Psychological Association.

Gendlin, E. T. (1982). *Focusing.* New York, NY: Bantam Books.

Ghetti, C. M. (2011a). Active music engagement with emotional-approach coping to improve well-being in liver and kidney transplant recipients. *Journal of Music Therapy, 48*(4), 463–485.

Ghetti, C. M. (2011b). *Effect of music therapy with emotional-approach coping on pre-procedural anxiety in cardiac catheterization* (Unpublished doctoral dissertation). Lawrence, KS: University of Kansas.

Ghetti, C. M. (2012). Music therapy as procedural support for invasive medical procedures: Toward the development of music therapy theory. *Nordic Journal of Music Therapy, 21*(1), 3–35.

Ghetti, C. M. (2013). Effect of music therapy with emotional-approach coping on preprocedural anxiety in cardiac catheterization: A randomized controlled trial. *Journal of Music Therapy, 50*(2), 93–122.

Gioia, T. (2006). *Healing songs.* Durham, NC: Duke University Press Books.

Goleman, D. (2013). *Focus: The hidden driver of excellence.* New York, NY: Harper Paperbacks.

Haase, J. E., Kintner, E. K., Monahan, P. O., & Robb, S. L. (2014). The resilience in illness model, part 1: Exploratory evaluation in adolescents and young adults with cancer. *Cancer Nursing, 37*(3), 1–12.

Hanh, T. N. (2011). *Peace is every breath: A practice for our busy lives.* New York, NY: HarperOne.

Hanser, S. [Samuel]. (2004). *Proposal for Senior thesis: The healing empowerment center.* New York, NY: Parsons The New School for Design.

Hanser, S. [Samuel]. (2009). *Growth and grace: Human becomings.* California institute of Integral Studies, San Francisco, CA.

Hanser, S. [Samuel]. (2010). *Many blessings: The remembrance of one.* Boston, MA: Sands Creative Group.

Hanser, S. B. [Suzanne]. (2014). Cognitive-behavioral music therapy. In B. Wheeler (Ed.), *Music therapy handbook* (pp. 161–171). Guilford, NJ: Guilford Press.

Hanser, S. B. [Suzanne], & Mandel, S. E. (2010). *Manage your stress and pain through music.* Boston, MA: Berklee Press.

Harrington, A. (2009). *The cure within: A history of mind-body medicine.* New York, NY: W. W. Norton & Company.

Harris, K. M. (2010). An integrative approach to health. *Demography, 47*(1), 1–22.

Hay, L. L. (1999). *You can heal your life.* Carlsbad, CA: Hay House Inc.

Hersey, B. (2014). *The practice of nada yoga: Meditation on the inner sacred sound.* Rochester, VT: Inner Traditions.

Huddleston, P. (2012). *Prepare for surgery, heal faster: A guide of mind-body techniques.* Cambridge, MA: Angel River Press.

Huron, D. (2006). *Sweet anticipation: Music and the psychology of expectation.* Cambridge, MA: MIT Press.

Iwanaga, M., Kobayashi, A., & Kawasaki, C. (2005). Heart rate variability with repetitive exposure to music. *Biological Psychology, 70*(1), 61–66.

Jacobson, E. (1938). *Progressive relaxation.* Oxford, UK: Oxford University Press.

Jahnke, R. (1997). *The healer within: Using traditional Chinese techniques to release your body's own medicine, movement, massage, meditation, breathing.* San Francisco, CA: HarperOne.

Jerath, R., Edry, J. W., Barnes, V. A., & Jerath, V. (2006). Physiology of long pranayamic breathing: Neural respiratory elements may provide a mechanism that explains how slow deep breathing shifts the autonomic nervous system. *Medical Hypotheses, 67*(3), 566–571.

Judith, A. (1987). *Wheels of life: A user's guide to the Chakra system.* St. Paul, MN: Llewellyn Publications.

Jung, C. G., & Franz, M.-L. (1964). *Man and his symbols.* New York, NY: Dell Publishing.

Juslin, P. N., & Sloboda, J. (2010). *Handbook of music and emotion: Theory, research, applications.* Oxford, UK: Oxford Univ. Press.

Kabat-Zinn, J. (1994). *Wherever you go, there you are.* New York, NY: Hachette Books.

Kaptchuk, T. (2000). *The web that has no weaver: Understanding Chinese medicine.* Chicago, IL: McGraw-Hill.

Kaslewicz, T. (2014). *Drummassage.* Unpublished manuscript, Music Therapy Department, Berklee College of Music, Boston, MA.

Katiyar, S. K., & Bihari, S. (2006). Role of pranayama in rehabilitation of COPD patients—a randomized controlled study. *Indian Journal of Allergy, Asthma, & Immunology, 20*(2), 98.

Keyes, L. E., & Campbell, D. (2008). *Toning: The creative power of the voice.* Camarillo, CA: Devorss & Co.

Khaw, K.-T., Wareham, N., Bingham, S., et al. (2008). Combined impact of health behaviours and mortality in men and women: The EPIC-Norfolk prospective population study. *PLoS Med, 5*(1), e12.

Kierkegaard, S. (1980). *The concept of anxiety: A simple psychologically orienting deliberation on the dogmatic issue of hereditary sin* (trans: Thomte, R.). Princeton, NJ: Princeton University Press.

Knutson, B., Burgdorf, J., & Panksepp, J. (2002). Ultrasonic vocalizations as indeces of affective states in rats. *Psychological Bulletin, 128,* 961-977.

Koelsch, S., Fritz, T., Schulze, K., Alsop, D., & Schlaug, G. (2005). Adults and children processing music: An fMRI study. *NeuroImage, 25*(4), 1068–1076.

Koopsen, C., & Young, C. (2009). *Integrative health: A holistic approach for health professionals.* Sudbury, MA: Jones & Bartlett.

Kornfield, J. (2011). *A lamp in the darkness: Illuminating the path through difficult times.* Boulder, CO: Sounds True.

Krishnananda, S. (1996). *The Mandukya upanishad.* Rishikesh, India: The Divine Life Society.

Langevin, H. M., & Yandow, J. A. (2002). Relationship of acupuncture points and meridians to connective tissue planes. *The Anatomical Record, 269*(6), 257–265.

Lazarus, R. S., & Folkman, S. (1984). *Stress, appraisal, and coping.* New York, NY: Springer.

Leardi, S., Pietroletti, R., Angeloni, G., et al. (2007). Randomized clinical trial examining the effect of music therapy in stress response to day surgery. *The British Journal of Surgery, 94*(8), 943–947.

Lee, C. A. (2003). *Architecture of aesthetic music therapy.* Gilsum, NH: Barcelona Publishers.

Liao, J., Yang, Y., Cohen, L., Zhao, Y., & Xu, Y. (2013). Effects of Chinese medicine five-element music on the quality of life for advanced cancer patients: A randomized controlled trial. *Chinese Journal of Integrative Medicine, 19*(10), 736–740.

Linehan, M. M. (1993). *Skills training manual for treating borderline personality disorder.* New York, NY: Guilford Press.

Loewy, J. V., MacGregor, B., Richards, K., & Rodriguez, J. (1997). Music therapy pediatric pain management: Assessing and attending to the sounds of hurt, fear and anxiety. In J. V. Loewy (Ed.), *Music therapy and pediatric pain* (pp. 45–56). Cherry Hill, NJ: Jeffrey Books.

Macdonald, R., Kreutz, G., & Mitchell, L. (2012). *Music, health, and wellbeing.* Oxford, UK: Oxford University Press.

MacLean, P. D. (1958). Contrasting functions of limbic and neocortical systems of the brain and their relevance to psychophysiological aspects of medicine. *The American Journal of Medicine, 25*(4), 611–626.

Madsen, C. K., & Madsen, C. H. (1981). *Teaching/discipline: A positive approach for educational development.* Raleigh, NC: Contemporary Publishers.

Maisel, E. (2002). *The Van Gogh Blues: The creative person's path through depression.* Novato, CA: New World Library.

Mandel, S. E., Hanser, S. B., Secic, M., & Davis, B. A. (2007). Effects of music therapy on health-related outcomes in cardiac rehabilitation: a randomized controlled trial. *Journal of Music Therapy, 44*(3), 176–197.

Maslow, A. H. (1943). A theory of human motivation. *Psychological Review, 50*(4), 370.

Mathieu, W. A. (1991). *The listening book: Discovering your own music.* Boston, MA: Shambhala.

Matthews, E. E., & Cook, P. F. (2009). Relationships among optimism, well-being, self-transcendence, coping, and social support in women during treatment for breast cancer. *Psycho-Oncology, 18*(7), 716–726.

Mayer, D. J. (2000). Acupuncture: An evidence-based review of the clinical literature. *Annual Review of Medicine, 51*, 49–63.

Mayyim Hayyim Sixth Day Group. (2009). *Blessings for the journey: A Jewish healing guide for women with cancer.* Newton, MA: Mayyim Hayyim.

McKay, M., Wood, J. C., & Brantley, J. (2007). *The dialectical behavior therapy skills workbook: Practical DBT exercises for learning mindfulness, interpersonal effectiveness, emotion regulation & tolerance.* Oakland, CA: New Harbinger Publications.

Melzack, R. (2001). Pain and the neuromatrix in the brain. *Journal of Dental Education, 65*(12), 1378–1382.

Miner, H. M. (1956). Body ritual among the Nacirema. *The American Anthropologist, 58*, 503–507.

Montello, L. (2002). *Essential musical intelligence: Using music as your path to healing, creativity, and radiant wholeness.* Wheaton, IL: Quest Books.

Montello, L. (2005). *Music and sound awareness journal.* New York, NY: Performance Wellness, Inc.

Morrison, J. (1995). *The book of Ayurveda: A holistic approach to health and longevity.* New York, NY: Touchstone.

Naperstek, B. (1997). *Your sixth sense: Unlocking the power of your intuition.* New York, NY: HarperCollins.

Ni, M. (1995). *The Yellow Emperor's classic of medicine: A new translation of the Neijing Suwen with commentary.* Boston, MA: Shambhala.

Nicolai, J. (2013). *Integrative wellness rules: A simple guide to healthy living.* Carlsbad, CA: Hay House.

NIH Consensus Conference. (1998). Acupuncture. *Journal of the American Medical Association, 280*(17), 1518–1524.

Nordoff, P., & Robbins, C. (1977). *Creative music therapy.* New York, NY: John Day & Co.

O'Brien, E. (2005). Songwriting with adult patients in oncology and clinical haematology. In F. Baker & T. Wigram (Eds.), *Songwriting methods, techniques and clinical applications for music therapy clinicians, educators and students* (pp. 180–205). London, UK: Jessica Kingsley Publishers.

O'Callaghan, C. C. (1996). Lyrical themes in songs written by palliative care patients. *Journal of Music Therapy, 33*(2), 74–92.

Orman, E. K. (2011). The effect of listening to specific musical genre selections on measures of heart rate variability. *Update: Applications of Research in Music Education, 30*(1), 64–69.

Osho. (2004). *Zen: Its history and teachings.* Lewes, UK: Bridgewater Book Co.

Pearsall, P. D. P. (2007). *Awe: The delights and dangers of our eleventh emotion.* Deerfield Beach, FL: Health Communications, Inc.

Peate, W. (2003). *Listening with your heart: Lessons from native America.* Tucson, AZ: Rio Nuevo Publishers.

Plato. (1999). *Great dialogues of Plato* (trans: Rouse, W. H.). New York, NY: New American Library.

Razzaque, R. (2014). *Breaking down is waking up: Can psychological suffering be a spiritual gateway?* London, UK: Watkins Publishing.

Reznikovitch, L. (2014). *Thou shalt not diet.* Charleston, SC: ClearSpace.

Robb, S. L., Burns, D. S., Stegenga, K. A., et al. (2014). Randomized clinical trial of therapeutic music video intervention for resilience outcomes in adolescents/young adults undergoing hematopoietic stem cell transplant: A report from the children's oncology group. *Cancer, 120*(6), 909–917.

Roque, A. L., Valenti, V. E., Guida, H. L., et al. (2013). The effects of auditory stimulation with music on heart rate variability in healthy women. *Clinics, 68*(7), 960–967.

Rosenbaum, E. (2005). *Here for now: Living well with cancer through mindfulness.* Hardwick, MA: Satya House Publications.

Rumi, J. (1994). *The essential Rumi* (trans: Barks, C.). San Francisco, CA: HarperSanFrancisco.

Saarikallio, S. (2012). Development and validation of the brief music in mood regulation scale (B-MMR). *Music Perception: An Interdisciplinary Journal, 30*(1), 97–105.

Sacks, O. (2015, February 19). Oliver Sacks on learning he has terminal cancer. *The New York Times.* Retrieved from http://www.nytimes.com/2015/02/19/opinion/oliver-sacks-on-learning-he-has-terminal-cancer.html

Salzberg, S. (1995). *Lovingkindness: The revolutionary art of happiness.* Boston, MA: Shambhala.

Scheier, M. F., Matthews, K. A., Owens, J. F., et al. (1989). Dispositional optimism and recovery from coronary artery bypass surgery: The beneficial effects on physical and psychological well-being. *Journal of Personality and Social Psychology, 57*(6), 1024–1040.

Scolastico, R. (1997). *Doorway to the soul.* New York, NY: Gallery Books.

Sendrey, A., & Norton, M. (1964). *David's harp.* New York, NY: New American Library.

Segerstrom, S. C., & Sephton, S. E. (2010). Optimistic expectancies and cell-mediated immunity: The role of positive affect. *Psychological Science, 21*, 448–455.

Shapiro, M., & Vivino, B. L. (2014). *Freedom from anxiety: A holistic approach to emotional well-being.* Berkeley, CA: North Atlantic Books.

Shrestha, S. (2009). *How to heal with singing bowls: Traditional Tibetan healing methods.* Boulder, CO: Sentient Publications.

Siegel, B. (1986). *Love, medicine and miracles.* New York, NY: Harper & Row.

Silverman, M. J. (2009). A descriptive analysis of music therapists working with consumers in substance abuse rehabilitation: Current clinical practice to guide future research. *The Arts in Psychotherapy, 36*(3), 123–130.

Silverstein, S. (1981). *A light in the attic.* New York, NY: HarperCollins.

Singer, B. H., & Ryff, C. D. (2001). *New horizons in health: An integrative approach*. Washington, DC: National Academies Press.

Singer, M. (2007). *The untethered soul*. Oakland, CA: New Harbinger Publications.

Sommerfeld, S. (n.d.). *We can turn DNA into music*. http://www.inlander.com/spokane/we-can-turn-dna-into-music/Content?oid=2155321. Date accessed 29 June 2015.

Song, B. (2014). *Flaws of five-element music therapy*. Paper presented at the 12th annual conference of the Chinese Music Therapy Association, Beijing, China.

Stefano, G. B., Fricchione, G. L., Slingsby, B. T., & Benson, H. (2001). The placebo effect and relaxation response: Neural processes and their coupling to constitutive nitric oxide. *Brain Research Reviews, 35*(1), 1–19.

Stevens, C. (2012). *Music medicine: The science and spirit of healing yourself with sound*. Boulder, CO: Sounds True.

Stillwater, M., & Malkin, G. (2003). *Graceful passages: A companion for living and dying*. Novato, CA: New World Library.

Summer, L. (1996). *Music: The new age elixir*. Amherst, NY: Prometheus Books.

Taylor, E. I. (2002). The relaxation response and its possible corollary in the shamanic trance. *Journal of Ritual Studies, 16*(2), 108–111.

Thaut, M., Gardiner, J. C., Holmberg, D., et al. (2009). Neurologic music therapy improves executive function and emotional adjustment in traumatic brain injury rehabilitation. *Annals of the New York Academy of Sciences, 1169*, 406–416.

Thaut, M. H. (2005). The future of music in therapy and medicine. *Annals of the New York Academy of Sciences, 1060*, 303–308.

Tick, H. (2013). *Holistic pain relief: Dr. Tick's breakthrough strategies to manage and eliminate pain*. Novato, CA: New World Library.

Toskar, C., & Toskar, A. (2011). *Health as a path: A guidebook for spiritual healing and health-care in everyday life*. Zurich, Switzerland: Spiritual Health Foundation.

Tse, M. M. Y., Chan, M. F., & Benzie, I. F. F. (2005). The effect of music therapy on postoperative pain, heart rate, systolic blood pressure and analgesic use following nasal surgery. *Journal of Pain & Palliative Care Pharmacotherapy, 19*(3), 21–29.

Ullmann, G., Williams, H. G., Hussey, J., et al. (2010). Effects of Feldenkrais exercises on balance, mobility, balance confidence, and gait performance in community-dwelling adults age 65 and older. *The Journal of Alternative and Complementary Medicine, 16*(1), 97–105.

Umemura, M., & Honda, K. (1998). Influence of music on heart rate variability and comfort: A consideration through comparison of music and noise. *Journal of Human Ergology, 27*(1–2), 30–38.

Vatanasapt, P., Vatanasapt, N., Laohasiriwong, S., & Prathanee, B. (2014). Music speaks the words: An integrated program for rehabilitation of post laryngectomy patients in Khon Kaen, Thailand. *Music and Medicine, 6*(1), 7–10.

Vaughan, F. (1995). *The inward arc: Healing in psychotherapy and spirituality.* Boston, MA: Shambhala.

Vishnu-Devananda, S. (1995). *Meditation and mantras.* Delhi, India: Motilal Banarsidass.

Weintraub, A. (2012). *Yoga skills for therapists: Effective practices for mood management.* New York, NY: W. W. Norton & Company.

Weiss, R. (2015). How therapists mourn. *The New York Times.* http://mobile. nytimes.com/blogs/opinionator/2015/07/04/how-therapists-mourn. Date accessed 14 July 2015.

Wigram, T. (2004). *Improvisation: Methods and techniques for music therapy clinicians, educators, and students.* London, UK: Jessica Kingsley.

Wigram, T. (2005). Songwriting methods—similarities and differences. In F. Baker & T. Wigram (Eds.), *Songwriting methods, techniques and clinical applications for music therapy clinicians, educators and students* (pp. 246–271). London, UK: Jessica Kingsley Publishers.

Wilbur, K. (Ed.). (1984). *Quantum questions.* Boulder, CO: New Science Library/Shambhala.

Yinger, O. S., & Gooding, L. F. (2015). A systematic review of music-based interventions for procedural support. *Journal of Music Therapy, 52*(1), 1–77.

Websites

American Cancer Society. http://www.cancer.org/treatment. Date accessed 15 Sept 2014.

American Psychological Association. http://www.apa.org/helpcenter/road-resilience.aspx. Date accessed 28 Jan 2015.

Bonny Method of Guided Imagery and Music. http://ami-bonnymethod.org. Date accessed 12 Oct 2014.

Hanser, S. [Samuel]. (2008). *The healing empowerment center.* http://www. healingempowermentcenter.org. Date accessed 15 Jan 2012.

HeartMath Institute. http://www.heartmath.org. Date accessed 15 Sept 2014.

Institute for Healthcare Improvement. http://www.ihi.org/Engage/Initiatives/TripleAim. Date accessed 15 Sept 2014.

Mind and Life Institute. https://www.mindandlife.org. Date accessed 28 Jan 2015.

National Institutes of Health. (2012). *Clinical neurocardiology section.* http://intra.ninds.nih.gov/Lab.asp?Org_ID=82. Date accessed 8 June 2015.

Rabbi Shefa Gold. http://www.rabbishefagold.com/nitzavim. Date accessed 28 Jan 2015.

Therapeutic Touch International Association. http://therapeutic-touch.org. Date accessed 29 Jan 2015.

Index

© The Editor(s) (if applicable) and The Author(s) 2016
S.B. Hanser, *Integrative Health through Music Therapy*,
DOI 10.1057/978-1-137-38477-5

cognitive-evaluative domain, 234
comfort
    breathing into, 155–8
    defined, 153–4
comforting companion, 154–5
comforting effect, 168
comforting imagery, 162–4
comforting songs, 167–71
    lullabies, 171
    singing, 169–70
comforting sounds
    listening, 166
    toning, 166–7
comforting the body, 158–62
    drummassage, 161–2
    facial massage, 159–60
    progressive muscle relaxation
        (PMR), 160–1
comforting the mind, 164–6
    mantra, 165–6
    meditation, 164
companion, 102–5, 113, 121,
    154–5, 183, 185–7, 192, 204,
    220, 226, 229
complementary therapies, 24–5
composure, 77–8
contemporary ethnomusicologists,
    65
conventional medicine, 38
Conway, Suzy, 254–5
COPD. *See* chronic obstructive
    pulmonary disease (COPD)
Cope, Stephen, 75
    *The Great Work of Your Life: A
    Guide for the Journey to Your
    True Calling*, 74–5
coping
    committing to, 224–5
    emotional-approach, 230–2

heart of, 238
with pain, 232–4
removing obstacles on the path to,
    223–4
with stresses of illness, 228–30
through head and heart, 218–19
Cousins, Norman, 27
    New England Journal of Medicine,
    27
Crowe, Barbara
    *Music and Soulmaking: Toward a
    New Theory of Music Therapy*, 252
Csikszentmihalyi, Mihaly, 75
    *Flow: The Psychology of Optimal
    Experience*, 18

D

Dabhade, A. M., 156
Dalai Lama XIV, 100
D'Angelo, James
    *The Healing Power of the Human
    Voice*, 187
Daniélou, Alain, 57, 62
darshanas, 47
Das, Kalani, 161
Huron, David
    *Sweet Anticipation: Music and the
    Psychology of Expectation*, 167
Davis, Lydia
    Head, Heart, 218
DBT. *See* dialectical behavior
    therapy (DBT)
Debra, 73, 74, 133, 134
Debussy, 109, 244
breath
    deep, 155–8
Dharana, 48
dharma, 74

Made in the USA
Monee, IL
11 June 2020